GREAT SHORTER WORKS *of* PASCAL

GREAT SHORTER WORKS *of* PASCAL

Translated with an Introduction by

EMILE CAILLIET

and

JOHN C. BLANKENAGEL

WIPF & STOCK · Eugene, Oregon

Wipf and Stock Publishers
199 W 8th Ave, Suite 3
Eugene, OR 97401

Great Shorter Works of Pascal
By Pascal, Blaise and Cailliet, Emile
ISBN 13: 978-1-5326-4627-0
Publication date 12/27/2017
Previously published by Westminster Press, 1948

CONTENTS

		Page
	CHRONOLOGICAL REFERENCE TABLE	9
	INTRODUCTION	15
1	LETTER FROM PASCAL TO MLLE [MRS.] PERIER (January 31, 1643).	39
2	LETTER TO THE CHANCELLOR, DEDICATING THE CALCULATING MACHINE (1645).	40
3	REPLY BY PASCAL TO FATHER NOËL [October-November, 1647].	42
4	FRAGMENT OF A PREFACE TO THE TREATISE ON THE VACUUM [October-November, 1647?].	50
5	LETTER FROM PASCAL TO MONSIEUR PERIER (November 15, 1647).	56
6	FRAGMENT OF A LETTER FROM PASCAL TO MADAME PERIER (January 26, 1648).	59
7	LETTER FROM PASCAL TO MONSIEUR LE PAILLEUR [February-March, 1648].	61
8	FRAGMENT OF A LETTER FROM PASCAL TO MADAME PERIER (April 1, 1648).	76
9	LETTER FROM PASCAL TO MADAME PERIER (November 5, 1648).	79
10	LETTER FROM PASCAL TO MONSIEUR AND MADAME PERIER (October 17, 1651) ON THE DEATH OF HIS FATHER.	82
11	LETTER FROM PASCAL TO QUEEN CHRISTINE OF SWEDEN [About June, 1652].	92
12	EXCERPT FROM A LETTER BY PASCAL TO MONSIEUR PERIER (June 6, 1653).	95
13	POTESTATUM NUMERICARUM SUMMA (SUMMATION OF POWERS OF NUMBERS) [1654?].	95
14	LETTER FROM PASCAL TO MONSIEUR DE FERMAT (July 29, 1654).	103
15	LETTER FROM PASCAL TO MONSIEUR DE FERMAT (August 24, 1654).	110
16	LETTER FROM PASCAL TO FERMAT (October 27, 1654)	116
17	LETTER FROM PASCAL TO MADAME PERIER [October-November, 1654?].	116
18	PASCAL'S MEMORIAL (Night of November 23, 1654).	117

		Page
19	WRITING ON THE CONVERSION OF THE SINNER [November-December, 1654?].	118
20	PASCAL'S CONVERSATION WITH MONSIEUR DE SACI ON EPICTETUS AND MONTAIGNE (EXCERPT FROM FONTAINE'S MEMOIRES) [January, 1655?].	121
21	THE MYSTERY OF JESUS [1655?].	133
22	[A SHORT EXPOSITION OF THE PROBLEM OF GRACE] [1656?].	136
23	EXCERPT FROM A LETTER BY PASCAL TO MONSIEUR AND MLLE DE ROUANNEZ [September, 1656].	142
24	EXCERPT FROM A LETTER BY PASCAL TO MONSIEUR AND MLLE DE ROUANNEZ [September 24, 1656].	144
25	EXCERPT FROM A LETTER BY PASCAL TO MONSIEUR AND MLLE DE ROUANNEZ [October, 1656] (?).	145
26	EXCERPT FROM A LETTER BY PASCAL TO MONSIEUR AND MLLE DE ROUANNEZ [October 27(?), 1656].	146
27	EXCERPT FROM A LETTER BY PASCAL TO MONSIEUR AND MLLE DE ROUANNEZ [Sunday, November 5, 1656].	147
28	EXCERPT FROM A LETTER BY PASCAL TO MONSIEUR AND MLLE DE ROUANNEZ [November, 1656] (?).	149
29	EXCERPT FROM A LETTER BY PASCAL TO MONSIEUR AND MLLE DE ROUANNEZ [November or December, 1656] (?).	151
30	EXCERPT FROM A LETTER BY PASCAL TO MONSIEUR AND MLLE DE ROUANNEZ [December, 1656(?)].	152
31	EXCERPT FROM A LETTER BY PASCAL TO MONSIEUR AND MLLE DE ROUANNEZ [December 24(?), 1656].	154
32	EXCERPT FROM A LETTER BY PASCAL TO A FRIEND IN CLERMONT [April-May, 1657] (?).	155
33	[COMPARISON OF THE CHRISTIANS OF THE EARLIEST TIMES WITH THOSE OF TODAY] [1657(?)].	156
34	LETTER FROM A LAWYER IN PARLIAMENT TO ONE OF HIS FRIENDS CONCERNING THE INQUISITION WHICH THEY WANT TO ESTABLISH IN FRANCE AS A RESULT OF A NEW BULL OF POPE ALEXANDER VII (June 1, 1657).	160
35	[AN IMPORTANT DOCUMENT. EXCERPT FROM THE DECREE OF THE INDEX, CONDEMNING THE PROVINCIAL LETTERS (September 6, 1657)].	172
36	FACTUM FOR THE PRIESTS OF PARIS (January 25, 1658).	173
37	[SUGGESTED PRONOUNCEMENT AGAINST THE APOLOGY FOR THE CASUISTS] (1658).	183
38	THE MIND OF THE GEOMETRICIAN [1658 or 1659] (?).	189
39	THE ART OF PERSUASION [1658 or 1659] (?).	202

		Page
40	THREE DISCOURSES BY PASCAL ON THE STATION OF NOBLEMEN. [REDACTION BY NICOLE] [End of 1659] (?).	211
41	LETTER FROM PASCAL TO FERMAT (August 10, 1660).	216
42	LETTER FROM PASCAL TO MADAME DE SABLÉ [End of 1660] (?).	217
43	WRITING BY PASCAL ON THE SIGNATURE OF THE FORMULARY [End of November or December, 1661] (?).	218
44	PRAYER BY PASCAL ASKING GOD TO USE ILLNESSES TO A GOOD END [Between 1659 and 1661] (?).	220
45	PASCAL'S WILL (August 3, 1662).	228

CHRONOLOGICAL REFERENCE TABLE

Blaise Pascal (1623–1662)

1588 Etienne Pascal, the father of Blaise, born in Clermont (Auvergne).
1616? Etienne Pascal marries Antoinette Begon.
1617 Birth of Anthonia Pascal who dies shortly after her baptism.
1619 Etienne Pascal buys the Langhac mansion, close by the Abbey in Clermont.
1620 Birth of Gilberte Pascal, who became Madame Perier.
1623 June 19. Birth of Blaise Pascal.
June 27. Christening of Blaise.
1625 October 5. Birth of Jacqueline Pascal, who later entered Port Royal and became Sister Saint Euphemia.
1626 Death of Antoinette (Begon) Pascal.
1631 Etienne Pascal sells his post of Second President of the Cour des Aides to a brother, converts his property into Government bonds, and settles in Paris with his three children.
1633 Saint Cyran appointed Confessor at Port Royal de Paris by Mother Superior Angélique, one of Antoine Arnauld's daughters.
1635 Young Blaise reveals the precocity of his scientific genius; he is said to have rediscovered by himself the thirty-second proposition of the First Book of Euclid. Advised by his learned friend Le Pailleur, Etienne Pascal allows his son Blaise to accompany him to the weekly gatherings of the Académie Mersenne. (Father Mersenne, a friend of Descartes, was always on the watch for new publications and new talent in the field of science.) Members of this group were Desargues, a geometrician, who suggested to Blaise the idea of starting from his knowledge of perspective and reducing the properties of conic sections to a small number of propositions; the epicure Le Pailleur, a self-taught man, who proved his competence by solving some of the most difficult problems; Roberval, professor of mathematics at the Collège de France, opponent of Descartes and precursor of Newton, one of the celebrities of French science; Carcavy, a mathematician, correspondent of Descartes; Mydorge, maker of lenses; Hardy, a mathematician versed in Oriental languages; the illustrious Fermat, one of the greatest mathematicians of all times. Blaise Pascal subsequently shared with him the honor of discovering the calculus of probabilities. Hobbes visited the Académie Mersenne in the winter of 1636–37.
1637 Descartes's *Discourse on Method*.

1638 Saint Cyran imprisoned for disruption of ecclesiastical peace. The *solitaires* of Port Royal move to the original home of their community at Port Royal in the Fields (abandoned since 1626 when malaria compelled transfer of the convent to Paris). Only the nuns remain in Paris. Death of Jansen.

1640 Publication of Jansen's *Augustinus*.

Appointed by Richelieu to be Deputy Commissioner in Upper Normandy for the levying of taxes and duties, Etienne Pascal arrives in Rouen.

Barely sixteen years old, Blaise Pascal produces an *Essay on Conic Sections* later discussed by Leibnitz, a fervent admirer of Pascal.

1641 June 15. Gilberte Pascal marries Florin Perier.

1642 Birth of Etienne Perier who later becomes a priest. (To him we owe the attestation of the authenticity of Pascal's *Memorial* as well as the copy of the same document published as *Text* 18. Only Perier's copy gives the last three lines whose authenticity remains a matter for speculation.)

Death of Galileo.

1642 or 1643 Blaise Pascal discovers the principle of the calculating machine and begins experimenting with over fifty models until the machine is built to his own satisfaction (although Pascal continues for at least ten years to plan new devices for dealing with fractions and for extracting square roots).

1645 Letter to the Chancellor, dedicating the calculating machine (*Text* 2).

1646 The Pascal family is quickened by Jansenist doctrine.

April 5. Birth of Margaret Perier.

Blaise Pascal begins research on the problem of the vacuum.

1647 Death of Torricelli.

Blaise Pascal goes to Paris for his health.

Descartes calls on him on September 23 and 24. A few days later Pascal returns Descartes's visit. (Subsequently Descartes claims that he had suggested to Pascal the idea of using a Torricellian tube at the foot and then at the top of a mountain to settle the question of atmospheric pressure. Pascal maintains that the idea was his own.) (*Text* 5).

Controversy with Father Noël, a Jesuit, who opposes to Pascal's experimental method a method of authority based on Aristotle (*Texts* 3, 5, 7).

Birth of Marie Perier.

1648 Misunderstandings between Blaise Pascal and Monsieur de Rebours of Port Royal (*Text* 6).

September 1. Death of Mersenne.

September 19. Following the directions of Blaise Pascal, Florin Perier performs the great experiment on the vacuum at the base of the Puy de Dôme. On receipt of his report, Blaise Pascal repeats the experiment at the top and foot of the old Saint James tower in Paris; probably also in a tower of Notre Dame; also in a tall private house. The question of atmospheric pressure thus settled, Blaise Pascal proceeds with generalizations from physics to mechanics and statics. (Pascal is credited with the invention of the syringe, the barometer, and the hydraulic press.)

1649 Jansen's *Augustinus* is denounced at the Sorbonne.

1650 Death of Descartes.

1651 August 22. The Duke of Rouannez is appointed Governor and Lieutenant General of Poitou.

September 24. Death of Etienne Pascal (*Text* 10).

September 27. Birth of Louis Perier.

1652 Jacqueline Pascal enters Port Royal in Paris.

Beginning of Pascal's "worldly period."

June (?). Letter from Pascal to the Queen of Sweden (*Text* 11).

1653 (?) Trip to Poitou (during the spring?) in the company of Méré, Miton, and the Duke of Rouannez. Initiation into the famous distinction between the geometrical mind (esprit géométrique) and the intuitive mind (esprit de finesse). Great scientific activity.

June 3. Five propositions of Jansen said to be found in the *Augustinus* are condemned by Pope Innocent X.

June 5. Profession of faith of Jacqueline Pascal at Port Royal. After these final vows she becomes Sister Saint Euphemia.

August. Birth of Blaise Perier.

1654 Pascal completes his treatises on the equilibrium of liquids and the weight of a mass of air; with Fermat he studies the calculus of probabilities (*Texts* 13–16).

End of September. Pascal turns more and more to the problem of religion (*Text* 17).

November 23. Pascal's night of religious ecstasy and conversion (*Memorial, Text* 18).

Retreat with the Port Royalists. An edifying convert.

1655 January (?). Famous conversation with his spiritual director Monsieur de Saci on Epictetus and Montaigne (*Text* 20).

The Mystery of Jesus (*Text* 21), probably written at Port Royal at that time on the occasion of a monthly meditation.

Nicolas Cornet, syndic of the Sorbonne had, in 1649, summarized the contents of Jansen's *Augustinus* in five propositions; these were submitted to Rome and condemned by Pope Innocent X in 1653. Port Royal greeted the condemnation with silence. Arnauld, without protesting publicly, was content to say that he too with Rome, condemned the condemned proposition—a matter of *Doctrine*, but that those propositions were not in the *Augustinus*—a matter of *Fact*.

The question of the Jesuits' influence in Rome remains an open problem.

1656 The Jesuits obtain a condemnation of Arnauld in the Sorbonne by a
1657 vote of 124 to 71 with 15 abstentions; now a second and final judgment is to be pronounced. In the person of Arnauld, its head, the whole Jansenist party, whose seat is at Port Royal, is threatened with a verdict of heresy.

At the request of Arnauld and the gentlemen of Port Royal, Pascal enters the lists on the side of his friends. Under the pseudonym of Louis de Montalte he writes the *Provincial Letters* (January 1656 to March 1657), the first great masterpiece of modern French prose.

March 24, 1656. Pascal is greatly encouraged by the miraculous healing of his niece Margaret Perier at Port Royal; this cure is always referred to as the Miracle of the Holy Thorn.

Meanwhile Pascal plays his role as a Christian layman. His letters of direction to the Duke of Rouannez and his sister (*Texts* 23–31) throw precious light on the frame of mind and the state of conscience of the man who, in the thick of the fight, is now writing the *Provincial Letters* (See *Text* 33 in this connection).

December 6, 1657. The *Provincial Letters* are condemned in Rome.

Pascal subsequently resumes his attacks on the Jesuits under cover of the intervention of Churchmen (*Texts* 34–37).

1658 To widen the influence of his guidance, Pascal contemplates writing a great work for the vindication of the Christian religion. Toward 1658 his design assumes more definite form in his mind; he consents to sketch the outline of his projected work for some of his Port Royal friends. He does this in about two hours. About eight years later Filleau de la Chaise undertakes to edit the *Discourse on the Pensées* in which Pascal's design appears. This he does on the basis of Pascal's oral exposé and with the aid of Pascal's notes. By his own admission, Pascal would have needed ten years of good health to carry out this plan. But after the spring of 1658, his health, which had never been good, became very poor.

While writing his *Pensées*, Pascal continued his collaboration with the French clergy against the casuistry of the Jesuits.

In order to distract his mind from excruciating headaches Pascal turns again to mathematics and solves the problem of the cycloid.

1659
1660 A very sick man, Pascal simultaneously carries on the activities related to the great causes to which he is committed.

Probably at this time he formulates in two great essays his views on the *Mind of the geometrician* (*Text* 38) and on the *Art of persuasion* (*Text* 39).

Evidently his concern is to make use of them for the vindication of Christianity on which he is working also (*Pensées*).

His letter to Fermat, dated August 10, 1660, now clearly indicates a final shift from geometry to an almost exclusive concern for religion and for his own soul.

In the midst of great suffering, Pascal truly becomes a hero and a saint (*Text* 44).

He denounces the expediency of Arnauld's ambiguous formula of appeasement when the Church of Rome requires from the clergy and from monastic orders the signature of a formulary (*Text* 43).

He faints during a last debate with the Port Royalists.

October 4. Jacqueline (Sister Saint Euphemia), his younger sister, dies of a broken heart three months after the signature has been wrested from her.

1662 March 18. Vehicles carrying passengers at five sous a ride start to run in the streets of Paris. Having invented the omnibus and organized the first Bus Company, Pascal asks for a thousand francs in advance for his share, in order to send the money to the poor of Blois who have suffered severely from a bitter winter.

August 3. Pascal's will (*Text* 45).

August 19. Pascal dies at the age of thirty-nine in the home of his brother-in-law Florin Perier in Paris, after having turned over his own home to an impoverished family.

August 21. Funeral rites in the Church of Saint-Etienne-du-Mont.

INTRODUCTION

Blaise Pascal, a genius of remarkable range, has suffered greatly from the analytical tendency of modern times. Arbitrary selections from his writings have been treated as isolated units rather than in full perspective. As a result, pearls of great price have remained in obscurity. Under the title GREAT SHORTER WORKS OF PASCAL we are presenting a rich treasure of such jewels.

1. THE PLACE OF THESE WRITINGS AMONG PASCAL'S WORKS

At the hands of specialists Pascal has been dealt with arbitrarily in fragmentary fashion as child prodigy, mathematician, physicist, man of the world, philosopher, theologian, polemicist, author, and saint. In his life, epochs of his thinking have been isolated. In his thinking, systems have been blocked off arbitrarily, despite the fact that from the very beginning Blaise had acquired a method quite his own which once and for all implied the renunciation of any system. In dealing with his works, writers have given primary consideration to striking inventions such as the calculating machine, the syringe, the hydraulic machine, the barometer, and the omnibus — in fact, an omnibus company.

At the same time scientists have incorporated in the body of human knowledge entire sections from his physics, such as the treatises on the equilibrium of liquids, which were perfected to such a degree that their presentation by Pascal remained definitive. Mathematicians wrestled with methods of his which in part were so difficult that a certain number of them had to be abandoned. Scholars of great breadth were introduced by Pascal to most complicated solutions of problems of integral calculus. With Fermat, but independently of him, Pascal grappled with the theory of probability and the problem of points. He paved the way for the authors of infinitesimal calculus.

Theologians, philosophers, and men of letters have long turned to the *Provincial Letters* and to the *Pensées* [Thoughts]; they have edited and re-edited these writings again and again in most varied editions. In doing this they doubtless showed good taste, but Pascal might well have said to them in the manner of the poet who was eternally praised for one of his works: "I did something else."

The edition of the *Œuvres de Blaise Pascal* by Brunschvicg, Boutroux, and Gazier in the collection *Les Grands Ecrivains de la France* numbers fourteen volumes. Of these fourteen, three are devoted to the *Pensées*, and the major portion of three others to the *Provincial Letters;* this leaves approximately eight other volumes. A considerable portion of these is devoted to the scientific works which we have mentioned. The *Œuvres* also echo the life of his family, of its members, of friends, and of social, scientific, and religious relationships. Abundant documents, and ample and very erudite introductions, enrich this veritable Pascalian encyclopedia.

In this impressive mass there are writings of the highest order. Naturally, they are not of uniform value, but who would claim anything different for the *Pensées* or for any great work considered as a whole? Certain letters have their place in the present collection primarily because of their documentary importance. This is true of the first document, a letter written by Pascal at the age of nineteen years, the oldest autograph of his which we possess. Other texts are highly specialized, such as *Text 22, A short exposition of the problem of grace*, whose publication here is intended to clarify Pascal's attitude toward religion and the significance of his intervention in the quarrel between the Jesuits and Jansenists. This is not to imply that the general level of these works is at all inferior to the classical excellence of his works as a whole. The infinite variety of Pascal's genius is clearly manifest in these shorter treatises. Some of these reveal a Pascal who is at the zenith of his powers; they are likely to mark just so many dates in the intellectual history of the reader who encounters them for the first time. This is true of *Text 4, Fragment of a preface to the treatise on the vacuum*. But for that matter, to choose here would be the equivalent of a betrayal.

2. Characterization of the Present Edition

The admirable *Mystery of Jesus*, one of the gems of religious literature, has been set apart from the *Pensées*, where too often it remains hidden, and has been included here. On the other hand, we have omitted shorter writings which some informed readers may judge essential.

Thus we have refrained from including the *Discourse on the passions of love*. Not that we doubt its attribution to Pascal; yet the fact remains that it presents a manuscript problem not unlike that once presented by the *Conversation with Monsieur de Saci*, the text of which Joseph Bédier had to establish according to an exacting method which remains a model of its kind.

The *Epitome of the life of Jesus Christ*, whose authenticity was established by Faugère, likewise raises a textual problem which is all the more difficult because only one manuscript is known. Nevertheless, we would have included its translation here, if the length of the text and its special character had not led us to decide in favor of a separate edition.

We shall doubtless be reproached by Pascalians for other omissions. However, we beg them to consider that apart from the *Discourse on the passions of love*, to which we have already referred, the present edition omits none of the shorter writings regarded as essential by Brunschvicg in his small edition; moreover it practically doubles the content of the small edition by adding texts of the first order chosen from the large edition. The text of the latter has been followed throughout in the present collection.

We have likewise followed the chronological order established by Brunschvicg, though his has been modified here and there in an attempt to insert into the chronology the undated writings on the basis of data at our disposal. In every case the reasons for doing so are to be found either in an earlier work (Emile Cailliet, *Pascal, Genius in the Light of Scripture*, The Westminster Press, 1945. 383 pages) or in the course of this introduction.

Since the present collection is a continuation of a Pascalian series, with its long, amply documented, and annotated presentation, it will be unnecessary for us to provide the usual apparatus of footnotes here.

Our foremost aim has been practical. We have tried to make essential classical Pascalian literature other than the *Provincial Letters* and the *Pensées* available to discriminating readers who might find the original texts difficult and discouraging.

3. Description of the Present Edition

Pascal was born in the old city of Clermont in Auvergne, whose practically minded inhabitants had transformed its moats into vegetable gardens. All his life he remained a native of Auvergne. His genius was eminently practical.

In the Family Circle

At the time when he wrote the letter with which the present collection begins (*Text* 1), Blaise Pascal, almost twenty years old, had just completed the calculating machine the purpose of which was to afford relief to his father, who spent his nights computing. We read that during the last four months Etienne has not gone to bed six times before two o'clock in the morning. Although at that time the rigid discipline of patriarchal tradition was very stern, the strength of affection reflects profound human tenderness. Though for the people of Upper Normandy Pascal's father was His Majesty's Deputy Commissioner for the levying of taxes and duties, he reports news and various happenings to his daughter, and he speaks of marriages which never fail to interest Gilberte, who herself had recently been married. Blaise's older sister had married Florin Perier on June 15, 1641; in 1642 a son was born to them and was christened Etienne in honor of his grandfather. Subsequently, we enjoy the touching note with which the grandfather's postscript, appended to the same letter, concludes: "Your little son slept here last night. Thanks to God he is very well." And the end of the letter, "Your good and excellent friend," well characterizes the nature of the family relations in this Christian home. The fact that this letter is addressed to "Mademoiselle" Perier need not lead us into error. Our celebrated contemporaries who like to call themselves "Miss" after having become "Mrs." are simply following an old and very bourgeois tradition which thus designates women even after their marriage.

No justification is needed for a method of chronological classification which brings together texts of different kinds in the manner of everyday life where tasks and preoccupations likewise are so varied. Such variety is well indicated by the rapprochement of the *Letter to Madame Perier* (*Text* 1) with the *Letter to the chancellor, dedicating the calculating machine* (*Text* 2). Incidentally, it is not merely the machine which is to aid Etienne Pascal, the father. The letter in which it is dedicated to the chancellor will serve, if necessary, to appease this high personage with whom Etienne previously had had some difficulties.

An Inventor's Pride

Even though it is marked by the hyperbolic style which was obligatory under such circumstances, the *Letter to the chancellor, dedicating the calculating machine*, reveals to us a Pascal who was aware of his genius and who was content with himself. He is not aware, as was the author of the *Ethica Nicomachea* (1124a), that "it is hard to be truly proud."

Here we are far from the self-abasement which the *Memorial* (*Text* 18) reveals, and which subsequently consecrates the admirable *Prayer asking God to use illnesses to a good end* (*Text* 44).

Experimental Realism

The same experimental realism which hitherto had guided Pascal in his labors and in his mathematical inventions comes to his aid in the realm of physics, and particularly so in his research on the question of a vacuum. Pascal's method, which is alert to the vicissitudes of research while directing it, is based on contact with facts. In his most penetrating generalizations he never loses this contact, for it is correct to say that the truly scientific mind does not proceed from the real to the intelligible except to return from the intelligible to the genuinely real, then to grapple all the more profoundly with reality.

Once more chronology comes to our aid in allowing the present collection to give to the *Fragment of a preface to the treatise on the vacuum* (*Text* 4) a pertinent preface in the form of a *Reply by Pascal to Father Noël* (*Text* 3). This letter to the learned Jesuit is more than an initiation into the twofold technical and methodological problem; it is a masterful lesson which concludes with a masterful rebuke. The fact is that from a purely empirical point of view adopted by the physicist Pascal, truth is that which everyone has been in a position to debate and that which no one can any longer debate; like the combat between Corneille's Rodrigue and the Moors, it is a combat which ends because there are no more warriors left on the battlefield. Indeed, when Pascal has finished with Father Noël we have the impression of seeing the latter disappear through a trap door. These clear, penetrating pages were written by a pen that is now ironical and now "truly eloquent"; it is the pen that ten years later produced the *Provincial Letters*. These were to proceed from a profound disagreement between Pascal and the Jesuits as he saw them.

Jurisdiction in Regard to Method

This disagreement was of long standing. Seventeen years earlier, in 1630, Pascal's father had protested against the founding of a Jesuit college in Clermont. But we are now concerned with a question of method or rather of competence in matters of method. Pascal's father was a jurist. Hence it is not at all surprising that his son, whom he himself had educated, should be impressed by the notion of competence in the juridical sense of the word, and even and above all in scientific matters.

The question of a vacuum is specifically one of rational and experimental method. The authority of Aristotle has nothing to do with it. But in the last analysis Father Noël proceeds from this authority, and it is fundamentally this usurpation of authority to which Pascal objects. Though he pays tribute to the efforts of preceding generations, he defines the measure of independence of his own generation. For him the true way of recognizing our indebtedness to our forerunners and of keeping faith with them is precisely to continue their reasoned efforts without ever being shackled by their errors.

In this domain Pascal is quite as rationalistic as Descartes. He knows that to judge means to affirm or to deny, and that consequently judgment is opposed to doubt. The *Reply to Father Noël* (*Text* 3) declares specifically that we should never pass a decisive judgment against or for a proposition without affirming or denying certain conditions. One of these is that it must seem "so clearly and so distinctly evident to the senses or to the reason, as the case may be, that the mind has no grounds for doubting its certainty." This is almost word for word Descartes's formulation of his famous criterion of evidence in the *Discourse on method* and the third *Meditation*.

Divergence Between Pascal and Descartes

Yet a growing divergence appears between these two great men. It first comes to light in the form of petty jealousy of the older man towards a newcomer of the rising generation — a very human situation. It should be recalled that at the age of fifteen years Pascal had planned a *Treatise on conic sections*, unfortunately lost, at which Descartes had taken umbrage when Father Mersenne had presented it to him in manuscript (1639). It is true that it was no secret among the latter's entourage that the young author "had walked all over all those who had treated the subject." Now after having published his *Discourse on method* (1637) two years previously, Descartes was busied with a work on a universal, analytical, and abstract mathematics which his optimism regarded as destined to penetrate the intelligibility of the universe. Thus conceived, his geometry was presented as a general science, more concerned with the analysis of algebraic relations than with the direct study of geometric figures. Somewhat in the manner of Plato, Descartes took delight in conceiving reality in the image of the human intellect. Pascal, even as an adolescent, was already concerned with safeguarding the reality of the data of experience and the concrete character of a geometry which would take full cognizance of its subject. This was his way of being faithful to the spirit of an Aristotle whom he scarcely knew. He safeguarded the integrality of human nature and the reality of the world of sense experience in the face of Descartes as Aristotle had done with Plato.

In this we see a striking illustration of a significant contrast recently established by Anton C. Pegis in his Introduction to the *Basic Writings of Saint Thomas Aquinas* (vol. I, p. xlii. Random House):

"Whatever errors they may have in common, it yet remains that Plato and Aristotle represent the two basically different approaches to reality that are philosophically possible. The great concern of Plato had been to give to knowledge a sure and firm foundation in reality. But as St. Thomas looked at Plato, what he saw was that Plato had succeeded, not in founding knowledge in reality, but in putting it there. From this point of view the Platonic error would consist in supposing that the intellect's picture of reality *was* reality; and to St. Thomas this meant, at once, the destruction of reality and the permanent dislocation of the human intellect in the presence of reality. The great virtue of Aristotle as a philosopher (granting his errors) was that he did not allow the human intellect to impose itself upon the world. In this fact lay the strength and significance of his anti-Platonism. The Aristotelian man has always lived in a genuine world of things; the Platonic man has always been, as a philosopher, the victim of his own intellect. So, at least, St. Thomas leads us to think."

It is more important to grasp a similar divergence between the outlook of Descartes and that of Pascal than to speculate as to whether it was Descartes who suggested to Pascal the idea of resolving the problem of the vacuum experimentally. We should also agree that Descartes was much more given to experiment than is generally admitted. Nevertheless the paths of Descartes and Pascal diverge from their point of departure.

Pascal Modern Without Being a Modernist

Behind this divergence we shall recognize fundamentally in Descartes a mind which has proclaimed its independence, and in Pascal a reverent mind which will find its freedom in careful obedience to jurisdiction and competence.

That is why Pascal goes infinitely beyond Descartes. Descartes wrote a *Discourse on method* and embarked upon a system. From the very outset Pascal renounced all system and lived with a method. Descartes's disciples soon renounced his reservations as to the laws and customs of his country which constituted an *hors d'œuvre* in his system. The fact is that he himself qualified them as provisional after having borrowed them from Montaigne, who appreciated their convenience. In the manner of Condillac these same disciples of Descartes were led to multiply the

Treatises on Systems for the very simple reason that their point of view condemned them to live from system to system. Unto our day Pascal remains a solitary figure in the modern world in which he has managed to live without being of it. Pascal was modern without being a modernist. That is why we ever return to him as one returns to that which is normal — after a fever.

An Essential Distinction

Faithful to the spirit of Aristotle even though he denounces the letter of Aristotle, Pascal gets the better of the Aristotelianizing Father Noël just as he gets the better of Descartes, who denounces Aristotle. Often a position in the middle of the road conjures up apparent contradictions. While we "pity the blindness of those who offer only authority as their proof in matters of physics, instead of setting forth proofs based on reasoning or experimentation," we must now be filled "with horror at the malice of others who, in theology, resort solely to reasoning instead of to the authority of the Scriptures and the [Church] Fathers." Such is the intolerable confusion of jurisdiction which the *Fragment of a preface to the treatise on the vacuum* exposes. The denunciation of innovations in matters of practical morals, and then of theology, such as we shall find on every page of the *Provincial Letters*, thus proceeds from the taking of a fundamental position.

This fundamental position, now clearly formulated by Pascal, is the necessity of tracing a line of demarcation between purely scientific matters pertaining to reason and experiment on the one hand, and the realities of religion on the other hand — realities which in the last analysis are found to be a question of authority.

What Is Its Present-Day Value?

What is the present-day value of this Pascalian distinction? In our opinion the fact that the line of demarcation suggested by him should be shifted today does not at all affect its validity. The domain which he would have considered as pertaining to theology has been invaded, above all since the beginning of the nineteenth century, by such disciplines as exegesis, comparative linguistics, archaeology, mythology, comparative religion, sociology, psychology, pathology, psychoanalysis, and even by the biochemistry of glands. What has happened, however, in the case of Catholic modernism and of Protestant liberalism shows well enough that Pascal's reservations on the subject of competent authority in matters of religion remain the order of the day.

It is noteworthy that Kierkegaard, the Danish Pascal, was led to draw a dividing line similar to that drawn in the *Fragment of a preface to the treatise on the vacuum*. Kierkegaard distinguishes between scientific matter, which naturally becomes an object of acquisition to which the personal life of the teacher is accidental, and ethicoreligious matter, Christian realities wherein commitment is the essential thing. Such an analogy in the formulation of a particular problem draws our attention to a deeper analogy between Pascal and Kierkegaard which will soon come to light in this introduction. But we now revert to the question of the vacuum.

Pascal's Versatility

An excellent popularization of this question is presented in the *Letter from Pascal to Perier* (*Text* 5). This letter is of particular interest because it contains the instructions for the celebrated experiment of Puy de Dôme which was to clarify the problem, lead to the invention of the barometer and of all its applications, and to allow the definitive redaction of a whole section of physical science.

The *Letter from Pascal to Le Pailleur* (*Text* 7) about Father Noël takes up the whole question again from the point of view of the scholar. Compared with the preceding letter, it gives evidence of Pascal's versatility. We admire the perfect courtesy of the gentleman of culture, as well as the compellingly logical reasoning, the thorough demonstration, and the lucid exposition.

The same qualities lend a classical purity to the *Letters to Fermat* on the question of probability and the rule of points (*Texts* 14, 15, and 16), to the fragments on *The mind of the geometrician* (*Text* 38), and *The art of persuasion* (*Text* 39). We shall have occasion to revert to these important texts which follow from six to ten years after the epoch we are now considering.

Misunderstanding with the Jansenists

It will be recalled that, after the middle of the year 1647, Blaise had left Rouen to establish himself at Paris with his young sister Jacqueline. On September 23 and 24, he had had visits from Descartes. Jacqueline and Blaise had taken advantage of their sojourn in Paris to establish personal contacts with the Jansenists, whom they had admired ever since the "Jansenist quickening" (cf. Emile Cailliet, *op. cit.*, pp. 53 ff.). In the case of Jacqueline, her experience had been particularly happy. Her admiration for Monsieur Singlin had clarified her desire to become a nun. Since Monsieur Singlin was in charge of the convent of Port Royal she, like the genuine Pascal that she was, had concluded that one could "be a nun *reasonably* in such a place as that." The experience of Blaise had been less fortunate and the *Fragment of a letter to Madame Perier* (*Text* 6) about his visits to Monsieur Rebours (January 26, 1648) explains to us the genesis of a long misunderstanding between Pascal and Port Royal. For a time Blaise and Jacqueline pursued their religious meditations along the same course and shared their readings and their experiences with their older sister. Their letter on this subject (*Text* 8) indicates, however, that there is a misunderstanding: "We have begun several times to write to you, but I have been prevented by the attitude [of Monsieur de Rebours] and by the discourses or, if you like, by the rebuffs of which you know."

A Cloud Over the Home

Etienne Pascal, the father, who had returned from Rouen to Paris after having resigned from his post, had dreamed of a peaceful retreat with Blaise and Jacqueline. When the announcement of the latter's decision to enter the convent upset this happy project, a misunderstanding had resulted which a mutual frank explanation had removed. But now the older sister, in a letter to her father, had unintentionally brought up the difficulties anew. Blaise and Jacqueline explain matters to her in a letter dated November 5, 1648 (*Text* 9).

Death of Pascal's Father

The crisis which precedes the "worldly period" of Pascal was precipitated by the death of his father and the settlement of his complicated estate, by the growing financial needs of Blaise, and the receiving of Jacqueline into Port Royal. The latter step normally entailed providing a dowry. The death of his beloved father, tutor, adviser, and constant friend, upset Blaise and led him to interpret the blow, which struck him and his sister, in the light of Scripture and of his own conscience, that is to say, in the light of his whole religious and moral experience. The *Letter from Pascal to Monsieur and Madame Perier* (October 17, 1651) *on the death of his father* (*Text* 10) is a classic in its very formality and in its rare dignity.

God and Mammon

After having lost his father, he had to "lose" his particularly beloved sister Jacqueline when, having entered the convent of Port Royal, she took her final vows and became Sister Euphemia. The touching fragment of the *Letter from Pascal to Perier* (*Text* 12) reveals the profound distress of its author. The fact that the letter is incomplete, that it was written by a Pascal who had become "worldly" and concerned with money to the point of having contested Jacqueline's dowry, all this reveals a Pascal henceforth at variance with himself. Although the compensations he found in the world were considerable, nevertheless he soon became aware of their vanity. Now he is engaged in repeating in the spiritual world the equivalent of the experiment of the vacuum which he had made in the physical world. These remarks made in the light of what we know about the subsequent experience of Pascal must not cause us to lose sight of the fecundity of his "worldly period."

The Three Orders of Reality

The proud *Letter to Queen Christine of Sweden* (*Text* 11), when he sent her the calculating machine, again reveals the continuity of Pascal's thinking; he continues to live with an idea in the back of his mind. This idea is that of the three orders which is to be formulated subsequently in the text which we find in fragment 793 of the *Pensées:*

"All bodies together, and all minds together, and all their productions, are not equal in value to the least feeling of love. This is of an order infinitely more exalted.
"From all bodies together one cannot draw forth one tiny thought; that is impossible, and of another order. From all bodies and minds one cannot draw forth a feeling of true love; that is impossible and of another order, supernatural."

It has already been shown (Emile Cailliet, *op. cit.*, especially pp. 174–179) that the maturation of the idea of the three orders reflects the entire evolution of Pascal. This idea goes back to a principle taught him in his childhood by his father. Etienne had taught Blaise that by its very nature an object of faith could not be an object of reason, still less could it be subordinated to the dictates of reason. On the other hand, he maintained that faith had no competence whatever in the field of natural phenomena. This principle, it will be recalled, dominated the controversy with Father Noël and the *Fragment of a preface to the treatise on the vacuum* (*Texts* 3 and 4). It is this that we find again in the *Letter to Queen Christine of Sweden* (*Text* 11). Superiority in the order of politics is but an image of intellectual superiority, that is to say, in the order of minds.

Pascal Among the Great of This World

Without doubt Pascal's worldly speculation is not disinterested. At any rate there is one thing that we are certain of finding in the world; that is, causes for spite. Henceforth, Pascal has to learn in the hard school of experience that "we distinguish men by external appearances rather than by inward qualities. Which of us two shall have precedence? Who will give place to the other? The least clever? But I am as clever as he is. We should have to fight over this. He has four lackeys, and I have only one. This can be seen; we have only to count. It falls to me to yield, and I am a fool if I contest the matter." And again: "Men would not have me honor a man clothed in brocade, and followed by seven or eight lackeys! Why! He will have me thrashed if I do not salute him. This costume, 'tis a force" (*Pensées*, frs. 319, 315).

The reader may compare with these fragments the second of the *Three discourses on the station of noblemen* (*Text* 40). There he will find, considered at a later date with great calmness and maturity of mind, this same consciousness of problems posed by birth and by merit in the framework of reminiscences of vexations undergone earlier by a worldly Pascal: "It is not necessary that I esteem you because you are a duke; but it is necessary that I salute you. . . . But if you were a duke without being a gentleman, I should still do you justice; for in rendering you the outward homage which the order of men has attached to your birth, I should not be lacking in the inward contempt for you which the baseness of your spirit merited." At that epoch (1659?) Pascal's aim is to remedy the failings common to nobles.

In the year 1652, Pascal merely seeks compensations in the matter of greatness. If we may be permitted to use the expression, in the presence of Her Most Serene Highness, the queen of Sweden, he indulges in what we call "wishful thinking." In his own words, what has really impelled him to offer his "extraordinary" machine to Her Majesty is the union in her sacred person "of two things which fill me equally with admiration and respect, namely, sovereign authority and sound science. For I have a very special veneration for those who have attained the highest rank, whether in power or in knowledge. If I am not mistaken, these latter may be considered as sovereigns quite as well as the former."

Pascal Returns to Mathematics

The difficulty in following Pascal arises from the fact that he pursues the most diverse tasks and preoccupations at the same time. Any chronological consideration of his life and of his work becomes all the more complicated because of this. Already weary of the world, Pascal gives the final touches to the redaction of the *Treatises on the equilibrium of liquids and the weight of the mass of air* (1654?), and returns to mathematics. A letter from Huygens to Shooten, dated December 27, 1654, informs us that a list of treatises on arithmetic and geometry undertaken by Pascal at that time mentions the summation of numerical powers. At the hands of Pascal the formulation of this question will continue to gain in precision and in new insight. His *Potestatum numericarum summa* (*Text* 13) seems to be a sequel to a first sketch presented to the Paris Academy under the title *De numericarum potestatum ambitibus*, and to be in preparation for the *Treatise on the arithmetical triangle* (end of 1654?) where the form of reasoning known as *recurrence* or *Fermation* appears.

It is interesting to note that prior to his exchange of letters with Fermat at the end of 1654, Pascal was unaware of the latter's research on the subject ever since 1636, as well as the formulation of the problem by Sainte-Croix to which Fermat was a party. What we have in the *Summation of powers of numbers* is an absolutely original demonstration which is subsequently to culminate in the eleventh proposition of the *Treatise on numerical orders*, namely: "A number of any given order, when multiplied by the preceding root and divided by the exponent of its order, will have for its quotient the number of the next order which follows from that root." However, the reader who is not a specialist will appreciate all the more the *Summation of powers of numbers* (*Text* 13). There, in a complete piece of research, he will see a Pascal who is at grips with the complexity of data, and who is waiting until the final paragraph for a new vista on the problem of orders. Having shown that lower orders are of no value, and may therefore be disregarded, he finally brings out "the ever admirable relationship which nature, charmed with unity, establishes between things outwardly far apart." How true it is that the genius who is the bearer of an idea recognizes its manifestation in the most diverse fields!

Pascal is particularly indebted to Chevalier de Méré for having been led to concentrate his attention on the question of probability; he admitted in his *Letter to Fermat* of July 29, 1654 (*Text* 14) that "Monsieur le Chevalier de Méré ... is the one who proposed these questions to me." The initial problem is as follows: In eight trials a player at dice attempts to throw a one; now in the midst of the game he is deprived of one of the throws to which he is entitled. For example, let us suppose that the player has had three trials without succeeding and that he is deprived of his fourth trial; how should he be indemnified? Pascal and

Fermat differed on the manner of rating the fourth trial. From there they went on to the division of the stakes which the players must adopt if they separate without finishing the game. This time Pascal and Fermat differed on the question of method; in the three *Letters to Fermat* (*Texts* 14, 15, and 16) we follow the elegance of Pascal's method while we admire the vigor of his intellect.

The Mind of the Geometrician Distinguished from the Intuitive Mind

It is this same Chevalier de Méré, companion of his "worldly period," who had suggested to Pascal the existence of an intuitive mind as distinguished from the mind of the geometrician. Geometry proceeds from definitions given once and for all; it adheres to exact combining of very simple characters whose number is strictly limited. To succeed in it, one need merely be interested in it, omit nothing, and have an accurate mind. But just because geometricians are accustomed to clear-cut principles, which they manipulate after having gained a full view of them, they are likely to lose themselves in those things that do not permit of such treatment and are all the more difficult to see clearly and to enumerate. The thing that makes many a geometrician appear ridiculous is that in the midst of the complexity of life he does not see what is in front of him. And so it was that, during a trip to Poitou, Méré had made fun of Pascal's long chains of reasoning and had pitied him as being a geometrician who is nothing but a geometrician. Pascal was not slow to grasp the point at issue. He soon became instinctively aware that matters are felt rather than seen. Later on, he himself explained why it is so difficult to suggest them to those who do not perceive them: "These principles are so subtle and so numerous that a very delicate and very clear sense is needed to perceive them, and to judge rightly and justly when they are perceived. And it is difficult to do this when so often we are unable to demonstrate them *in proper order* as in mathematics, since the principles are not known to us in the same way, and since it would be an endless matter to understand" (*Pensées*, fr. 1, vol. XII, 11, 12). This is the context in which one must read the famous fragment 277 (vol. XIII, 201) which is often misconstrued: "The heart has its reason which reason does not know."

An Antinomy Resolved on a Higher Level

Although the Pascalian distinction between the mind of the geometrician and the intuitive mind has been clearly established, nevertheless, many people have lost sight of the manner in which Pascal himself resolved this antinomy, as he did so many others, on a higher level. On this score it is necessary to supplement the *Pensées* by the fragments which our collection presents under the titles *The mind of the geometrician* (*Text* 38) and *The art of persuasion* (*Text* 39); yet it should be noted carefully that these texts presented here in an extended consideration of Pascal's "worldly period" were not merely written several years later, but that they follow upon his remarkable religious experiences, beginning with the night of November 23, 1654 (cf. *Memorial, Text* 18). Let us repeat that in the case of Pascal more than of anyone else, with the possible exception of his master, Saint Augustine, the treatise must be read against the background of his life.

This relation to Saint Augustine is not fortuitous. In *Text* 38 we find a very remarkable meditation on the notion of time which calls to mind a similar one in the *Confessions* in chapter XV of Book XI (especially chapters XIII, XIV, XV, and XVI). For Pascal as for Saint Augustine — to whom we owe the formulation of a Christian philosophy of history — the notion of time is inseparable from the Biblical dogma of creation by God, who remains apart from the creation which he controls. This point is fundamental for the understanding of Pascal as well as for that of Saint Augustine, and, in our opinion, this point has not been sufficiently noted. If Pascal was modern while escaping modernism, he owes this to the God of the Bible, and not to the God of philosophers and scholars whose monotheism is at best but a metaphysical persuasion of the intellect. The Aramaic verse of Jer. 10:11 would sum up his position on this point: "The gods that have not made the heavens and the earth, these shall perish from the earth and from under the heavens." Pascal does not speculate on the existence of God; he proceeds from the *reality* of God, which is entirely different.

Our Most Elementary Principles Are Beyond Verification

Henceforth, Pascal notes that in the final analysis geometry is based on unverifiable propositions, and that we must be content to accept them as such. This is the case with our idea of time. We avail ourselves of these notions because they are convenient. Pascal is already doing for fundamental notions of geometry what our contemporary physicists have been led to do with fundamental scientific ideas in their origin and in their effects. Thus Max Planck admits that "the law of causality cannot be demonstrated any more than it can be logically refuted: it is neither correct nor incorrect; it is a heuristic principle; it points the way, and in my opinion it is the most valuable pointer that we possess in order to find a path through the confusion of events, and in order to know in what direction scientific investigation must proceed so that it shall reach useful results. The law of causality lays hold of the awakening soul of the child and compels it continually to ask why; it accompanies the scientist through the whole course of his life and continually places new problems before him." (*The Philosophy of Physics*, pp. 82, 83, W. W. Norton and Co., 1936.) The same applies to Pascal with regard to the notions of "space, time, motion, number, equality." Henceforth, the approach of the geometrician consists essentially in "the art of demonstrating those truths that have already been discovered, and of clarifying them in such a manner that their proof is incontrovertible" (*Text* 38). It is instructive to note that this is also the approach of the theologian according to Saint Thomas (*Summa contra gentiles*, 1, 9). Any proof of the existence of God presupposes faith in God.

The Mind of the Geometrician Is Inseparable from the Intuitive Mind

Nevertheless, Pascal the geometrician is careful not to pass from one extreme to the other. According to the same *Text* 38 on *The mind of the geometrician*, "it is a natural weakness of man to believe that he possesses truth directly. For that reason he is always ready to deny anything which is incomprehensible to him. Yet, in fact, by nature he knows delusions only, and he ought to regard as genuine only the opposite of those things that seem to him to be false. That is why, whenever a proposition is inconceivable, we should suspend judgment and not deny it because of that." The fact is that man begins to know only inasmuch as he begins to know his own limitations. "Submission is the use of reason; this is what constitutes genuine Christianity," declares fragment 269 of the *Pensées*. The fact that geometry does not give us the last word about anything does not mean that it serves no end. After the manner of causality, according to Max Planck, it is an "orderly procedure, the most perfect known to men." Its principles are felt and not demonstrated. This does not prevent "the knowledge of first principles such as space, time, movement, and numbers from being as sound as any of those which our reasoning provides. And it is on such knowledge which comes from the heart and from instinct that reason must lean and on which it must base its whole argument. (The heart feels that there are three dimensions in space, and that numbers are infinite; reason then demonstrates that there are no two squares of numbers, one of which is double the other. Principles are felt, propositions are concluded; and all this with certainty although in different ways.)" (*Pensées*, fr. 282.) Once more the analogy between geometry and theology is manifest, since, according to fragment 278 of the *Pensées*, "the heart, and not reason, senses God." It is in this sense that Pascalian geometry becomes Christian at the higher level where the mind of the geometrician appeals the case to the intuitive mind, because in the latter it has found its very soul.

Confirmation by the Art of Persuasion

Henceforth, *The art of persuasion* (*Text* 39) will give the reader a counterproof of *The mind of the geometrician* (*Text* 38), but the limitations of this introduction do not permit us to give it in detail. He will have to be content with a "direction of methodically perfect proofs" after resigning himself to accept certain "principles which, once agreed to, remain fixed and . . . never contradicted." But Pascal forthwith admits that "there are few principles of this kind, and, apart from geometry, which considers only very simple figures, there is scarcely a truth upon which we always agree, and there are even fewer objects of pleasure toward which we do not constantly change." The essential thing about an art of persuasion would be an art of pleasing, but such an art is beyond reasoning because men are governed largely by their caprices. Pascal must also omit consideration of divine truths, "for they have their place infinitely above nature. God alone can place them in the soul and do this in a manner pleasing to Him. I know that He has wished them to enter the mind from the heart and not into the heart from the mind." In other words, they constitute an Act of God. Through human infirmity such an Act of God had already been misunderstood of old, as can be seen in the rejoinder of the Jews to Moses: "Tell us agreeable things and we shall listen to you." Thus the Act of God collides with the same obstacle as the art of persuasion. The mind of the geometrician loses its prerogatives at the point where the intuitive mind becomes infirm in a perverted creation.

Pascal's Final Word as a Geometrician

The geometrician in Pascal then speaks his final word in the *Letter to Fermat*, dated August 10, 1660 (*Text* 41): "For to speak to you frankly about geometry, I consider it to be the highest exercise of the mind, but at the same time I know it to be so unprofitable that I make little distinction between a man who is merely a geometrician and a skillful artisan. Therefore I call it the most beautiful trade in all the world, but after all it is only a trade, and I have often said that it is good to test but not to employ our capacities."

On the Heights

It becomes clear that the evolution of Pascal the geometrician on the morrow of his "worldly period" reflects his religious concern on the morrow of the *Memorial*. It is without doubt the history of a "liberator of intelligence," if we were to repeat part of a beautiful designation of Paul Desjardin's (*Rev. hebd.*, 1923, 230), yet it would be more exact to say that it is the history of a liberated man who "was not disobedient unto the heavenly vision" (Acts 26:19).

The history of this liberation was the essential theme of *Pascal, Genius in the Light of Scripture;* it is a history that would have to be repeated here at length in its laborious complexity if one were to lay claim to any accuracy. Hence we take the liberty of referring the reader to this volume. And so two undated texts, the *Letter to Madame Perier (Text* 17) and *On the conversion of the sinner (Text* 19), will gain by being read in the context of chapter VI, "Pascal's hour of agony"; moreover the *Memorial (Text* 18) is discussed at length in chapter VII, "Fire in the night." The *Conversation with Monsieur de Saci on Epictetus and Montaigne (Text* 20) and the *Mystery of Jesus (Text* 21) are likewise integrated in the context of Pascal's experience in chapter IX, "The new vista." The memorable mystic night of November 23, 1654, and the subsequent retreat to Port Royal were not destined to end in serenity. Pascal was not to enjoy that rest which was promised to the people of God in *The Epistle to the Hebrews*. "Not peace, but a sword" is the title of chapter X. Called upon for help by his Jansenist friends, Pascal entered the lists.

In our present collection of GREAT SHORTER WORKS OF PASCAL the change of climate is clearly noticeable when the elevated *Mystery of Jesus (Text* 21) is followed by the matter-of-fact *Short exposition of the problem of grace (Text* 22). We have placed it here because it seems to correspond well to the period of initiation of the "Provincial" who was to write the famous *Letters*.

A Committed Christian

Let us not lose sight of the fact that the publication of the *Provincial Letters* (1656–1657) falls between *Text* 22 and the *Letter from a lawyer in Parliament to one of his friends concerning the inquisition which they want to establish in France on the occasion of a new Bull of Pope Alexander VII*, dated June 1, 1657 (*Text* 34). This means that the present collection is an important supplement to the *Provincial Letters* at a time when the hostilities, interrupted after the partial redaction of a nineteenth *Provincial* (April-May, 1657?), were resumed under cover of the intervention of Churchmen. Stirred by the display of Jesuit abuse which had been exposed by Pascal and by the resounding triumph of the anonymous *Apology for the Casuists*, the clergy of France swung into action. Assembled in synod on January 7, 1658, the priests of Paris intervened at the same time before Parliament, the faculty of theology and the vicars-general. In addition, their commission submitted to the synod of February 4 a *Factum* which was found to have come from the pen of Pascal (*Text* 36). Here he encouraged resistance to the Bull of Alexander VII, *Ad Sanctam*, whose publication had been ordered by the Assembly of the Clergy on March 14, 1657. As for the prophetic *Suggested pronouncement against the Apology for the Casuists* (*Text* 37), it has been found among Pascal's papers in his own handwriting. The same applies to other analogous writings. We have chosen these two because they fully reveal Pascal's "true eloquence" which scorns eloquence because it was nourished on the substance of the Bible. Like the *Provincial Letters*, these masterpieces truly reveal Pascal as the last prophet of Israel.

Pascal's holy indignation in the course of these years of controversy, and the irony with which he lashes his adversaries, certainly inspired the eloquence of Bossuet and also the comedy of Molière. To be sure, the burlesque irony of such attacks upon Churchmen came as a shock to many a Christian, and first of all to Pascal himself. There is but little doubt that it took nothing less than the miracle of the Holy Thorn to confirm Pascal in the necessity and the relevance of his intervention. Numerous also are the readers of the *Provincial Letters* who think of their author as a fanatic who has lost contact with prayer and meditation.

The Provincial Letters Illumined by the Letters of Spiritual Guidance

Once more chronology comes to our aid at this point in the concordance it reveals between the *Provincial Letters* and the *Letters to Monsieur and Mlle de Rouannez* (*Texts* 23-31). The Duke of Rouannez had been led to God by Pascal. Subsequently he had given up his government of Poitou and marriage with a rich heiress, Mademoiselle de Mesme. The duke's sister herself had refused the hand of the Marquis d'Alluyre, and was to enter the convent of Port Royal in 1657 in spite of the violent objections of her family. Her trials after Pascal's death need not detain us here any more than the suppositions, gratuitous for the most part, with which Chamaillard has salaciously regaled the readers of his *Pascal mondain et amoureux* (1923).

What interests us here is that Pascal had become the spiritual director of the brother and sister. His letters, it should be carefully noted, are always addressed to Monsieur *and* Mlle de Rouannez. They are written with noble Christian dignity, and are richly nurtured by Scripture. Now chronology establishes the fact that these letters of spiritual guidance were written in the heat of the battle. For example, at the beginning of the twelfth *Provincial Letter* Pascal had taken from the replies of his Jesuit adversaries the appellations "impious," "buffoon," "ignoramus," "bad joker," "impostor," "slanderer," "cheat," "heretic," "disguised Calvinist," "disciple of Du Moulin," and "possessed by a legion of devils" — "And anything you want," he added. Soon, however, the amused tone of the opening paragraph was tinged with bitterness. An examination of the *Impostures* of the Jesuits had given way to a free-for-all that was only too painful for a Christian to follow. Now this twelfth *Provincial Letter* was of September 9, 1656; that is to say, it is contemporaneous with the first letters to Monsieur and Mlle de Rouannez. Since the second one of these (*Text* 24) is of September 24, and the first (*Text* 23) bears merely the word "September," it is more than probable that it was written at the same time as the *Provincial Letter* in question. In other words, the man who is here at grips with the Jesuits in the midst of the worst abuse is the same man who wrote, "A little while ago I was reading the thirteenth chapter of Saint Mark and so I shall tell you what I found there." And a consideration of what he found in his Bible, according to this and the following letters, shows us not only a man who is calm at the center of his being because he is in close contact with his God, but the author, as well, of the *Provincial Letters*, asking of the Scriptures the profound meaning of this mystery of iniquity with which he is at grips. Similarly the reader will bear in mind that the second *Letter to Monsieur and Mlle de Rouannez* (*Text* 24) is dated September 24, 1656; that is to say, it was written by the Pascal who had just finished writing the terrible thirteenth *Provincial Letter* on homicide. And so the correlation continues up to the last two *Letters to Monsieur and Mlle de Rouannez* (*Texts* 30 and 31) which are inserted chronologically between the sixteenth and seventeenth *Provincial Letters*. However, the interest aroused by these personal letters is far more important than the fact that they shed new light on the *Provincial Letters*. The intrinsic value of their spiritual guidance is all the more precious because Pascal was one of the first to inaugurate the great tradition of lay Christians.

This same tradition is equally in evidence in the *Letter from Pascal to a friend in Clermont* (*Text* 32), already mentioned in this introduction apropos of Perier. Brunschvicg inserted it in volume ten of the works of Blaise Pascal at a date presumed to be 1660. Now Domat was in Paris at the end of 1661, and Perier seems to have sojourned there in November, 1661. Hence we concur with a suggestion made by Brunschvicg himself (vol. X, p. 151, n. 1) who states that this letter alludes to the difficulties which Perier had in 1657 with some Sulpicians of the Seminary of Clermont. As regards Pascal's wrath, which this letter echoes, it probably was this wrath which inspired the very lively notes in the margin of the nineteenth *Provincial*.

Where We Re-encounter Kierkegaard, the Danish Pascal

Though it too is undated, the short treatise entitled *Comparison of the Christians of the earliest times with those of today* (*Text* 33) seems to us to belong to the context which has just been considered. We have already had occasion to compare Kierkegaard, the Danish Pascal of the first half of the nineteenth century, with Pascal. Those who have read Walter Lowrie's translation of Kierkegaard's *Attack upon Christendom* (Princeton University Press, 1944), studded with fragments chosen from the *Journals*, will find there ample matter for comparison and reflection. Pascal's theme and that of Kierkegaard are the same, that is to say, the Christianity of the New Testament no longer exists. But, in addition, one parallel after another can be pointed out. Yet we must limit ourselves here to a few indications in expectation of the book which must some day be written on "Pascal and Kierkegaard."

Both of these men expose the growing compromise between the Church and the world. With this widening of the "narrow path," Christianity is made easy, and therefore becomes meaningless.

At the time of the birth of the Church, writes Pascal, "people entered the Church only after long toil and long desire."

"Today people find themselves there without any trouble, without any care, and without toil."

"People were admitted to the Church only after a rigid examination."

"People are received into it now before being ready to be examined," etc.

The *Instant No. 2* of Kierkegaard has an article "We are all Christians" (p. 107) which asserts that "we are Christians to such a degree that, if among us there lived a Free-thinker who in the strongest terms declared that the whole of Christianity is a lie, *idem* in the strongest terms that he was not a Christian — there is no help for him, he is a Christian."

The *Instant No. 4* takes up the same assertion under a longer title where it is summed up as follows: "In 'Christendom' all are Christians; when all are Christians, the New Testament *eo ipso* does not exist; yea, it is impossible" (p. 149).

The *Instant No. 5* is even more emphatic in two articles entitled respectively "We are all Christians — without having so much as a suspicion what Christianity is" (pp. 157, 158), and "When all are Christians, Christianity *eo ipso* does not exist" (pp. 166, 167), etc.

If we ask how we have come to such a pass and what are the sad results of such an anomaly, Pascal and Kierkegaard again are in accord. Both present the Church as having ceased to be the salt of the earth, as having become a vague mass of amorphous non-Christians, as having lost what once made it attractive, namely, the respect of the world in which it is spread out. This situation must be all the more serious for Pascal and Kierkegaard, since both of them are familiar with the Biblical point of view, according to which the Gentiles are drawn to the Church as to a center of attraction. According to I Peter 2:9, 10, the Church has been called out of darkness *into* a marvelous light: those who in time past *were* not a people, *are* now the people of God.

At the Sources of Existentialism

Like Pascal, Kierkegaard is fundamentally interested in the concrete implications of life for the individual. As David F. Swenson says so excellently in his penetrating *Something about Kierkegaard* (Augsburg Publishing House, 1941), "the problem of the existential thinker is namely to understand himself as an existing human being, essentially like all other human beings in status and task. His thought is thus a concrete thought, in that it has essential reference to the thinker and deals with a particular something which the thinker seeks to apprehend" (pp. 72, 73). This is why Kierkegaard turned from Hegel just as Pascal turned from Descartes. Although Kierkegaard's readings brought his existentialism more closely akin to Socrates, the fundamental truth is that this existentialism is already complete in Pascal, because he had proceeded from Biblical realism in his concern for the individual soul of flesh and blood. If the Christians of today are no longer those of the earliest times, if the Christianity of the New Testament no longer exists, it is because this fundamental consideration has been lost sight of. Now this is what constitutes the *raison d'être* of the Gospel; and this is what constitutes the aim of Christ's sacrifice.

Appeasement Exposed

Because they have seen these vital truths, albeit from different angles, both Pascal and Kierkegaard have a horror of the form of compromise which we have come to denounce under the name of appeasement. Without pursuing our parallel between Pascal and Kierkegaard any farther in this introduction, we must hasten to make a reservation: Pascal is tolerant. His *Letter to Madame de Sablé* (*Text* 42) on Menjot, a Protestant, is particularly precious to those who are alert to the veritable terror with which heresy filled him: "Although I already esteemed him highly because of the things my sister said of him, I am unable to express to you with what joy I received the favor which he wished to do me. One need merely read his letter to see how much wit and judgment he has." No principle is at stake here, and no religious conviction. The only thing involved is Christian charity, the source of all genuine tolerance. This letter is kindred in spirit to the conclusion of *A short exposition of the problem of grace* (*Text* 22), where he shows his Church extending her arms to separated brothers to form a happy union. But peace is never bought by Pascal at the price of compromise. He has an epithet for that kind of peace: he calls it a false peace. There is a true peace and a false peace, just as there is a true charity and a false charity. According to Pascal, false charity is one that leaves the wicked at peace in their vices, while true charity is the one that troubles such wretched tranquillity. For Pascal, one of the chief verities of the Christian religion is that there are moments when it becomes necessary to disturb this possession of error which the wicked call peace. A fragment of the *Pensées* declares, "It is false piety to preserve peace at the expense of truth" (fr. 930, *Œuvres*, vol. XIV, 371).

When in 1661 the Church of Rome required the signature of the monastic orders to a formulary condemning Jansen, Jacqueline Pascal — now Sister Euphemia — made her memorable declaration: "Since the bishops have the courage of maidens, maidens should have the courage of bishops. It is not our task to defend the truth; it is ours to die for the truth and rather to suffer everything than to abandon it." The voice of a Pascal, indeed! To Sister Angélique of Saint John, Jacqueline confesses her excessive grief upon signing under coercion. With death gripping her heart, she nevertheless had to sign, but only a little later, on October 6, 1661, she died. At the news of her death, which he received without flinching, Pascal remarked simply, "God give us grace to die as well as that." He knew that his cross was awaiting him too. With the exception of Domat, the Duke de Rouannez, and his own nephew, Etienne Perier, his Jansenist friends were ready to compromise in the wake of a meeting called at Pascal's home. Pascal made a last appeal. Heads were lowered. Everything grew black before his eyes. He fainted. When he regained consciousness he explained painfully to his older sister, Madame Perier:

"When I saw all those very persons waver and succumb who should have been the defenders of the truth and to whom God had made the truth known, I confess that I was so overcome with grief that I could not endure it, and so I collapsed."

It is against such a background that we must read the *Writing by Pascal on the signature of the formulary* (*Text* 43). It is by no means an exaggeration to say that Pascal wrote it with his blood. From every viewpoint it is one of the writings that does the highest honor to a redeemed race.

Pascal in Prayer

The *Mystery of Jesus*, as, by the same token, the *Prayer by Pascal asking God to use illnesses to a good end* (*Text* 44), needs no commentary. Nourished by the very marrow of the Bible, and expressing a faith that has reached its full maturity, it belongs to Pascal's last years. On this point we are in accord with Bishop, Brunschivcg, and Pascal's older sister, Madame Perier herself. Pascal had been sick all his life, and this fact must never be lost sight of by anyone who approaches him. The end of his life was of a saintliness that has drawn cries of admiration from even those witnesses who were farthest removed from the Christian religion. It is this saintliness that speaks so strongly in the *Prayer by Pascal;* the faith expressed here is that of a Saint Paul or of a Saint Augustine. Hence across the ages it will inspire Christians who in their turn will ask God to use illnesses to a good end.

Looking Beyond This Wilderness

Pascal's will, August 3, 1662 (*Text* 45), in its legalistic terms, gives a sober but faithful epitome of the man who fought the good fight and is now ready to enter into the joy of his Lord.

Blaise Pascal died August 19, 1662.

1. LETTER FROM PASCAL TO MADEMOISELLE PERIER, COUNSELOR AT CLERMONT

Rouen, Saturday, the last of January, 1643.

My dear sister:

I do not doubt that you have been uneasy because of the long time in which you have received no news from these quarters. But I believe you well suspected that the journey of the assessors was the cause of it, as it actually was. Otherwise I should not have failed to write to you oftener. I must tell you that since the Commissioners were at Gisors, my Father had me take a trip to Paris where I found a letter which you had written to me, in which you let me know that you are surprised because I reproach you for not writing often enough, and in which you say that you are writing to Rouen once every week. If that is the case, it is certain that your letters are being lost, for I do not receive one every three weeks. On my return to Rouen I found a letter from Monsieur Perier who reports that you are sick. He does not state whether your illness is dangerous, nor whether you are better; since then, a regular courier has passed by without our receiving a letter, so that we are in a state of uneasiness from which I am requesting you to free us as soon as possible. But I believe the request I am making here will be needless, for before you receive this letter I hope we shall have had letters from you or from Monsieur Perier. The division is taking place, thank God! If I knew anything new, I should let you know. I am,

    My dear sister,

Your very humble and very affectionate servant and brother

                                              PASCAL

Here is a postscript in the handwriting of Etienne Pascal, the father:
My good daughter will excuse me if I do not write to her as I should like to, if I had time. For I have never been in one sixth of the difficulties

in which I am at present. I could not be in greater difficulties without having too many; for four months I have not gone to bed six times before two o'clock in the morning.

I recently began a bantering letter to you on the subject of your last letter about the marriage of Monsieur Desjeux, but I have never had time to finish it. As regards news, the daughter of Monsieur de Paris, auditor, bookkeeper, married to Monsieur de Neufville, likewise auditor, died, as did also the daughter of Belair who was married to little Lambert. Your little son slept here last night. Thanks to God, he is very well. I am ever,

  Your good and excellent friend

              PASCAL

2. DEDICATORY LETTER TO THE CHANCELLOR ON THE SUBJECT OF THE MACHINE RECENTLY INVENTED BY B[LAISE] P[ASCAL] ESQUIRE, TO PERFORM ALL SORTS OF OPERATIONS IN ARITHMETIC BY A REGULATED MOTION WITHOUT A PEN OR COUNTERS WITH NECESSARY DIRECTIONS FOR USE BY THOSE WHO WILL BE CURIOUS TO SEE THE AFORESAID MACHINE AND TO USE IT

1645

To
His Lordship
the
Chancellor

Sir:

If the public derives any benefit from the invention which I have made to perform all sorts of operations in arithmetic by a method which is as new as it is convenient, it will be under greater obligation to Your Highness than to my slight efforts, since I can never boast of having conceived it and since it owes its birth entirely to your honored commands. The length and the difficulties of the ordinary means in use led me to think about some shorter and easier aid to give me relief in the lengthy calculations in which I have been engaged for some years in several matters that are dependent on the employment with which you have been pleased to honor my father in the service of His Majesty in

Upper Normandy. In this search I used all the knowledge which my bent and the work in my early studies have led me to acquire in mathematics. After profound meditation I recognized that it was not impossible to find this aid. The knowledge of geometry, of physics, and of mechanics furnished me with the plan, and assured me that its use would be infallible if some artisan could make the instrument whose model I had conceived. But it was at this point that I encountered obstacles as great as those that I wanted to avoid and for which I was seeking a remedy. Since I lacked the skill to manipulate metal and a hammer as I do pen and compass, and since the artisans had more knowledge and practice in their art than in the sciences on which it is based, I saw myself reduced to giving up my whole enterprise, which brought only a great deal of weariness without any degree of success. But, Sir, Your Highness kept up my courage, which was waning, and did me the favor of speaking of the simple draft which my friends had presented to you in terms which led me to see it quite differently from what it had previously appeared to me. As a consequence, with the new strength which your praises gave me, I made new efforts, and, giving up all other activities, I no longer thought of anything but the construction of this little machine which I have ventured, Sir, to present to you, after having put it in condition to perform by itself, and without any mental effort, the calculations of all phases of arithmetic, as I had intended. It is then to you, Sir, that I owe this little attempt, since you are the one who led me to make it; it is, moreover from you, too, that I am hoping for its honorable protection. Unknown inventions always have more censors than approvers. Those who have made them are blamed because they are not fully understood, and because of unjust prejudice, the imagined difficulty of extraordinary things causes people to charge them with being impossible. They do this instead of considering them so as to be able to appreciate them; the result is that they subsequently reject them as inapplicable. Moreover, Sir, I expect, indeed, that among so many scholars who have penetrated into the ultimate secrets of mathematics there may be some who will at first consider my deed to be bold, because, young and weak as I am, I have ventured upon a new path in a field bristling with thorns, and without having a guide to break a trail for me. But let them accuse me and even condemn me if they can prove that I have not fulfilled exactly what I had promised. The only favor I ask of them is that they examine what I have done, and not the favor' of approving it without knowing it. Moreover, Sir, I may say to Your Highness that I already have the satisfaction of seeing my little work authorized with the approbation of some of the leaders in this veritable science which, by quite special preference, has the advantage of teaching only what it demonstrates; in addition, this science has the honor of their esteem and of their recommendation. And I may add that even the one man among them, whom the others admire daily and whose findings they accept, has not considered it beneath him to take the trouble, in the midst of his great duties, to teach both its construction and its use to those who have some desire to use it. These are, indeed, Sir, great rewards for the time I have devoted to it and for the expense to which I have gone in order to put the thing into the condition in which you find it at present. But permit me to flatter my vanity to the point of saying that they would not entirely satisfy me, if I had not received a much more important and delightful reward from Your Highness. In fact, Sir, when I reflect that this same tongue, which daily pronounces oracles on the throne of Justice, has deigned to praise the first attempt of a man of twenty years, that you have deemed it worthy of being the subject of your conversation more than once, and to see it placed in your cabinet among so many other rare and precious things with which it is filled, I am covered with glory, and I find no words to show my gratitude to Your Highness and my joy to everybody. In this impotence into which the excess of your kindness has placed me, I shall content myself with revering it in silence. Since the whole family, whose name I bear, is as much interested as I am, through this kindness and through various other favors, in making good wishes for you and for your prosperity every day, we do this with all our heart. We do this so ardently and continually that no one can glory more in being attached to your service than we. Nor, Sir, can anyone glory any more than I in being your very humble and very obedient servant.

B. PASCAL

3. REPLY BY BLAISE PASCAL TO THE VERY REVEREND FATHER NOËL, RECTOR, OF THE SOCIETY OF PARIS IN PARIS

[October-November, 1647]

My very Reverend Father:

The honor you have done me by writing to me leads me to break with the intention I had of resolving the difficulties which I had reported in my epitome only in the complete treatise on which I am working.

But, in order that I may do it more systematically, allow me to quote to you a universal rule which applies to all specific subjects in which it is a matter of recognizing the truth. I do not doubt that you will agree with it, since it is generally accepted by all those who look at things without prejudice. Moreover, it provides the basis for the manner in which science is treated in the schools and which is employed by people who seek what is genuinely sound and what fills and satisfies the mind completely. This is that we should never pass a decisive judgment against or for a proposition without affirming or denying one of the following two conditions. Either, of itself, it seems so clearly and so distinctly evident to the senses or to the reason, as the case may be, that the mind has no grounds for doubting its certainty; this is what we call *principles* or *axioms*, such as, for example, *if equals are added to equals, the sums will be equal*. Or it is deduced by infallible and necessary conclusions from such principles or axioms on whose certainty depends the full certainty of the conclusions which are carefully drawn therefrom. An example of this kind is that *the three angles of a triangle are equal to two right angles;* this, though self-evident, is clearly demonstrable by infallible conclusions from such axioms. Everything based on one of these two conditions is certain and authentic, and all that is based on neither of them passes for doubtful and uncertain. We pass decisive judgment on things of the first kind, and leave the others in a state of indecision, so that, according to their merit, we call them now *vision*, now *caprice*, at times *fancy*, sometimes *idea* and at most a *fine thought;* and because we cannot affirm them without temerity we incline rather to the negative, though we are quick to revert to a positive assertion if an obvious demonstration leads us to regard it as true. And we reserve for the mysteries of faith, which the Holy Spirit himself has revealed, this submission of spirit which directs our belief to mysteries that are hidden from the senses and from reason.

Having posited this, I turn to your letter, in the first lines of which, in order to prove that this space is corporeal, you employ the following terms: *I say that it is a body, since it has the properties of a body, it transmits light with refraction and reflection, and it brings about retardation of the motion of another body.* Here I would remark that in your intent to prove that it is a body you regard two things as principles. The first is, that it transmits light with refractions and reflections; the second is, that it retards the motion of a body. Of these two principles the first has not seemed true to any of those who wanted to ascertain it; on the contrary, we have always observed that the ray which penetrates the glass and this space has no refraction other than that caused by the glass, and that consequently, if it is filled with any matter, the glass in no way breaks the ray, or its refraction is not perceptible. Thus since, beyond doubt, you have proved nothing to the contrary, I see that the meaning of your words is that the ray, reflected or broken by the glass, passes through this space. From this and from the fact that bodies fall in time, you wish to conclude that it is filled with a matter which conducts this light and causes this retardation.

But, my Reverend Father, if we relate this to the method of reasoning of which you have spoken, we shall find that first of all it would have had to remain in accord with the definition of an empty space, of light, and of motion, and to show by the nature of these things a manifest contradiction in the following propositions: "That light penetrates an empty space, and that a body moves in time." Your proof cannot be carried to this point. Moreover, since the nature of light is unknown to you and to me, and since not one of all those who have tried to define it has satisfied any of those who search for palpable truths, and since it will probably remain unknown to us forever, I foresee that this argument will remain for a long time without receiving the support it needs to carry conviction.

For consider, I beg of you, how it is possible to conclude infallibly that the nature of light is such that it can exist in a vacuum, when we are ignorant of the nature of light. If our knowledge of it were as great as our ignorance of it, we might perhaps know that it would exist in a vacuum with greater brilliance than in any other *medium*, since we see that its power increases as the medium in which it is becomes more rarefied, and as in some manner the medium approaches nothingness. And if we knew the nature of motion I have no doubt at all that it would perforce seem to take place in a vacuum in the same time as in the air whose lack of resistance is apparent in the falling of bodies of different weights.

That is why, in view of our slight knowledge of the nature of these things, if I take a similar liberty of regarding a thought as a principle, I may say with equal reason: Light exists in a vacuum, and motion takes place in a vacuum in time; or light apparently penetrates empty space, and motion apparently takes place in a vacuum in time; therefore it may in reality be empty.

So let us postpone this proof to a time when we shall have understanding of the nature of light. Until then I shall be unable to admit your principle, and it would be difficult for you to prove it. Let us not, I beg of you, draw infallible conclusions from the nature of a thing when we are ignorant of it. Otherwise I should fear that you would not be in agreement with me on the conditions necessary to make a demonstration perfect, and you would merely call that certain which we merely call doubtful.

In the course of your letter, as if you had invincibly established that this empty space is a body, you merely labor to determine what this body is. In order to decide in the affirmative what matter fills it, you begin with these words: "Let us presuppose that just as blood is a mingling of several liquids which compose it, so the air is composed of air and fire, and of the four elements which enter into the composition of all bodies in nature." You subsequently *presuppose* that this fire can be separated from air, and that being separated from it, it may penetrate the pores of glass; furthermore you *presuppose* that, when separated from it, it has a tendency to return to it, and even that it is constantly attracted to it; and you explain this discourse, which is intelligible enough in itself, by comparisons that you add to it.

But, Father, I believe that you give this out as a thought and not as a demonstration; and no matter what difficulty I have in accommodating the thought I have of this with the end of your letter, I believe if you gave me proofs, they would not have so slight a foundation. For at this time when so large a number of learned persons are trying so arduously to find what matter fills this space, and when this difficulty is today troubling so many minds, I should find it difficult to believe that in order to bring about so desirable a solution of so great and so honest a doubt you would postulate not merely the properties of a new matter, but indeed its very existence. As a result, whoever presupposes the contrary, will also have to draw a contrary conclusion. If this method of proving is accepted, it will no longer be difficult to solve the greatest difficulties. And the flux of the sea and the attraction of the magnet will become easy to comprehend if one is permitted to postulate matters and their properties to suit.

For all things of this nature, whose existence is not manifest to any of the senses, are as difficult to believe as they are easy to invent. Many persons, and among them the most learned of our times, have raised objections to me on this same matter before you (but as a mere assumption and not as an unvarying truth), and that is why I have mentioned it in my propositions. Others, in order to fill empty space with some matter, have imagined one with which they fill the entire universe, because it is a characteristic of the imagination to produce big things with as little effort as small things. Some people have pronounced it to be the same substance as the sky and the elements; others have made of it a different substance, according to their fancy, because they disposed of it as their creation.

But if anyone asks of them, as of you, that they show us this matter, they reply that it is invisible; if they are asked to make it give forth a sound, they say it cannot be heard, and so on for all the other senses. And they think they have done much, when they have found that others are incapable of showing that it does not exist, though they arrogate to themselves full authority for showing that it does exist.

But we find more grounds for denying its existence, because one cannot sanction belief in it for the mere reason that one cannot show that it does not exist.

For we cannot believe them all without making nature out to be a monster, and because reason does not incline toward the one any more than to the other — since it finds them equally foreign — reason rejects them all in order to keep from making a wrong choice.

I know you may say that you have not invented this matter all alone, and that numerous physicists had already worked on it, but as regards this matter, we have no basis in authority for it. When we quote the authors, we cite their demonstrations and not their names; we are concerned here only with matters of history, and so much so that if the authors whom you cite said that they have seen these small igneous bodies mingled with the air, I should have enough deference for their sincerity and their integrity to believe these to be genuine and I should believe the authors as historians of fact. But, since they merely say they think the air is composed of them, you will permit me to retain my first doubt.

Finally, Father, I beg you to consider that all these men together could not demonstrate that any body succeeds the one which leaves an apparently empty space, and that it is moreover impossible for all these men to show that when water rises in such a space some body has left it. According to your maxims would that not suffice to assure that that space is empty? Yet I simply say, in my opinion it is empty, and you may judge whether those who speak with so much restraint of a thing about which they have a right to speak with so much assurance, are able to pass decisive judgment on the existence of this igneous matter which is so dubious and so vaguely established.

After having supposed the existence of this matter with all the properties you have chosen to assign to it, you give an account of some of my experiments. It is not a very difficult thing to explain how an effect can be produced when one supposes the matter, the nature and the definition of its cause. Nevertheless, it is difficult for those who imagine them to defend themselves against vain complacency, and against a secret charm which they find in their invention, above all when they have adjusted them so well that from the fictions which they have supposed they necessarily conclude truths as already evident.

But I feel obliged to tell you something on this subject, namely, that whenever one sets up an hypothesis in order to find the cause of several known phenomena, this hypothesis may be of three kinds.

For sometimes we reach a manifestly absurd conclusion from the negation of an hypothesis, and then the hypothesis is true and constant; or we reach a manifestly absurd conclusion from its affirmation, and then the hypothesis is held to be false. And when we have been unable to draw an absurd conclusion either from its negation or its affirmation, the hypothesis remains dubious. Consequently, to have an hypothesis seem obvious, it is not sufficient that all phenomena follow from it; whereas if something follows from it which is contrary to a single one of these phenomena, that suffices to assure its falseness.

For example, if we find a hot stone without knowing the cause of its heat, would anyone be regarded as having found the true cause, if he reasoned in this fashion: Let us presuppose that this stone had been put into a big fire from which it had been withdrawn after a short time; then this stone must still be hot; now it is hot, and consequently it had been put into the fire. If that were to be true, fire would have to be the sole cause of its heat; but since the latter may come from the sun and from friction, the conclusion would have no validity. For just as the same cause may produce several different effects, so the same effect may be produced by several different causes. It is thus that, when we discourse humanly about motion and about the stability of the earth, all the phenomena of the movements and the retrogradation of the planets follow perfectly from the hypotheses of *Ptolemy*, of *Tycho*, of *Copernicus* and of many others that one may name, among all of which only a single one can be true. But who will dare to make such a great distinction, and who can, without courting error, uphold one at the expense of the others; just as in the analogy of the stone who can, without making himself ridiculous, stubbornly maintain that fire had caused its heat?

You see from this that even though all the phenomena of my experiments followed from your hypothesis, it would still be of the nature of other hypotheses; and even though it always remained within the bounds of probability, yet it would never rise to the level of a demonstration. But some day I hope to show you at greater length that things which are absolutely contrary to experiment follow from the affirmation of your hypothesis. I shall touch on one of them here briefly. If it is true, as you suppose, that this space is full of this more rarefied and igneous air and that it has the tendency you ascribe to it of returning into the air from which it has come, and that this outer air has the power to withdraw it *like a compressed sponge,* and that quicksilver is held in suspension by this mutual attraction, and that it causes quicksilver to rise even when we incline the tube; then it necessarily follows that when the apparently empty space is larger, a longer column of quicksilver must be held in suspension (contrary to what appears in experiments). For since all the parts of this interior and exterior air have the same quality of attraction, it is constant, according to all the rules of mechanics, that their quantity, when increased in the same measure as space, must necessarily increase their effect, just as a large sponge, when squeezed, draws more water than a small one.

Now if, to solve this difficulty, you make a second supposition and invent another property for the express purpose of saving yourself from this inconvenience, and if even that is not found to be satisfactory enough and it obliges you to imagine a third in order to save the other two without any proof and without establishing anything, then I should never have any reply for you other than what I have already told you, or rather I shall believe that I have already replied to it.

But, Father, when I say this and when somehow I anticipate these last suppositions, I myself am making a false supposition, for I am not doubting that if anything emanates from you, it will be supported by convincing reasons, since otherwise it would mean imitating those who merely want to show that they are not lacking in words.

Finally, Father, to bring my whole reply to a head, even if it were true that this space is a body (which I am very far from conceding to you) and if the air were filled with igneous spirits (which I do not consider very probable), and if they had the properties you attribute to them (this is a mere notion which is obvious neither to you nor to anybody), even then it would not follow from this that space is filled with it. And even if it were still true that by supposing space to be full of it (which in no way seems to be the case), we might deduct therefrom everything that appears in experiments, even then the most favorable judgment that one could pass on this opinion would be to rate it as one of several possibilities. But since we necessarily conclude things from it that are contrary to experiments, judge what place it must occupy among the three kinds of hypotheses of which we spoke a little while ago.

Toward the end of your letter, to define body you explain only some of its accidents, and even relative characteristics such as *high, low, right,* and *left,* which properly give a definition of space and which are not suited to a body, no matter how much space it occupies. For in conformity with your very authors, a body is defined as *that which is composed of matter and of form;* whereas what we call an *empty space* is a space having length, width and depth, motionless and capable of containing a body of like length and shape; that is what is called a *solid* in geometry, where we consider only abstract and incorporeal things. Consequently the essential difference to be found between an empty space and a body which has length, breadth and depth, is that the one is immovable and the other can be moved, that the one may receive into itself a body which penetrates its dimensions whereas the other cannot do this; for the maxim that penetration of dimensions is impossible extends only to the dimensions of two material bodies, otherwise it would not be universally accepted. From this we can see that there is as much difference between nothingness and an empty space, as there is between an empty space and a material body, and that thus an empty space is in the middle between matter and nothingness. That is why the maxim of Aristotle, of whom you speak, namely that *nonbeings are not different,* applies to real nothingness and not to any space.

I shall finish with your letter in which you say that no physicist could possibly have made the fourth of the objections which I raised, namely that a matter, which is unheard of and unknown to all the senses, fills this space. To this I must reply that I can assure you of the contrary, since this statement to the contrary is by one of the most famous physicists of our time, and you have been able to look into his writings; in the whole universe he establishes a universal matter which is imperceptible and unheard of, and similar in substance to the sky and the elements. Moreover, in examining yours, I have found it is so imperceptible, and that it has such unheard of properties, that is to say, properties which had never been ascribed to it, that I find it to be of the same nature.

The sentence which precedes your last civilities, defines light in these terms: *Light is a luminary motion of rays composed of lucid bodies, that is to say, luminous bodies.* Here I must say to you that it seems to me it would have been necessary first of all to define what *luminary* is and what a *lucid* or *luminous body* is, for up to that point I am unable to understand what light is. And since in definitions we never use the term to be *defined*, I should have difficulty in accommodating myself to yours, which says that *light* is a *luminary* motion of *luminous* bodies. . . . These, Father, are my opinions which I shall always submit to yours.

As for the rest, one cannot deny you the fame of having upheld a peripatetic physics as well as that can be done; and I find that your letter is no less a mark of the weakness of the opinion which you defend than of the vigor of your intellect.

And certainly the skill with which you have defended the impossibility of a vacuum on the slender grounds that remain to support it, makes it easy to judge that with similar effort you would have incontrovertibly established the contrary opinion in view of the vantage-ground which experiments provide.

An indisposition has prevented me from having the honor of seeing you as well as from writing to you with my own hand. That is why I beg of you to excuse the mistakes which are to be found in this letter, above all in spelling.

I am very cordially, my very Reverend Father,
    Your very humble and very obedient servant
PASCAL

Paris, October 29, 1647

4. FRAGMENT OF A PREFACE TO THE TREATISE ON THE VACUUM

[October-November, 1647?]

The respect for antiquity has today come to such a point in matters where it should have least influence that all its thoughts, its mysteries, and even its obscurities have been turned into oracles. Indeed, one can no longer submit innovations without jeopardy, and the text of an author suffices to bring the most cogent reasoning to naught.

Not that I would correct matters by substituting one vice for another or profess no esteem for the ancients because others hold them in too high esteem. I do not pretend to banish their authority in order to elevate reasoning alone, although there are those who desire to establish their authority solely at the expense of reasoning. . . .

In order to make this important distinction with proper care we must consider that some matters of knowledge depend on memory alone and are purely historical. Here the sole concern is to know what authors have written. Other matters of knowledge depend only on reasoning, and are entirely dogmatic. Here the aim is to seek and to discover hidden truths. Those which come under the first heading are as limited as the books that contain them.

On the basis of this distinction the extent of this respect for authority must be appraised. The respect which one should have for . . . [sentence incomplete].

In matters where we merely seek to know what authors have written, as in history, geography, jurisprudence, languages, above all in theology, and finally in all those which have as their basic principle either simple facts or divine or human institutions, we must of necessity have recourse to their books, since these contain all that we can know about such matters.

If it is a matter of knowing who was the first king of France, in what place geographers located the prime meridian, what words are used in a dead language, and all such things, what means other than books can lead us to this knowledge? And who can add anything new to what they teach us about them, since we wish to know merely what they contain? It is authority alone that can enlighten us. But it is in theology that this authority has greatest weight because there it is inseparable from truth, and because only through it do we know truth. For if we desire to give complete assurance about matters which are most incomprehensible to reason, we need merely point to them in sacred books (similarly, when we wish to call attention to the uncertainty of the most plausible things, we need merely point out that they are not contained in these books). This is because these principles transcend nature and reason, and since the human mind is too feeble to arrive by its own efforts, it cannot attain such high understanding if it is not carried aloft by a force which is omnipotent and supernatural.

It is not the same with subjects which are self-evident to the senses and to reasoning; there authority is unnecessary; reason alone suffices to know them. Each has its separate jurisdiction; now the one has the advantage, and now the other reigns in its turn. But since subjects of this kind are adjusted to the range of the mind, it is entirely free to extend this range; its inexhaustible fecundity is constantly productive, and the sum total of its inventions may be without end and without interruption. . . .

It is thus that geometry, arithmetic, music, physics, medicine, architecture, and all the sciences, which are subject to experiment and to reasoning, must be augmented to become perfect. The ancients found them but roughly sketched by their predecessors, and we shall leave them to those who come after us in a better state than we received them. Since their perfection depends on time and toil, it is evident that our toil and our time would have achieved less for us if the labors of the ancients had been divorced from ours. Joined together, however, the two must produce a greater result than each by itself.

The clearing up of this difference must make us pity the blindness of those who offer only authority as their proof in matters of physics, instead of setting forth proofs based on reasoning or experimentation. And the clearing up of this difference must fill us with horror at the malice of others who, in theology, resort solely to reasoning instead of to the authority of the Scriptures and the [Church] Fathers. We must give heart to those timid people who dare not invent anything in physics, and we must confound the insolence of those foolhardy people who bring forth innovations in theology. Nevertheless, the misfortune of our world is such that we encounter many new opinions on theology that were unknown to antiquity, but which are now upheld with obstinacy and received with applause. On the other hand, though their number is small, new opinions advanced in physics seem perforce to be convicted of error as soon as they shock accepted opinions. It is as if the respect we have for ancient philosophers were a duty, and the respect we have for the most ancient of the Church Fathers were merely a courtesy. I leave it to judicious persons to note the full import of this abuse which perverts the order of the sciences so unjustly; and I believe that very few of them would wish to see this [liberty] extended to other matters, since new inventions are infallibly errors in matters which we debase with impunity. Yet they are absolutely necessary for the perfection of so many subjects which are incomparably inferior, but which we would not dare to infringe upon.

Let us distribute our credulity and our distrust with greater justice, and let us limit this respect which we have for the ancients. Since reason gives rise to this respect, reason should be the measure of it. Let us bear in mind that, if the ancients had been so reluctant, and had not dared to add to the knowledge transmitted to them, and if their contemporaries had opposed the same obstacles to the adoption of proposed inventions, they would have deprived themselves and posterity of the fruits of their inventions. Just as they make use of what was bequeathed to them as a means of gaining more, and just as their happy daring paved the way for great things, so we should do the same with what they have acquired for us. Following their example, we should make this the means and not the end of study, and thus endeavor to surpass them by imitating them. For what is more unjust than to treat our ancients with greater restraint than they had for their predecessors, and to have this inviolable respect for them which they do not deserve from us, since they did not have a similar respect for those who had the same advantage over them? . . . [five or six lines missing]

The secrets of nature are hidden; though she is ever active, we do not always discover her doings. Time reveals them from age to age and although nature constantly remains uniform, she is not uniformly known. The experiments which make her known to us are constantly being multiplied, and since they are the sole principles of physics, the results multiply in proportion. And so it happens that today we can progress toward other views and new opinions without scorn and without ingratitude, since the first knowledge the ancients gave us served as stepping stones to our own. To these advantages we owe the ascendancy that they have over us. For, having reached a certain level due to their efforts, we mount higher by the slightest exertion, and with less toil and glory we find ourselves above them. From such heights we can discover things that were hidden from their view. Our own view has wider sweep, and although they knew as well as we all that they were able to see in nature, we see more than they.

Nevertheless it is strange how we revere their opinions. We make it a crime to contradict them and a deed of violence to add to them, as if they had left no further truths to be ascertained. Is not this an affront to human reason, and are we not putting it on a level with animal instinct when we disregard the principal difference between them? The difference is this: the results of reasoning are constantly being augmented, whereas instinct always remains in *status quo*. Honeycombs were proportioned as well a thousand years ago as today, and each bee forms this hexagon as exactly the first time as the last. It is the same with everything produced by this mysterious urge. Nature instructs animals as necessity demands, but this fragile knowledge ends with the need they have of it. Since they receive it without study, they miss the joy that comes from conserving it. Each time that it is given to them, it is new to them, for since nature's only aim is to maintain animals on a limited scale of perfection, she endows them with this necessary knowledge; it is always the same, for fear that they may retrogress, and it cannot be augmented by them for fear that they might exceed the limits assigned to them.

It is not the same with man who is made for infinity. He dwells in ignorance during the first age of his life, but in his progress he is constantly instructing himself. For he profits not only by his own experience, but also by that of his predecessors, because he is constantly storing up in his memory the knowledge he has already acquired, and because the knowledge of the ancients is ever present for him in the books they have left him. And as he preserves this knowledge, he can easily add to it as well. Thus it is that, in a sense, men today are where the ancient philosophers would be, if these had lived on to the present day, and had added to their own knowledge all that their studies would have enabled them to acquire in the course of so many centuries. Hence by a unique prerogative each man not only advances in the sciences from day to day, but all men together make continual progress as the universe ages, because the same thing happens in the succession of men that happens in the different stages of an individual. Thus in the course of so many centuries the whole succession of men must be regarded like a single individual who lives on and who is constantly learning. Now it becomes obvious how wrongly we respect antiquity in its philosophers, for, since old age is the age farthest removed from childhood, who can fail to see that, in this universal man, old age must not be sought in the times near his birth but rather in those farthest removed from it? Those whom we call ancients were veritably new in all things, and actually constituted the childhood of mankind. Since we have added to their knowledge all the experience of the centuries that followed them, it is within ourselves that we can find the antiquity which we revere in others.

The ancients are to be admired for the conclusions they drew from the few principles known to them, and they are to be pardoned for those in which they lacked the good fortune of experience rather than the power of reasoning.

For, were they not excusable for their notion of the Milky Way when, invention not yet having come to the aid of their feeble eyesight, they attributed this color to greater density in that part of the sky which reflects light more strongly? But would we not be inexcusable if we adhered to the same notion, now, when with the advantages of the telescope, we have discovered an infinite number of small stars, whose more abundant splendor has brought us to a recognition of the real cause of this whiteness?

Moreover, did they not have cause for saying that all corruptible bodies are enclosed in the sphere of the moon, when during the course of so many centuries they had never yet noted corruption nor generation outside of that space? But why should we not assert the contrary when the whole world has actually seen comets burst into flames and disappear far beyond that sphere?

And so, on the subject of a vacuum, they were right in saying that nature does not tolerate a vacuum, because all their experiments had always led them to see that she abhors and does not tolerate it. But if the new experiments had been known to them, perhaps they would then have had grounds for affirming what they had cause to deny when a vacuum had not yet made its appearance; since to make a generalization it would not be enough to have seen nature constant on a hundred occasions, nor a thousand, nor any other number, however great it might be. For if a single case remained to be examined, it alone would suffice to prevent general definition, and if a single case were in disagreement, it alone . . . [two lines missing]. For in all matters where proof consists in experiments and not in [reasoned] demonstrations, we can make a general assertion only by the general enumeration of all parts and of all different cases. And so when we say that the diamond is the hardest of all bodies, we mean of all the bodies that we know, and we cannot, nor should we say that gold is the heaviest of all bodies; it would be temerity if we included in this general proposition those which we do not yet know, although there may be some in nature. Similarly, when the ancients asserted that nature tolerates no vacuum, they meant that she tolerated none in all the experiments they had seen, and without temerity they could not have included those of which they had no knowledge. For if these had existed, the ancients would doubtless have drawn the same conclusions as we, and by their approbation they would have invested them with the authority of this very antiquity which people wish to set up today as the sole principle of science.

And so, without contradicting them, we may assert the contrary of what they said, and no matter what influence this antiquity had, the truth must always prevail, even though it be newly discovered. For the truth is always older than all the opinions which men have held of it and we should be ignoring the nature of truth, if we imagined that truth began at the time when it began to be known.

5. LETTER FROM MONSIEUR PASCAL THE YOUNGER TO MONSIEUR PERIER

November 15, 1647

Sir:

I should not interrupt the continual work in which your duties engage you for the purpose of talking with you about meditations on physics, if I did not know that they serve to entertain you in your hours of relaxation and that whereas others might be embarrassed by them you will find them a diversion. I hesitate all the less because I know the pleasure you derive from this sort of conversation. This one is to be merely a continuation of those which we have had together about a vacuum. You know the opinion which philosophers have had on this subject. They all regarded it as a maxim that nature abhors a vacuum; and almost all of them, going still further, have maintained that she cannot permit one, and that she would destroy herself rather than to tolerate a vacuum. Thus opinions have been divided; some have been satisfied with saying merely that she abhorred it; others have maintained that she could not tolerate it. In my *Epitome of the treatise on the vacuum* I have labored to annihilate this latter opinion, and I believe that the experiments which I reported there suffice to make manifest that nature may tolerate and indeed does tolerate a space, as large as you will, which is empty of all the kinds of matter known to us and which are perceptible to our senses. I am now working on an investigation of the truth of the first opinion, and am on a search for experiments which will show whether the effects which are attributed to an abhorrence of a vacuum must really be attributed to this abhorrence of a vacuum, or whether they must be attributed to the weight and to the pressure of the air. For, to disclose my thought to you frankly, I find it difficult to believe that nature, which is not animate, nor sensitive, should be susceptible to abhorrence, since passions presuppose a soul capable of feeling them. I incline far more to attributing all these effects to the weight and to the pressure of the air, because I consider them merely as special cases of a universal proposition of the equilibrium of liquids which is to make up the larger part of the treatise that I have promised. Not that I did not have these same thoughts at the time of the production of my epitome. Nevertheless, for lack of convincing experiments, I did not then dare (and I do not yet dare) to deviate from the maxim in my epitome. For at that time I had no design other than to combat the opinion of those who maintain that a vacuum is absolutely impossible and that nature would rather tolerate her destruction than the slightest empty space. Indeed, I do not think that we should permit ourselves to deviate thoughtlessly from the maxims which we have from antiquity, if we are obligated to hold them by indubitable and compelling proofs. But in this case I hold that it would be extreme weakness to have the slightest scruples about doing so, and that in the end we ought to manifest more veneration for obvious truths than stubborn adherence to these opinions received from others. I could not show you any more clearly the circumspection I exercise before deviating from ancient maxims than by reminding you of an experiment which I performed some days ago in your presence. This was with two tubes, one within the other; it apparently shows a vacuum within a vacuum. You saw that the quicksilver in the inside tube remained suspended at the height where it stays in ordinary experiments when it was counterbalanced and pressed by the weight of the entire mass of the air. And you saw that, on the other hand, it fell completely without retaining any height nor suspension when, by means of the vacuum surrounding it, it was no longer pressed nor counterbalanced by any air; this having been removed on all sides. Next you saw that this height or suspension of quicksilver increased or decreased as the pressure of the air increased or decreased, and that in the end all these diverse heights of the quicksilver were always found to be proportional to the pressure of the air.

Certainly, after this experiment, there was cause for being persuaded that it is not abhorrence of a vacuum, as we thought, which causes the suspension of quicksilver in the ordinary experiment but rather the weight and the pressure of the air, which counterbalance the weight of the quicksilver. But because all the results of this last experiment with the two tubes — which are explained so naturally by the pressure and weight of the air alone — may still be explained plausibly enough by a horror of a vacuum, I am adhering to that ancient maxim. Nevertheless I am resolved to seek full enlightenment of this difficulty by a decisive experiment. I have imagined one which may alone suffice to give us the light we are seeking, if it is properly carried out. This is to perform the ordinary experiment of the vacuum several times in the same day, in the same tube, with the same quicksilver, now at the foot and now at the summit of a mountain, at least five or six hundred fathoms high, to determine whether the height of the quicksilver suspended in the tube will be found the same or different in these two locations. You will doubtless see that this experiment is decisive for the question, and that if the height of the quicksilver should be less at the summit than at the foot of the mountain (as I have many reasons to believe, although all those who have meditated on this matter are opposed to this belief), it will necessarily follow that the weight and the pressure of the air are the sole cause for this suspension of the quicksilver, and that it is not the horror of a vacuum. For it is quite certain that much more air bears down upon the foot of the mountain than upon its summit, whereas one could not say that nature abhors a vacuum more at the foot of the mountain than at its summit.

But since some difficulty ordinarily attaches to big things, I see great difficulty in the execution of this design. For an exceedingly high mountain must be chosen for it, near a city in which there is someone capable of bringing all the necessary precision to this test. For if the mountain were far away, it would be difficult to carry the vessels there, and the quicksilver, the tubes, and many other necessary things. And it would be difficult to undertake these laborious trips as many times as would be necessary, and to encounter at the top of these mountains the calm and favorable weather which is but rarely seen there. And since outside of Paris one finds people with these capacities just as rarely as one finds places where these conditions obtain, I have considered myself very fortunate to have found both on this occasion. For our city of Clermont is at the foot of the high mountain Puy de Dôme, and I hope that out of kindness you will do me the favor of undertaking this experiment yourself. On this assurance I have led all our curious people of Paris to hope for this. Among others there is also the Reverend Father Mersenne, who has already promised in letters which he has written to Italy, to Poland, to Sweden, to Holland, etc., to notify his friends whom he has won by his merits. I am not dwelling on the means of executing it, because I well know that you will not overlook any of the conditions necessary to do this with precision.

I request you merely that it be as soon as possible, and that you may pardon this liberty to which I am impelled by my impatience to learn of the success of the undertaking. Without it I cannot finish the treatise which I have promised to the public, nor satisfy the desire of so many persons who are waiting for it, and who will be infinitely obliged to you. Not that I wish to lessen my gratitude by reference to the number of those who will share it with me. For, on the contrary, I wish to share their gratitude toward you, and to remain all the more, Sir, your very humble and very obedient servant

PASCAL

Paris, November 15, 1647

6. FRAGMENT OF A LETTER FROM BLAISE PASCAL TO HIS SISTER MADAME PERIER

January 26, 1648.

My dear sister:

We have received your letter. I had intended to answer the first one which you wrote to me more than four months ago, but my indisposition and other matters prevented me from finishing it. Since that time I have not been able to write to you, either because of my illness, or because of lack of leisure, or for some other reason. I rarely have leisure hours and health at the same time. Nevertheless, I shall try to finish this letter without forcing myself; I don't know whether it will be long or short. My main design is to tell you about visits of which you know; in doing so I hope to have something to satisfy you and to answer your last letters. I can only begin by telling you of the pleasure they gave me; they brought me such a feeling of satisfaction, that I could not convey it to you by word of mouth. I beg you to believe, that though I have not written to you, there has not been an hour in which you were not in my thoughts or in which I did not wish for the continuation of the great design which God has inspired in you. I felt new transports of joy on receiving all the letters that bore any evidence of it, and I was delighted to see the continuation of it even though you had no news from us. That has led me to believe that this design had more than human support, since it had no need of human aid to maintain itself. Nevertheless, I should like to contribute something to it, but unfortunately I have no contribution to make at present. My weakness is so great that, if I undertook to do so, it would be an act of temerity rather than of charity, and I should have to fear for both of us the misfortune which threatens a blind leader of the blind. I have felt my incapacity incomparably more since the visits in question, and very far from having won from them enough light for others, I have carried away from them nothing but confusion and disturbance for myself which God alone can calm. I am working carefully, but without eagerness and without anxiety, knowing well, as I do, that both [my difficulties] will be removed. I say to you that God alone can soothe my troubles, and that I, too, shall work toward this end. For the very people from whom I had expected help in dissipating my troubles merely create situations which add to them and heighten them. And so, seeing that I am abandoned to my own devices, I can do nothing but pray to God to bless it [my labor] with success.

For my work I shall need to communicate with learned persons and with disinterested persons. The former will not enter into such communication; I no longer turn to any but the latter, and so I desire exceedingly to see you, for letters are long, inconvenient, and almost useless on such occasions. Nevertheless, I shall write you a little about it.

The first time I saw Monsieur Rebours, I introduced myself to him, and was received by him with as much courtesy as I could have desired. These courtesies were really bestowed on my father, since they were extended to me out of consideration for him. After the first exchange of civilities I requested his permission to see him again from time to time; this he granted to me. Thus I was at liberty to see him, for I do not count this first meeting as a visit, since it was but permission for visits. I went to him some time later, and among other things I said to him with my usual frankness and candor that we had seen their books [i.e., those of Port Royal] and those of their adversaries, and that this sufficed to make him understand that we shared their sentiments. He manifested some delight at this. I then told him that I thought, by following the same principles of common sense, one could demonstrate many things which his adversaries said were opposed to his views, and that well guided reasoning would lead to belief in them, although one should believe them without the aid of reasoning.

These were my very words, in which I do not believe there was anything to offend the most reserved modesty. But, as you know, all acts may have two sources, and this discourse might well spring from vanity and confidence in reasoning. Hence this suspicion which was increased by his knowledge of my study of geometry sufficed to make him consider my discourse strange. He manifested this by a reply so full of humility and modesty that it would doubtless have confounded the pride which he wished to refute. Nevertheless, I tried to acquaint him with my motive, but my self-justification undoubtedly heightened his doubt, and he took my excuses for obstinacy. I admit that his discourse was so beautiful, that if I had been in the state which he imagined, such a discourse would have cured me of it, but since I did not believe I had this malady, I opposed the remedy which he proffered to me. But he urged it all the more, since I seemed to shun it, for he took my refusal for obduracy. And the more he strove to continue, the more my thanks proved to him that I did not consider it necessary. Thus this entire interview took place in this equivocation and in an embarrassment which persisted in all the others and which has scarcely been cleared up. I shall not tell you about the others word for word, because it would be neither necessary nor pertinent. I shall merely tell you in substance the chief thing that was said or rather the chief thing that was held back.

But above everything I beg you not to draw any inference from all that I am writing to you, because it might happen that I was not telling things quite accurately, and that might give rise to some suspicion which would be as prejudiced as unjust. For after all, after having thought it over carefully, I find in it only a case of obscurity where it would be dangerous and difficult to decide. As for me, I am suspending my judgment completely, as much because of my weakness as because of my lack of knowledge . . . [sentence incomplete].

7. LETTER BY PASCAL TO MONSIEUR LE PAILLEUR ON THE SUBJECT OF FATHER NOËL, JESUIT

[February-March, 1648]

Sir:

Since you wish to know what has made me interrupt the exchange of letters in which the Reverend Father Noël did me the honor of engaging me, I shall satisfy you promptly. I do not doubt that if you disapprove of my procedure before knowing the cause of it, you will approve of it when you know the reasons which restrained me.

The strongest reason of them all is that the Reverend Father Talon, on taking the trouble of bringing me Father Noël's last letter, gave me to understand in the presence of three of your good friends, that Father Noël sympathized with my indisposition, that he feared my first letter had affected my health, and that he begged me not to jeopardize it by a second letter; that we could clear up the remaining difficulties by word of mouth: in a word he begged me not to reply to him. I was given to understand further that since he [Father Noël] had written this only for me, he wished no one else to see it, and since letters were individual matters, they would suffer violence if they did not remain secret.

I admit that if this proposition had come to me from any quarter other than that of these good Fathers, it would have seemed suspect to me, and I should have feared that whoever made it to me wished to take advantage of a silence in which he would have engaged me by a captious request. But I had so little doubt of their sincerity that I promised them everything without reserve and without fear. Accordingly I was particularly careful to keep his letter secret and unanswered. As a consequence of this, several persons and even some of these Fathers who were not well informed of Father Noël's intention took it upon themselves to say that, having found my opinions routed in his letter, I had concealed the beauties of his letter, for fear of uncovering my shame, and that my weakness alone had prevented me from replying to it.

You see, Sir, how adverse this conjuncture was for me, since I could neither conceal his letter without detriment nor publish it without being unfaithful; my honor was threatened equally by my reply and by my silence, inasmuch as the one was false to my promise and the other contrary to my interests.

Nevertheless, I have scrupulously kept my word. I put off replying to his letter until I should write the Treatise in which I must reply precisely to all the objections that have been raised against the following proposition. This proposition which I advanced in my epitome is to the effect "that this space is not full of any of the kinds of matter which are observed by the senses and which are known in nature." In this way I believed that nothing would oblige me to precipitate my reply, which I wanted to make more exact by deferring it for a time. To these considerations I add that, since all disputes of this sort continue forever if someone does not break them off, and since they cannot be settled if one of the two parties does not take the initiative in ending them, I thought that the age, the merits, and the station of this Father obliged me to yield to him the advantage of having written the final word on this subject. But beyond all these reasons I confess that his letter alone sufficed to dispense me from replying to him, and I am sure you will find that it seems to have been conceived expressly in terms which would not obligate me to reply to him.

To show this, I am going to call your attention to the points he has treated, but in a sequence which is different from his, and such as he would doubtless have chosen in a more elaborate treatise, but which he did not deem necessary in the informality of a letter; for every one of these points is to be found scattered in the whole body of his discourse, and stated in practically every part of it.

His intention here is to declare that my letter led him to give up his original opinion although he is unable to adjust himself to mine. So much so that we may consider it to be divided into two parts, one of which contains the things which prevent him from following my thought while the other contains those which support his second opinion. On each of these parts I hope to show you how little I was obligated to reply.

As for the first, which concerns the things that swerve him from my opinion, his first difficulties are that this space cannot be anything other than a body, since it bears and transmits light, and since it retards the motion of another body. But I thought that in my letter I had showed him well enough the weakness of these same objections in his first letter. For I had told him in clear enough terms that although bodies fall in time in this space, and although light penetrates it, we should not attribute these effects to a matter which necessarily fills it, since they may belong to the nature of motion and of light. Furthermore, as long as we remain in our present ignorance of the nature of these things, we should draw no conclusion from them, since a conclusion would be based merely on uncertainty. Moreover, since Father Noël concludes from the appearance of these effects that this space is filled by a matter which bears light and causes this retardation, we may with just as much reason conclude from these same effects that light exists in a vacuum and that motion takes place there in time. In addition, so many other things favor this latter opinion that in the judgment of scholars it was incomparably more plausible than the other, even before it had the support which these experiments lent to it.

But if he thus indicated that he had scarcely noticed this part of my letter, by the second of the things in my opinion which shock him he gives evidence of not having understood another part. For he imputes to me a thought which is contrary to the very terms of my letter and of my publication and utterly opposed to the foundation of all my maxims. It is this. He imagines that I have asserted in decisive terms the real existence of empty space. And on the basis of this fiction of his imagination which he takes for an invariable truth, he takes his pen to point out the weakness of my assertion.

Nevertheless, he was able to see what I put into my publication. There my conclusion is simply that my opinion will be "that this space is empty until someone has shown that a matter fills it." Now this is not a real assertion of the existence of a vacuum. He was also able to see that I put into my letter these words which seem to me clear enough: "Finally, my Reverend Father, I beg you to consider that all these men together could not demonstrate that any body succeeds the one which leaves this apparently empty space, and that moreover it is not possible for all these men to show that when water rises in such a space, a body has left it. According to your maxims, would that not suffice to assure that this space is empty? Nevertheless, I simply say that in my opinion it is empty. Judge whether those who speak with so much restraint of a thing about which they have a right to speak with so much assurance, are able to pass decisive judgment on the existence of this igneous matter which is so dubious and so vaguely established."

Moreover, I should never have imagined what gave rise to this thought in him, if he had not informed me about it himself on the first page where he faithfully reports the distinction about empty space which I made in my letter. It is this: "What we call empty space is a space which has length, breadth and depth; it is immovable and capable of containing a body of similar length and shape; and it is what we call a *solid* in geometry where we consider only abstract and incorporeal things." After having reported this definition word for word, he immediately draws this conclusion from it: "There is your thought of an empty space, Sir, very well explained; I desire to believe that all this is obvious to you, and that your mind is convinced and fully satisfied with it, since you affirm it."

If he had not quoted my own words, I should have believed that he had not read them well or that they had been badly written, and that instead of the first word, *I call*, he would have found this, *I assure*. But since he quoted my entire sentence, I can merely think that he perceived a necessary sequence among these words, and that he makes no difference between defining a thing and asserting its existence.

That is why from the very words which I defined for him he believed I had asserted the actual existence of a vacuum. I know that those who are not accustomed to see things treated in their proper order imagine that one may define a thing without being assured of its existence. But they ought to observe that one should always define things before trying to find whether they are possible or not, and that the stages which lead us to the knowledge of truths are definition, axiom and proof. For at first we conceive the idea of a thing, next we give a name to this idea, that is to say we define it, and finally we try to find whether this thing is true or false. If we find it is impossible, it passes for a falsehood; if we demonstrate that it is true, it passes for a truth; and as long as we can prove neither its possibility nor its impossibility, it passes for a notion. From this it is obvious that there is no necessary connection between the definition of a thing and the assurance of its existence, and that we may define an impossible thing as well as a real thing. Thus we may call a rectilinear and right-angled triangle what we would imagine as having two right angles, and then show that such a triangle is impossible; thus Euclid first defines parallels and shows afterward that they may exist; the definition of the circle precedes the *postulate* which proposes its possibility. Thus astronomers have given names to the concentric, excentric and epicylic circles which they imagined in the heavens without being assured that stars actually describe such circles in their movements; thus the Peripatetics gave a name to this sphere of fire whose truth it would be difficult to demonstrate.

That is why when I wished to oppose the decisions of Father Noël, who denied the existence of a vacuum in nature, I thought that I could not embark on this inquiry nor even say a word about it before I had declared what I mean by the word *vacuum*. This I felt obliged to do all the more by some passages in the first letter of this Father which led me to judge that the notion he had of it was not in conformity with mine. I saw that he could not distinguish between dimensions and matter, nor between immateriality and nothingness, and that this confusion led him to conclude that when I assigned length, breadth and depth to this space, I was taking it upon myself to say it was a body, and that as soon as I pronounced it to be immaterial I was reducing it to nothingness. In order to disentangle these ideas, I gave them this definition from which he can see that the thing we conceive and express by the word *empty space* is in the middle between matter and nothingness, without participating either of the one or of the other; that it differs from nothingness by its dimensions; and that its lack of resistance and its immovability distinguish it from matter to such an extent that it remains between these two extremes without any possibility of being confused with either one of the two.

Toward the end of his letter, in one sentence, he brings together all his difficulties in order to give them more forcefulness by combining them. These are his words (p. XI): *This space is neither God, nor creature, nor body, nor spirit, nor substance nor accident; it transmits light without being transparent, it resists without resistance, it is immovable and is transported with the tube, it is everywhere and nowhere, it does everything and does nothing. Such are the admirable properties of empty space. Insofar as it is space, it is and performs wonders; insofar as it is empty, it is and does nothing; insofar as it is space, it is long, wide, and deep; insofar as it is empty, it excludes length, breadth and depth. If necessary, I shall show all these beautiful properties as derived from empty space.*

Since a long succession of beautiful things finally becomes boresome because of its own length, I believe Father Noël grew weary of having produced so much, and that, anticipating boredom on the part of those who had seen them, he wanted to step down from a heavier to a less serious style in order to afford them relief by this pleasantry, so that after having provided so many things which called for laborious admiration he would, out of benevolence, give them an entertaining subject. I was the first to feel the effect of this kindness, and those who will next see his letter, will likewise experience it. For there is no one, who after having read what I wrote to him, will not laugh at the conclusions he draws from it and at these antitheses which are so aptly set forth, that it is easy to see that he made a much more studious effort to place his words in opposition to each other than to choose them in conformity with reason and truth.

Let us scrutinize the objections singly. *This space*, says he, *is neither God nor creature*. The mysteries which are the concern of the Deity are too sacred to be profaned by our disputes. We should make them the object of our worship and not the subject of our conversations; so much so, that without discussing them in any way, I yield entirely to whatever those may decide about them who have a right to such decision.

Neither body nor spirit. It is true that space is neither body nor spirit; but it is space. Thus time is neither body nor spirit, but it is time. And since time nevertheless exists, even though it is neither one of these things, so empty space may well exist, without necessarily being either body or spirit.

Neither substance nor accident. This is true, if by the word *substance* we mean that which is either body or spirit. For in this sense, space is neither substance nor accident, but it is space; just as in the same sense, time is neither substance nor accident, but it is time; because in order to be, it is not necessary to be substance or accident, just as several of their Fathers maintain that God is neither the one nor the other, although he be the sovereign Being.

Which transmits light without being transparent. This discourse has so little light that I am unable to perceive it, for I do not understand what meaning this Father gives to this word *transparent*, since he finds that empty space is not so. For, if by transparence he means, as all opticists do, the absence of every obstacle to the passage of light, I do not see why he robs our space of it which allows it to pass freely. And so, speaking on this subject with my slight knowledge, I would have said that these words *transmit light*, which are suited only to his way of imagining light, have the same meaning as the words *to allow light to pass;* also the same meaning as *it is transparent*, that is to say, that it presents no obstacle to light. In this I find neither obscurity nor contradiction.

It resists without resistance. Since he judges the resistance of this space only by the time which bodies require in it for their motion, and since we have discoursed at such length on the nullity of this conclusion, one will see that he has no reason for saying that it resists. On the contrary, it will be found that this space does not oppose resistance or that it is without resistance, in which I see nothing but full conformity with reason.

That it is immovable and is transported with the tube. Here Father Noël shows how little he penetrates into the opinion which he wishes to refute. I should have to request him to note on this subject that when an opinion is accepted by a number of scholars, one should not make much of the objections which seem to undermine it when these are easy to foresee. For we should believe that those who uphold them have already been mindful of them, and that since these objections are easily discovered, scholars have found the solution for them, because they persevere in this thought. Now, to examine this difficulty in particular, if these antitheses or contrarieties had not dazzled his mind as much as they charmed his imagination, he would doubtless have had in mind that, despite appearances, the vacuum is not transported with the tube, and that immobility is as natural to space as motion is to a body. To make this truth obvious, it must be observed that space in general embraces all bodies in nature, each of which occupies a certain part of it. Yet, although all of them are movable, the space which they fill is not so, for when a body is moved from one place to another, it merely changes place without taking with it the place it occupied at the time it was at rest. Indeed, what does it do other than to leave its first immovable place in order successively to take other places which are likewise immovable? But the one it has left, always remains fixed and unshaken, so that it becomes either filled with another body if one succeeds it, or empty if no other body offers to succeed it. But whether it be empty or filled, this vast space, which is ever in like repose, and whose amplitude embraces everything, is as stable and motionless in each of its parts as it is in its totality. Consequently I do not see how Father Noël could claim that the tube communicates its motion to the empty space, since, having no consistence to be pushed, having no handle to be pulled, and being affected neither by weight nor by any power of attraction, it is clear that we cannot make it change. What deceived him is that when the tube was carried from one place to another, he saw no change in it. That is why he thought that this space was always the same, because it was always similar to itself. But he ought to observe that the space which the tube encloses in one position is not the same as that which it includes in the second, and that in the course of its motion the tube is continually taking over new spaces. And so it happens that the space which was empty in the first of its positions becomes filled with air when it sets out to take the second position in which it makes the space empty that it encounters, whereas this was full of air beforehand. But both of these spaces, which are alternately full and empty, always remain equally motionless. From this it is evident that it is beside the point to believe that the empty space changes place; and the strangest thing is that the matter with which the good Father fills it is such that even according to his very hypothesis it could not be transported with the tube. For since it would enter and leave through the pores of the glass with full ease without adhering to the glass in any way — just like water in a vessel which is pierced on all sides — it is obvious that the matter would not be carried with it [the tube] since we see that the same tube does not transport light because it pierces it without difficulty and without holding it. And it is obvious that our very space, when exposed to the sun, changes rays when it changes place without carrying with it to the second place the light which filled it in the first, and that in the different positions it receives different rays as well as different spaces.

Finally, Father Noël is surprised *that it does everything and does nothing; that it is everywhere and nowhere; that it exists and performs wonders, although it does not exist; that it has dimensions without having them.* If this discourse has meaning, I confess that I do not understand it; that is why I do not consider myself under obligation to reply to it.

These, Sir, are the difficulties and the things which shock him about my opinion. But since they give evidence that he does not understand my thought rather than that he contradicts it, and since it seems that he finds obscurity rather than flaws in it, I thought he would find it clarified in my letter, if he took the trouble to look at it with greater care. And I thought I was not obligated to reply to him, since a second reading would suffice to resolve the doubts to which the first had given rise.

As for the second part of his letter which concerns the change from his first thought and the statement of his second proposition, he declares first of all his reason for denying the existence of a vacuum. The reason he advances for this is that a vacuum cannot be perceived by any one of the senses. This leads him to say that, since I deny the existence of matter for the simple reason that it gives no perceptible sign of its existence and that the mind conceives no necessity for it, he may with equal and even greater authority deny the existence of a vacuum, because the two have one thing in common: neither one of them can be perceived by any one of the senses. Here are his words: *"We say that water exists because we see it and touch it; we say there is air in an inflated balloon because we feel the resistance; there is fire because we feel heat; but a true vacuum does not reach any one of the senses.*"

But I am astounded that he would draw a parallel between such disparate things, and that he failed to bear in mind, that since there is nothing so contrary to being as nothingness, nor so contrary to affirmation as negation, we proceed to the proofs of both by contrary means, and that what establishes the one overthrows the other. For what is needed to arrive at a knowledge of nothingness other than to recognize an utter lack of all kinds of properties and effects? Whereas if a single one of these should appear, we would, on the contrary, conclude the real existence of a cause which produced it. And then he says: "*Behold, Sir, which one of us two is to be believed more, you who affirm a space which is not perceptible to the senses, which is of no value either to art or to nature, and which you employ only to decide a very dubious question, etc.*"

But, Sir, I leave you to judge, when we see nothing, and when the senses perceive nothing in a place, who is on more solid ground: he who affirms that there is something, although he perceives nothing, or he who thinks there is nothing, because he sees nothing.

After, as we have just seen, Father Noël stated the reason why he rules out a vacuum and that he has grounds for debarring it because of this same deprivation of properties which so justly lead others to believe in it and which are the only perceptible means of arriving at its proof, he now undertakes to prove that it is a body. To this end he imagined a definition of a body which he expressly conceived so that it will suit our space, in order that he might draw his conclusion from it easily. These are his words: "*I define body as that which is composed of parts that are outside of each other, and I say that every body is space when we consider it between its extremities, and that every other space is a body, because it is composed of parts that are outside of each other.*"

But here it is not a question of showing that our space is not empty, and of calling it body, as Father Noël has done, but rather of showing that it is a body, as he has claimed to do. Not that he should not be permitted to give any name he pleases to whatever has parts which are outside of each other, but he will gain no great advantage from this liberty. For the word *body*, through the choice which he has made of it, becomes ambiguous, so that there are two kinds of entirely different and even heterogeneous things which are called *body:* one, which has parts outside of each other and which according to Father Noël will be called *body;* the other, a material substance, movable and impenetrable which will ordinarily be called *body*. But from this resemblance in names he cannot conclude a resemblance of properties in these things; nor can he, by this means, show that whatever has parts outside of each other is the same thing as a material, immovable and impenetrable substance, because it is not in his power to make their nature agree as readily as their names. Let us assume that he had given to whatever has parts outside of each other the name of *water*, of *mind*, of *light*, which he could have done as easily as to call it *body;* then he could not have concluded therefrom that our space is any one of these things. Moreover, when he called *body* whatever has parts outside of each other and when by virtue of this definition he said, *I say that all space is body*, then we must take the word *body* in the sense which he just gave to it. And so, if we substitute the definition for the thing defined, which can always be done without changing the sense of a proposition, he will find that this conclusion, that every space is a body, is nothing other than this: that every space has parts that are outside of each other but not that all space is material, as Father Noël has imagined. I shall not dwell any longer on a conclusion whose weakness is so obvious, since I am talking to an excellent geometrician, and since you have as much skill in discovering errors in reasoning as you have strength to avoid them.

Going still further, the Reverend Father Noël wishes to show what a body is. To establish his thought, he begins with a long discourse, in which he claims to prove a continual and necessary mingling of elements; in this he shows nothing except that some parts of one element are to be found among the parts of another and that they are jumbled by accident rather than by nature. And so it might happen that they would separate without violence, and that they would return of their own accord to their former simplicity; for the natural mingling of two bodies means that their separation makes both of them change their name and their nature, as in the case of all metals and all mixtures. Because when we take from gold the mercury, which entered into its composition, what remains is no longer gold. But in the mixture which Father Noël imagines for us, we see only a violent confusion of some vapors scattered in the air which are suspended in it like dust, without seeming to enter into the composition of the air; the same holds for his other mixtures. As regards the mixture of water and air, he considers it to be demonstrated best, and he says it is proved conclusively by the bellows caused by the falling of water in a chamber which is almost entirely closed, and which you see explained at length in his letter. It is strange that this Father did not bear in mind that this air, which he says comes out of the water, is nothing other than the outer air which is carried with the falling water and which is fully capable of entering the chamber by the same aperture, because it is larger than that through which the water flows away. And so the water which is dispersed while falling through this aperture, carries into it all the air it encounters and envelops and whose escape it prevents by the violence of its fall and by the impulsion of its motion. Accordingly, the air which continually enters through this aperture without ever being able to escape through it, rushes violently through the opening which it finds to be free. Since this proof is the only one by which he proves the mixture of air and water, and since it does not show it in any way, it turns out that he does not prove it at all.

The mixture which he proves least and of which he makes most is that of water with the other elements; for all that one can conclude from the experiment with the handkerchief and the cat is that some of their fattiest and oiliest parts, already so disposed by heat, are kindled by friction. Then he states it to be his opinion that our space is full of this igneous matter, expanded and mixed with all the elements, as he assumes without proofs, and disseminated throughout the whole universe. That is the matter which he puts into the tube, and as for the suspension of the liquid, he ascribes it to the weight of the outer air. I was delighted to see him thus join in the opinion of those who have examined these experiments with the greatest penetration. For you know that the letter of the great Torricelli, written more than four years ago to Signor Ricchy, shows that since then he has been of the same thought and that all our scholars are in agreement with it, and more and more confirmed in it. Nevertheless, we are counting on the confirmation from the experiment which is to be performed on one of our high mountains; but I expect to receive a report on it only after some time, because in reply to letters which I wrote about it more than six months ago, I was always informed that snow makes their summits inaccessible.

That, then, is his second, and although it seems that there is little difference between this matter and what he put into his first letter, nevertheless it is greater than it seems, and it is as follows.

In his first thought, nature abhors a vacuum and makes her abhorrence of it felt; in the second, nature gives no sign of the abhorrence which she has for a vacuum, and does nothing to avoid it. In the first, he established a mutual adherence among all bodies in nature: in the second he removes all this adherence and all this desire for union. In the first, he gave the faculty of attraction to this subtle matter and to all the other bodies;

in the second, he abolishes all this active and passive attraction. Finally' he assigned many properties in his first of which he deprived it in the second; so that if it takes a few degrees to fall into nothingness, it is now exceedingly close to nothingness, and it would seem that only a bit of preoccupation prevents it from being precipitated into nothingness.

But I should like very much to hear from this Father where he got this ascendant which he has over nature, and this empire which he exercises so absolutely over the elements which serve him with so much dependence that they change their properties in proportion as he changes his thoughts, and that the universe accommodates its effects to the inconstancy of his intentions. I do not comprehend what blindness may be put to the test of such a light and how one can give any credence to things to which one has given birth and which one can destroy with the same facility.

But the greatest [difference] which I find between these two opinions, is that Father Noël assures and affirms the truth of the first and that he merely proposes the second as a simple idea. That is what my first letter obtained from him, and the principal effect which it had on his mind; so that if to his first opinion I replied that I did not believe it had the data necessary to assure a thing, I shall say to the second that since he gives it out only as an idea, and since neither reason nor the senses bear witness to the matter he establishes, I shall leave him to his opinion just as I leave to their opinions those who think the moon is inhabited and that in polar and inaccessible lands there are men entirely different from others.

Thus, Sir, you see that Father Noël puts into the tube a subtle matter which is distributed over the whole universe, and that he assigns to the outer air the power to uphold the suspended liquid. From this it is easy to see that this thought is in no way different from that of Monsieur Descartes, since he agrees on the question of the suspension of quicksilver as well as on the matter which fills this space, as is seen in his own words on page six, where he says that this matter, which he calls *subtle air*, is the same as what Monsieur Descartes has named *subtle matter*. That is why I felt less obligated to reply to him, since I ought to address this reply to him who is the inventor of this opinion.

As I was writing these last lines, Father Noël did me the honor of sending me his book on another subject which he entitles *The fullness of the vacuum*. He charged the person, who took the trouble to bring it, with assuring me that there was nothing in it against me, and that all the words which seemed harsh were not addressed to me but to the

Capuchin Reverend Father Valerianus Magnus. And the reason he gave me for this is that this Father upheld and affirmed the existence of a vacuum, whereas I merely professed to oppose those who have decided this question. But Father Noël would have exonerated me better, if he had made this testimony as public as the suspicion he has aroused.

I have glanced through this book, and I have found that here he has a new idea, and that in our tube he puts a matter which approaches the first, but that he attributes the suspension of quicksilver to a property which he assigns to it, which he calls *mobile lightness*, and not to the weight of the outer air, as he did in his letter.

And to give a little succinct survey of the book, the title, first of all, promises the demonstration of the fullness [of the vacuum] through new experiments and its confirmation by mine. At the beginning of the book he sets himself up as a defender of nature, and by an allegory which is perhaps a bit too protracted, he brings a suit in which he makes nature complain against the opinion of a vacuum as calumny. And without having had nature manifest her resentment and without her having charged him with defending her, he sets himself up as her advocate. And in this quality he guarantees to show the imposture and the false depositions of the witnesses with which he is confronted — this is what he calls our experiments — and he promises to provide witness against witness, that is to say, experiment for experiment and to demonstrate that ours have had very little recognition and are even less conclusive. But in the body of the book, when it comes to acquitting himself of his great promises, he merely speaks doubtfully; and after having led one to hope for such high vengeance, he merely brings conjectures instead of convictions. For in the third chapter, where he wishes to establish that it is a body, he simply says that he finds it more reasonable to say that it is a body. When it is a question of showing the mixture of the elements, he merely adds very feeble things to those which he had said in his letter. When it is a question of showing the fullness of the world, he gives no proof for it; and on these vain appearances he establishes his *ether*, which is imperceptible to all the senses, with the imaginary lightness which he attributes to it.

What is strange is, that after having stated doubts on which to base his opinion, he affirms it by false experiments. Nevertheless, he proposes them with such boldness that they would be accepted as genuine by all those who have not seen the contrary, for he says the eyes show it, that all this cannot be denied, that we see it with the eye, although our eyes make us see the contrary. So it is evident that he has seen none of the experiments of which he speaks; and it is strange that he should have spoken with so much assurance about things of which he was ignorant and of which he has made a report that is so highly inaccurate. For I desire to believe that he himself was deceived, and not that he wished to deceive others; the esteem in which I hold him leads me to judge that he has been too credulous rather than lacking in sincerity. Certainly he has grounds for complaining about those who told him that a bellows full of this seeming vacuum, if opened and promptly closed, pushes out a matter as perceptible as air, and that when a tube full of quicksilver and of this same emptiness is turned upside-down, the quicksilver falls as slowly in this vacuum as in the air, and that this vacuum retards its natural movement as much as the air. He has grounds, too, for complaining about many other things which he reports. Yet I assure him to the contrary, that the air enters there, and that the quicksilver falls in this vacuum with an extreme impetuosity, etc.

Finally, to show you that Father Noël does not understand the experiments in my epitome, I ask you to note this trait of his among others: I said in the first of my experiences which he reported, "that if a glass syringe with a tight fitting piston were plunged entirely into water with its mouth covered by a finger so that it touched the bottom of the piston — while the hand and the arm were put into the water for that purpose — one would need but mediocre force to withdraw it from the water and separate it from the finger without having any water at all enter it. This the philosophers believed could not be done with any finite force. In this way the finger often feels pulled painfully, and the piston leaves a space which apparently is empty, into which it seems that no body has been able to enter, since it is entirely surrounded by water which was unable to gain access, because the opening was stopped. Now if we pull the piston more, the apparent vacuum becomes greater, but the finger feels no greater pull from it." He believed that these words, *feels no greater pull from it,* have the same meaning as these words, *no longer feels any pull from it;* whereas according to all the rules of grammar it means that the finger does not feel a greater pull. And since he knows these experiments only from reading about them, he thought that in fact the finger no longer felt any pull, which is absolutely false, for it still feels it as much. But the hypothesis of this Father is so accommodating that he has proved by a necessary succession of his principles why the finger no longer feels any pull, although that is absolutely false. I believe that he could just as easily make the contrary seem reasonable by the same principles. But I do not know in what esteem judicious persons would hold his fashion of proving the affirmative and the negative of the same proposition with equal forcefulness.

You will see, Sir, from this that Father Noël bases this invisible matter on false experiments in order to explain by them others which he has misunderstood. Moreover, it is quite proper that he should avail himself of a matter which cannot be seen and which cannot be comprehended in order to reply to experiments which he has not seen and which he has not comprehended. When he is better informed, I have no doubt that he will change his mind and above all on his mobile lightness. That is why it is necessary to postpone the reply to this book until this Father has corrected it and when he has recognized the falsity of the facts and the imposture of the witnesses whom he cites in opposition, and when he no longer makes a case against an opinion on a vacuum as based on experiments which have had very little recognition and are even less conclusive.

Just as I was writing these words, I received a printed notice from this Father, which reverses the greater part of his book; he revokes the mobile lightness of the *ether*, by calling back the weight of the outer air to support the quicksilver. Hence I find it rather difficult to refute the thoughts of this Father, since he is the first to change them promptly, so that one cannot reply to him. I begin to see that his way of doing is very different from mine, because he produces his opinions as and when he conceives them. But their own inconsistencies suffice to show their unsoundness, since the authority with which he disposes of this matter clearly testifies that he is its author, and yet it exists only in his imagination.

All those who combat the truth are subject to similar inconstancy in their thinking, and those who fall into this variety are suspected of contradicting the truth. Moreover, it is strange to see among those who uphold the fullness of the earth the great number of opinions which clash with each other. The one supports the *ether* and excludes every other matter; another supports liquid spirits to the detriment of the *ether;* another supports air enclosed in the pores of bodies, and bans all other things; another supports air which is rarefied and devoid of all other bodies. Finally some have appeared who, not having dared to introduce the boundlessness of God, have chosen among men a person who is illustrious enough by his birth and by his merit to introduce his spirit here and to have it fill all things. Thus each one is the enemy of all the others, and since all of them conspire to destroy one, [he] necessarily [succumbs]. But since they merely triumph over each other, they are all victorious without any one being able to take advantage of his victory, because all this advantage is born of their own confusion. And so it is not necessary to combat them in order to overthrow them, since it suffices to abandon them to themselves, inasmuch as they are a divided body whose warring members rend each other from within. On the other hand, those who favor the vacuum remain in a union which is ever consistent and which by virtue of this has such relation to the truth that it must be followed until the truth appears to us uncovered. For it is not in this embarrassment and in this tumult that we must seek the truth; and we cannot find it outside of this maxim which merely permits decision on obvious things and which forbids us to assert or to deny those which are not obvious. It is this proper mean and this perfect temper in which you remain to such advantage and in which through a good fortune, which I cannot prize enough, I have always been brought up with a singular method and with more than paternal care.

These, Sir, are the reasons which restrained me and which I felt I should no longer conceal from you. Although it may seem that I present them in my interest rather than to satisfy your curiosity, I hope that this doubt may not extend to you, since you know that I am less concerned with these whimsical points of honor than with an eagerness for conversing with you. And I find much less charm in defending my opinions than in assuring you, Sir, that I am very cordially,

Your very humble and obedient servant

PASCAL

8. FRAGMENT OF A LETTER FROM PASCAL TO MADAME PERIER

April 1, 1648.

We don't know whether this [letter] will remain without end like many others, but we know well that we should like to write to you without end. We have here the letter of Monsieur de Saint-Cyran *On vocation*, which was recently printed without approval or permission, and which has shocked many people. We are reading it; we shall send it to you later. We shall be very glad to know your and my father's opinion of it. It is very elevated.

We have begun several times to write to you, but I have been prevented by the attitude [of Monsieur de Rebours] and by the discourses or, if you like, by the rebuffs of which you know. But after having clarified the matter as much as possible, one must approach it with a certain circumspection, and if there are occasions when one should not speak of such things, we may be dispensed from doing so. For since we do not doubt each other, and since we are mutually assured that in all these discourses our sole aim is the glory of God and that we have almost no communication with others, I do not see that we could have any scruples, so long as He gives us these sentiments. If to these considerations we add the bond between us which nature has made, and if to this bond we add the one which grace has made, I believe that far from finding in it a prohibition we will find an obligation in it. For I find that our happiness in being thus united has been so great that we must unite in recognizing and enjoying it. For we must confess that only since this time (which Monsieur de Saint-Cyran would have us call the beginning of life) can we consider ourselves as truly related, and that it has been God's pleasure to join us together in the new world in the spirit just as much as He has joined us on earth by ties of the flesh.

We entreat you to let no day pass without calling this to mind and ever to recognize the ways of God in this relationship in which He has not merely made us brother and sister but also children of the same father; for you know that my father has anticipated and, as it were, conceived us in this design. By virtue of this we must admire that God has given us both the foreshadowing and the reality of this union; for we have often said to each other that corporeal things are but the image of spiritual things, and that God has represented invisible things in the visible things. This thought is so general and so useful that we should allow no considerable period of time to pass without giving it due thought. We have said enough to each other with special reference to the relation of these two kinds of things. That is why we shall not speak of it here, for it is too long to write about, and too beautiful not to have been impressed on our memory; moreover, in my opinion, it is absolutely necessary. For our sins keep us entangled in corporeal and earthly things which are not merely the punishment of our sins, but also the occasion for committing new sins and the cause of our first ones. Hence, if we would arise from our fall, we must do so from the very place to which we have fallen. That is why we must be mindful of the advantage which the goodness of God has given us in ever leaving before our eyes an image of the blessings that we have lost. And in the very captivity to which His justice has reduced us we must surround ourselves with so many objects which serve us as an ever present lesson.

Hence we must consider ourselves as criminals in a prison completely filled with images of their liberator and with instructions necessary to be released from servitude. But we must confess that we cannot behold these holy images without a supernatural light. For just as all things speak of God to those that know Him, and just as they are revealed to those who love Him, so these same things are hidden from those who do not know Him. Accordingly we see that in the darkness of this world people follow them with brutish blindness, we see them become attached to them and make them the final goal of their desires; this cannot be done without sacrilege, for God alone must be the final goal as well as the sole and the true principle. To be sure, created nature has some resemblance with its Creator, and at least by their union with the rest of nature even the least things and the smallest and vilest parts of the world represent the perfect unity which is found only in God. Nevertheless, we cannot rightfully pay them sovereign respect because there is nothing so abominable in the eyes of God and men as idolatry, for idolatry renders to the creature the honor which is due solely to the Creator. Scripture is full of the vengeance of God on those who were guilty of idolatry, and the first commandment of the Decalogue, which embraces all the others, forbids adoration of the images of all things. But since He is far more jealous of our affections than of our respect, it is obvious that there is no crime which would be more injurious or more detestable than supreme love of created things even though they represent Him.

That is why those, to whom God has made these great verities known, must use these images in order to possess Him whom they represent, so that they may not remain forever in that carnal and Judaic blindness which leads men to take the shadow for reality. By regeneration God has freely withdrawn some from sin (which is veritable nothingness because it is contrary to God who is a veritable being) in order to give them a place in His Church which is His veritable temple. After He has freely withdrawn them from nothingness to the point of their creation in order to give them a place in the universe, they have a double obligation to serve Him and to honor Him. For inasmuch as they are creatures, they must remain in the order of creatures, and they must not profane the place they fill. And inasmuch as they are Christians they must, without ceasing, aspire to render themselves worthy to be members of the Body of Jesus Christ. Now the creatures who make up the world acquit themselves of this obligation by remaining in a limited perfection, inasmuch as the perfection of the world is also limited. But the children of God must impose no limits on their purity and their perfection because they are part of a body which is wholly divine and infinite in its perfection. So we see that Jesus Christ does not limit the commandment of perfection, and that He proposes a model of infinite perfection when He says: "Be ye therefore perfect, even as your Father which is in heaven is perfect." Moreover, a harmful and common error among Christians and even among those who profess piety lies in persuading themselves that there is a certain degree of perfection in which one is secure, and that it is unnecessary to go beyond this, since there is no wrong in stopping there, and since one may risk falling by ascending higher . . . [sentence incomplete].

9. LETTER FROM BLAISE PASCAL TO MADAME PERIER, HIS SISTER

Paris, November 5, 1648, afternoon.

My dear sister:
Your letter has called to our mind a misunderstanding which had been forgotten; so utterly does it belong to the past. The rather lengthy explanations which we received have brought out the old, general cause of our complaints, and the amends made to us for them have softened the bitterness which they had aroused in my father. We have said what you had already said without knowing that you had said it, and then we excused by word of mouth what you had since excused in writing without knowing that you had excused it. And we have found out what you have done only after we had done it ourselves, for just as we concealed none of it from my father, so he too disclosed everything to us and thereby ended all our suspicions. You know how these embarrassments disturb the peace of the household, both without and within, and how in such encounters one is in need of the warnings which you gave us too late.

We ourselves have some information to give you about your family. It seems that we have given you the information that you now give us in writing.

Firstly, I do not recall having talked to you about it, and in fact I have so little recollection of it, that it was quite new to me. Moreover, if it were true, I should fear you could not have humanly retained it, if you had not forgotten the person from whom you had learned it in order merely to remember God who alone can truly have taught it to you. If you remember it as a good thing, you could not think that you had it from anyone else; since neither you nor the others can learn it from anyone but God alone. For although in that kind of gratitude we do not stop with the men to whom we turn as if they were the authors of the benefits that we have received, nevertheless that does not fail to create a slight opposition in the sight of God. And it does so primarily in persons who are not entirely purged of carnal impressions which lead them to regard the objects which transmit benefits as the source of these benefits.

Not that we should not recognize and remember the persons from whom we have certain instructions when these persons have the right to give them, such as priests, bishops, and directors, because they are the masters of whom others are disciples. But as for us, that is a different matter; for as the Angel declines the adoration of a holy servant like himself, we shall say to you, in requesting you no longer to make use of these expressions of human gratitude, that you refrain from paying us similar compliments, because we are disciples just as you are.

The second has to do with your saying that it is not necessary to repeat these things to us, since we already know them well. This causes us to fear that here you are not differentiating enough between the things of which you speak and of which the world speaks. For beyond doubt, when we have learned these once and retained them well, we have no need of further instruction in them. On the other hand, it is not enough to learn those of the other kind once, and to have known them in the proper manner — that is to say through the inner working of God — for us to preserve their knowledge in the same way, even though we remember them well. Not that we cannot remember and retain an epistle of Saint Paul as easily as a book by Virgil. But the knowledge which we acquire in this way as well as its continuation is but a matter of memory. On the other hand, in order to understand [in St. Paul] this secret language which is foreign to those who are foreign to heaven, it is necessary that the same grace, which alone can give first intelligence of it, continue this intelligence. The same grace must make it ever present by retracing it without ceasing in the hearts of the faithful so as to make it live forever. Similarly, in the blessed, God continually renews their blessedness which is a result and a continuation of grace, just as the Church likewise holds that the Father continually begets the Son and maintains the eternity of His essence by an outpouring of His substance which is without interruption as well as without end.

Thus the continuation of the justice of the faithful is nothing but the continuation of the infusion of grace and not through one single grace which lives forever. It is this which teaches us perfectly our perpetual dependence on the mercy of God, since if He interrupts its flow ever so little, drought will necessarily set in. In view of this necessity, it is easy to see that we must continually make new efforts to acquire this continued renewal of spirit. For we can preserve the old grace only by acquiring a new grace, otherwise we will lose that which we think we retain, like those, who, wishing to shut in the light, merely shut in darkness. Thus we must unceasingly watch over the purification of our inner being, which is ever sullied by new stains while at the same time retaining the old ones, since without constant renewal we are incapable of receiving this new wine which will not be put into old bottles.

That is why you must not fear to place before our eyes the things which we have in our memory and which we must recall in our hearts. For beyond doubt your discourse may serve them better as an instrument of grace than can the idea of it which remains in our memory, since grace is granted especially in answer to prayer. Moreover, this love which you have had for us is one prayer among the number of those which should never be interrupted. And so it is that one should never refuse to read nor to hear these holy things, however familiar and generally well known they may be; for without the spirit which must vivify it, our memory as well as the teachings it retains is but an inanimate and Judaical body. And it happens very often that God avails Himself of these external means to make them understood and to leave all the less ground for the vanity of men when thus they receive grace within them. It is thus that a book and a sermon, however commonplace they may be, bring much more fruit to him who yields himself eagerly, than will the excellence of more elevated discourses which usually afford more pleasure than instruction. And we sometimes see that those who listen to them properly, no matter how ignorant and almost stupid they may be, are moved by the very name of God and by the very words which threaten them with hell, even though this be all they understand of them and although they knew this as well before.

The third has to do with your saying that you are writing these things only to make us understand that you are of this opinion. We have reason to praise you and to thank you equally in this matter; we praise you for your perseverance, and we thank you for the evidence of it which you give. We had already got that admission from Monsieur Perier, and the things which we had sent word of to him had assured us;

we can tell you how much they satisfied us only by describing to you the joy that you would have if you heard the same thing said of us.

We have nothing in particular to say to you excepting with regard to the plan of your house. We know that Monsieur Perier takes whatever he undertakes too seriously to think fully of two things at a time, and that this entire plan is so long that, in order to carry it out, he would have to go for a long time without thinking of any other thing. We know well also that his project is for only a part of the building; but besides being but too long in itself, it involves the completion of the rest as soon as there is no further obstacle in the way. And this despite every resolve which one may make to prevent it, particularly if it takes as much time to build it as to undeceive oneself of the hidden charms which are there. Consequently we have advised him to build much less than he meant to and nothing but what is plainly needed, though in line with the same plan, so that he will not become too heavily involved, and so that he will not deprive himself of the means of achieving it. We request you to think this over seriously, to make up your mind, and to advise him accordingly. This for fear that he may have too much prudence, and devote much more care and energy to the building of a house, which he is not obliged to build, than was devoted to the mystic tower. You remember the one of which Saint Augustine speaks in one of his letters that he promised to finish in his conversations.

Adieu. B[LAISE] P[ASCAL] — J[ACQUELINE] P[ASCAL]

Postscript by Jacqueline: I hope to be able to write to you myself about my own affair of which I shall give you details. Meanwhile pray to God for the outcome.

If you know some good soul, have him pray to God for me, too.

10. LETTER FROM MONSIEUR PASCAL TO MONSIEUR AND MADAME PERIER, AT CLERMONT, ON THE OCCASION OF THE DEATH OF MONSIEUR PASCAL, THE FATHER, WHO DIED AT PARIS, SEPTEMBER 24, 1651

Paris, October 17, 1651.

Since both of you have now been informed of our common sorrow, and since the letter we had begun has given you some consolation by its account of the blessed circumstances which accompanied our affliction, I cannot keep from you those which remain in my memory. I pray God to grant these consolations to me, and to renew for me several which in the past we received by His grace and which have been given to us anew on this occasion by our friends.

I no longer know where the first letter ended. My sister sent it without being aware that it was not finished. I seem to recall merely that in substance it contained some particulars on God's guidance in life and in illness. I have written them so indelibly in my heart and they bring such steadfast consolation that I should like to repeat them here in case you were unable to see them for yourself in the preceding letter and if my sister were not to give you a more detailed account at her first convenience. Therefore, I shall tell you here only about the conclusion which I draw from them. This is that the end of his life was so Christian, so happy, so holy, and so to be desired that beyond those whose interest arises from natural ties, there is no Christian who should not rejoice over it.

On this great foundation I shall begin what I have to say with a very consoling discourse for those whose minds are free enough to understand it at the height of their grief. This is that we must seek consolation for our ills not in ourselves, not in men, and not in all created things but rather in God. And the reason for it is that all creatures are not the primary cause of the accidents which we call evils; rather, since divine Providence is their sole and veritable cause, their arbiter and their sovereign cause, we must beyond doubt have direct recourse to the source, and we must reascend to the origin in order to find genuine relief. Let us follow this precept and let us envisage this end not as a result of circumstance, not as a fatal necessity of nature, and not as a puppet of the elements and of the parts which compose man (for God has not abandoned His elect to caprice and to chance). Rather let us envisage this end as an indispensable, inevitable, appropriate holy consequence, useful to the well-being of the Church and to the exaltation of the name and the greatness of God. Let us view it as a decree of God's providence, conceived in all eternity to be fulfilled in the fullness of His time, in such a year, on such a day, at such an hour, in such a place, and in such a manner. Finally, let us consider that everything which has happened has throughout all time been foreseen and foreknown by God. If, I say, by a transport of grace we consider this death not in itself and outside of God, but outside of itself and in the intimate will of God, in the justice of His decree, in the order of His providence which is its veritable cause, and without which it would not have happened, by which alone it has happened, and in the manner in which it has happened, then we shall adore in humble silence the inaccessible height of His hidden designs. Then we shall venerate the holiness of His decrees, we shall bless the course of His providence; by uniting our will with that of God Himself, we shall desire with Him, in Him, and for Him the thing He has desired in us and for us in all eternity.

Let us then view it in this light, and let us practice this lesson that I learned from a great man in the time of our greatest affliction, namely that there is consolation in truth alone. Beyond doubt Seneca and Socrates have nothing persuasive [or consoling to offer] on this occasion. They made the same error that at first blinded all men: they all regarded death as natural to man; and all the discourses which they based on this false principle were so futile that they merely served by their uselessness to show how feeble man is in general, since the highest achievements of the greatest among men are so low and so puerile.

This is not the case with Jesus Christ; it is not so with canonical books. There the truth is discovered and joined as infallibly as it is infallibly separated from error. Let us then consider death in the [light of] truth which Holy Writ has taught us. We have this admirable advantage of knowing that death is veritably and actually the penalty for sin, imposed on man to expiate his crime, and necessary to man to purge him of sin; death alone can deliver the soul from the lust of its members, without which the Saints do not live in this world. We know that life and the life of Christians is a perpetual sacrifice which can be made complete only by death; we know that Jesus Christ, by coming into the world, considered Himself and offered Himself to God as a sacrifice and as a living sacrifice. We know that His birth, His life, His death, His resurrection, His ascension and His presence in the Eucharist, His eternal seat at the right [of God] are but a single and unique sacrifice; we know that what has happened in Jesus Christ must happen in all His members.

Let us then consider life as a sacrifice, and that the accidents of life make their impress on the spirit of Christians only insofar as they interrupt or fulfill this sacrifice. Let us call evil only that which makes a victim of God into a victim of the devil; but let us call that good which makes the victim of the devil in Adam into a victim of God, and on this basis let us examine the nature of death.

According to this rule we must have recourse to the person of Jesus Christ, for everything in men is abominable. And just as God views men only through the Mediator Jesus Christ, so men likewise should regard others and themselves only through the mediation of Jesus Christ. For if we do not pass through this medium, we shall find in ourselves nothing but veritable misfortunes or loathsome pleasures, but if we consider all things in Jesus Christ we shall find every consolation, every satisfaction, every edification.

Let us then consider death in Jesus Christ and not without Jesus Christ. Without Jesus Christ it is horrible, it is detestable, and the horror of nature. In Jesus Christ it is entirely different; it is worthy of love, it is holy and the joy of the faithful. All is sweetness in Jesus Christ, even death; that is why He suffered and died to sanctify death and suffering. And that is why, as God and as man, He was all that is great and all that is abject in order to sanctify in Himself all things except sin and to be a model in all situations.

To consider the meaning of death and the meaning of death in Jesus Christ, we must see what place it holds in His continuous and uninterrupted sacrifice, and to do that we must note that in sacrifices the principal part is the death of the victim. The oblation and the sanctification which precede are merely the setting. The fulfillment, however, is death. By annihilating its life, the creature renders unto God all the homage of which it is capable. This it does by self-annihilation before the eyes of Divine Majesty and by adoring His sovereign existence which is the only true existence. It is true that there is still another part, after the death of the victim, without which its death is useless: this is the acceptance which God makes of the sacrifice. It is what the Scriptures say: *Et odoratus est Dominus suavitatem.* And God smelled and received the odor of sacrifice. This is what veritably crowns oblation, yet it is an act of God toward the creature rather than of the creature toward God, and it does not prevent the last act of the creature from being death.

All these things have been accomplished in Jesus Christ. By entering the world, He offered Himself: *Obtulit semetipsum per Spiritum sanctum. Ingrediens mundum, dixit: Hostiam noluisti. . . . Tunc dixi: Ecce venio. In capite, etc.* "He has offered Himself through the Holy Spirit. On coming into the world, He said: Lord, sacrifice Thou wouldest not, but a body hast Thou prepared me. Then said I, Lo, I come to do Thy will, O God, and Thy law is rooted in my heart." Here is His oblation. His sanctification followed immediately upon His oblation. This sacrifice continued throughout His whole life, and found its fulfillment in His death. He had to pass through suffering to enter into His glory. And although He was the son of God, He had to learn obedience. But in the days of His flesh, when He had offered up supplications with loud crying unto Him that was able to save Him from death, He was heard in that He feared. And God resuscitated Him and sent His glory, foreshadowed by fire from heaven which fell on the victims, to burn and consume His body, and to make it live spiritually of the life of glory. That is what Jesus Christ obtained and what was accomplished by His resurrection.

Since this sacrifice was completed by the death of Jesus Christ and consummated even in His body through the resurrection in which sinful flesh was consumed in glory, Jesus Christ had fulfilled everything on His part. Then there remained only the acceptance of the sacrifice by God, and as the smoke of sacrifice rose and carried its fragrance to the throne of God, Jesus Christ in this state of complete immolation was offered, carried aloft, and received at the very throne of God. And this is what was accomplished by the ascension in which He was elevated by His own strength and by the might of His [Holy] Spirit which completely surrounded Him. He was carried aloft like the incense of sacrifices, which foreshadow Jesus Christ; He was carried on high by the air that upheld Him, and that foreshadows the Holy Spirit. And for us The Acts of the Apostles marks the eagerness with which He was received in heaven, in order to assure us that this holy sacrifice accomplished on earth was acceptable to God and was received in God's bosom where it burns in glory, world without end.

This is the state of things in our sovereign Lord. Now let us consider them in us. The Church is the society of the faithful and above all the society of the elect, into which Jesus Christ, by special privilege as the only son of God, entered from the moment of His incarnation. From the moment when we enter the Church we are offered and sanctified. This sacrifice is continued in life and fulfilled in death. In death the soul, veritably forsaking all the vices and the love of earth, whose corruption constantly infects it during life, achieves its immolation, and is received in the bosom of God.

Let us then not be afflicted like the heathen who have no hope. We did not lose my father at the moment of his death. We had lost him, so to speak, as soon as he entered the Church through baptism. From then on he belonged to God. His life was consecrated to God; his acts concerned the world only through God. In death he was fully detached from sin; and this is the moment when he was received by God and when his sacrifice received its fulfillment and its crown. Thus he has done that to which he had consecrated himself; he has completed the work which God had given him to do; he has accomplished the one thing for which he was created. The will of God was accomplished in him, and his will was absolved in God. Let not our will take asunder what God has united; and let us suppress or moderate by the wisdom of truth those sentiments of corrupt and frustrated nature which has nothing but false images and whose illusions trouble the holiness of those sentiments which truth and the Gospel should give us.

Therefore let us no longer regard death as do the heathen, but rather as do the Christians, that is to say, with hope, as Saint Paul prescribes, since this is the special privilege of Christians. Let us no longer consider a body to be foul carrion, for deceitful nature regards it as such; but let us view it as the inviolable and eternal temple of the Holy Spirit, as faith teaches us. For we know that the bodies of the saints are inhabited by the Holy Spirit until the resurrection, which will take place by virtue of this Spirit which dwells in them to that end. This is the faith of the Church Fathers. For this reason we honor the relics of the dead. In accordance with this true principle the Eucharist was formerly placed in the mouth of the dead; for, since men knew that they were the temple of the Holy Spirit, they believed that they merited this union with the Holy Sacrament. But the Church has changed this custom, not because bodies are not holy, but because the Eucharist should not be given to the dead, since it is the bread of life and of the living.

Let us no longer consider a man as having ceased to live, even though nature suggests this, but rather as beginning to live, as truth assures us. Let us no longer consider his soul as having perished and as being reduced to nothingness, but rather as quickened and united with the living Lord. And, by attention to these verities, let us correct erroneous conceptions which have been so strongly impressed upon us, and impulses of horror which are so natural to man.

If we are to overcome this horror more fully we must indeed understand its origin. If I am to indicate it to you in a few words, I shall be compelled to tell you in general the source of all vices and of all sins. I have learned this from two very great and very holy persons. The truth which opens up this mystery is that God has created man with two loves, the love of God and the love of self; yet with this law that the love of God shall be infinite, that is to say, with no end other than God Himself, and that the love of self shall be finite and leading back to God.

In this state man not only loved himself without sin, but could love himself only without sin.

With the coming of sin, man has lost the first of these loves. And since love of self has remained alone in this great soul which is capable of infinite love, this self-love has spread and overflowed into the vacuum which the love of God has left. And thus he has loved himself and all things for himself, that is to say, infinitely.

That is the origin of self-love. It was natural for Adam and appropriate in his state of innocence; but it has become criminal and immoderate as a result of his sin.

That is the source of this love and the cause of its shortcomings and of its excess.

It is the same with the desire to dominate, with laziness, and others. This, too, could be developed easily. Let us return to our sole theme. The horror of death was natural to Adam while he was innocent, because, being very pleasing to God, his life could not be other than pleasing to him as a man. And death was horrible when it ended a life which was in conformity with the will of God. Then, when he had sinned, man's life became corrupt; his body and his soul became enemies, and both became the enemy of God.

Though this horrible change has infected so holy a life, love of life has nevertheless remained; the horror of death has likewise remained. This was right for Adam, but it is wrong and criminal for us.

That is the origin of the horror of death, and the cause of its deficiency.

Let us then clarify this error of nature by the light of faith.

The horror of death is natural for man in a state of innocence; death is indeed horrible when it ends a life that is wholly pure. We had good reason to hate it when it separated a holy soul from a holy body, but we have good reason to love it when it separates a holy soul from an impure body. We had good reason to flee from death when it disrupted the harmony between soul and body, but not when it calms irreconcilable strife. In short, we had reason to abhor death when it afflicted an innocent body, when it deprived the body of the freedom to honor God, when it separated the soul from a body that yielded itself and co-operated with His will, and when it ended all the good of which man is capable. But it is quite wrong to maintain these same sentiments when death ends an impure life, when it deprives the body of the freedom to sin, and when it delivers the soul from a very powerful rebel that opposes all its striving for salvation.

Then let us not abandon this love of life which nature has given us, inasmuch as we have received it from God; but let it be the love of the same life for which God has given it to us, and not the love of a contrary end.

While consenting to the love which Adam had for his life of innocence and to the love which Jesus Christ, who seemed to suffer death with repugnance, had for His own life, let us proceed to hate a life which is contrary to that which Jesus Christ loved. And let us fear only the death which Jesus Christ feared, the death which comes to a body that is pleasing to God. But let us not fear that other death which, by punishing a guilty body and by purging a vicious body, gives us quite different feelings if we have a bit of faith, hope, and charity.

One of the great principles of Christianity is that everything that happened to Jesus Christ must take place in the soul and in the body of every Christian. Just as Jesus Christ suffered during His mortal life, died unto this mortal life, was raised from death to a new life, ascended to heaven, and sits at the right hand of the Father, so the body and the soul must suffer, die, be raised, ascend to heaven, and sit at the right hand.

All these things are fulfilled in the soul during this life, but not in the body.

The soul suffers and dies of sin in penitence and in baptism; the soul is raised to a new life in the same baptism; the soul leaves the earth and ascends to heaven in the hour of death, and sits at the right hand in the time which God decrees.

None of these things happens in the body during this life, but the same things happen to it subsequently.

For at death, the body dies unto its mortal life; in the general judgment, it will be raised to a new life; after the judgment it will ascend to heaven, and will be seated at the right hand.

Thus the same things happen to the body and to the soul, but at a different time, and the changes in the body occur only when those in the soul have taken place, namely in the hour of death. And so death is the crowning of the soul with blessedness, and it is the beginning of the blessedness of the body.

These are the admirable ways of divine wisdom in the salvation of the saints; on this subject Saint Augustine teaches us that God has so ordered it for fear that if the body of man were dead and raised forever in baptism, we would have entered upon obedience to the Gospel only through love of life. Instead of that, the greatness of faith shines forth far more when we approach immortality through the shadows of death.

This is assuredly our belief, and the faith that we profess; I believe that all I have just said more than suffices to console you through my faint efforts. I should not undertake to extend this aid as coming from myself; but since I am but repeating what I have learned, I do so with assurance while praying God to bless these seeds, and to grant that they may grow, for without Him we can do nothing and His most holy words will not take root in us, as He Himself has said.

Not that I wish you not to resent this blow. It is too grievous; it would indeed be unbearable without supernatural aid. It is not meet for us to be without grief like the angels who have none of the feelings natural to man. Neither is it meet for us to be without consolation like the heathen who have no consciousness of grace. But it is meet that we should be afflicted and consoled like Christians, and that the consolation of grace should prevail over natural sentiments. We should say with the apostles: "We are persecuted and we bless," so that grace may not merely be in us, but may be victorious in us. Thus as we hallow the name of our Father, His will shall be made our will; may His grace reign and rule over nature, and may our affections be likened unto the substance of a sacrifice which His grace consummates and annihilates for the glory of God; and may these particular sacrifices honor and anticipate the universal sacrifice in which all nature shall be consummated by the power of Jesus Christ.

Thus we shall profit from our shortcomings, since they will serve as the substance for this burnt offering; for it is the aim of true Christians to profit from their own weaknesses because all things work together for good to the elect.

And if we take good care we shall find it most helpful to consider the matter in truth as we have just said. It is true that the death of the body is but the image of the death of the soul. Now since we build on the principle that in this occurrence we have every possible reason to hope for the salvation of the soul, it is certain that if we can stay the course of woe, we must profit thereby. For since the death of the body is so terrible that it causes us such feelings of grief, the death of the soul would indeed bring us even greater inconsolable grief. God has sent us the former; God has turned away the latter. Let us therefore consider the greatness of our blessings amid the greatness of our ills, and let the height of our sorrow be the measure of the height of our joy.

There is nothing which can moderate our grief, unless it be the fact that their souls may languish for some time in the punishments which are destined to purge the rest of the sins of this life; we must exert ourselves carefully to soften the wrath of God.

Prayer and sacrifices are a sovereign remedy in these troubles. But, in our afflictions, I have learned from a holy man that one of the most substantial and useful charities toward the dead is to do the things which they would want us to do if they were still in the world, and to put into practice the holy precepts which they gave us, and to place ourselves for them into the state which they now desire for us.

In so doing we somehow make them live again in us, since their counsels are still living and active in us; and just as the heresiarchs are punished in another life for the sins in which they have engaged their followers, in whom their venom still lives, so the dead are rewarded, beyond their own merit, for those to whom they have given consistency by their precepts and by their example.

Let us then do everything in our power to make our father live anew in us before God; and let us console ourselves in the union of our hearts where it seems to me he is still living; and let our reunion somehow return his presence to us, as Jesus Christ is present in the assembly of His faithful.

I pray God to mold us and to keep us in these sentiments and to continue those which He seemingly has given to me, that I may have greater tenderness for you and for my sister than ever. For it seems to me that the love which we had for my father must not be lost to us, and that we must unite ourselves anew, that we must above all inherit the affection which he bore for us, in order that we may love each other even more heartily, if that be possible.

I pray God to fortify us in these resolutions; in this hope I entreat your permission to state an opinion which you would indeed reach without me, but which I shall state nevertheless. This is that, after having found reasons to console ourselves about him, we shall not fail to find consolation for ourselves, as we foresee occasions where his presence would fill our needs and come to our aid.

I am the most interested party in this. If I had lost him six years ago, I should have been lost; and although at present I believe he is not quite so absolutely indispensable to me, I know he would still have been a necessity to me for ten years, and helpful to me all my life. But we must hope that since God has decreed his death in such a time, in such a place and in such a manner, it is doubtless most expedient for His glory and for our salvation.

Strange as it may seem, I believe that we should regard all happenings in this light, and no matter how sinister they may seem to us, we must hope that God will find in them the source of gladness for us if we but trust to His guidance.

We know certain noblemen who feared deaths in their household which God may have averted because of their prayer. But this has been the cause or occasion of so much misery, that one might well wish their prayer had not been granted.

Man is assuredly too infirm to be able to take a sane view of the course of future events. Let us then hope in God and let us not be wearied by indiscreet and foolhardy anticipation. Let us trust in God for the guidance of our lives, and may grief not have domination over us.

Saint Augustine teaches us that in every man there is a serpent, an Eve and an Adam. The senses and our nature are the serpent. Eve is lustful appetite, and Adam is reason.

Nature constantly tempts us, and lustful appetite often fills us with desire; but sin is not committed if reason does not consent. Therefore, let us leave this serpent and this Eve to their devices, if we cannot do otherwise; but let us pray to God that His grace may so strengthen us that Adam may remain victorious. Then let Jesus Christ be the victor over Adam, and let Him reign in us forever and ever. Amen.

11. LETTER FROM PASCAL TO HER MOST SERENE HIGHNESS, THE QUEEN OF SWEDEN

[About June, 1652]

Madame:

If I had as much good health as zeal I should go in person to present to Your Majesty a work to which I have devoted several years and which I venture to offer at this great distance. I should not permit hands other than mine to have the honor of placing it at the feet of the greatest princess of the world. This work, Madame, is a machine which performs arithmetical calculations without a pen and without counters. Your Majesty is not unaware of the labor and the time entailed in new productions, especially when their inventors themselves desire to bring them to their ultimate perfection. Consequently it would be needless to say how much I have worked on this one; I can do no more than say that I have devoted myself to it with as much ardor as if I had foreseen that some day it would be seen by so august a person. But, Madame, if this honor did not actually motivate my efforts, it will at least be their reward, and I shall consider myself but too fortunate, if in the wake of so many vigils it may give to Your Majesty a few moments of gratification.

Moreover, I shall not importune Your Majesty with details about the nature of this machine; if you have any curiosity about it, you may perhaps be content with a discourse about it which I addressed to Monsieur de Bourdelot. In this I touched briefly on the whole history of this piece of work, the aim of its invention, the occasion for my research, the usefulness of its activities, the difficulties of its execution, the stages in its progress, its successful completion, and the ways of using it. I shall state here only the reason which leads me to offer it to Your Majesty; I consider it the crowning and the final happiness of its undertaking. I know, Madame, that I might seem suspect of having sought my own fame by presenting it to Your Majesty. This machine might be considered extraordinary merely because it is seen to be addressed to you, and though it should be offered to you only by virtue of its excellence, people may judge it to be excellent for the sole reason that it is offered to you. Nevertheless this is not the hope which has inspired my design. It is too great, Madame, to have any object other than that of Your Majesty. What has really impelled me is the union in your sacred person of two things which fill me equally with admiration and respect, namely sovereign authority and sound science. For I have a very special veneration for those who have attained the highest rank, whether in power or in knowledge. If I am not mistaken, these latter may be considered as sovereigns quite as well as the former. The same degrees of rank may be encountered among geniuses as among nobles, and it seems to me that the power of kings over their subjects is but an image of the power of minds over those minds which are their inferiors, over those whom they have the right to lead by persuasion. Among them, this is similar to the right to command in political Government. Indeed, this second empire seems to me to be of an even more exalted order because the mind is of a higher order than the body; and it is all the more equitable because it can be exercised and preserved only through merit, whereas the other may depend wholly upon birth or fortune. Hence it must be admitted that each of these empires is great in itself. But, Madame, if you will permit me to say so, I am detracting nothing from Your Majesty when I state that the one seems to me to be imperfect without the other. No matter how powerful a monarch may be, his glory lacks something if he lacks pre-eminence of the mind, and no matter how enlightened a subject may be, his rank is always lowered by his dependence. Men, who naturally desire what is most perfect, have up to the present constantly aspired to find this sovereign par excellence. All kings and all scholars were but faint images that met their expectations only halfway; in the entire history of the world our ancestors could hardly find a king who was tolerably learned. This masterpiece was reserved to our century. And in order that this great marvel might seem to be accompanied by every possible astounding trait, a young queen fills this high place which men were unable to attain. In her are joined the advantage of experience with the tenderness of her years; leisure and study are joined with the duties attendant upon royal birth, and the eminence of science with the frailty of sex. It is Your Majesty, Madame, that has provided the universe with this unique example which it lacked. In Your Majesty power is dispensed through the light of science, and science is elevated by the luster of authority. By virtue of this marvelous union Your Majesty sees nothing higher than her power, neither does she see anything higher than her mind; in consequence she will be the marvel of all the centuries to come, as she has been the product of all the centuries that have preceded her. Reign therefore, incomparable princess, in a manner that will be entirely new; may your genius bring into subjection everything that is not subjugated by your arms; reign by the right of birth for a long succession of years and over as many triumphant provinces, but ever reign over the whole extent of the earth by the might of your merit. As for me, not having been born under the first of your empires, I desire all the world to know that I glory in living under the second; in testimony of this I dare raise my eyes to my Queen in giving her this first proof of my dependence.

This, Madame, is what leads me to make this present to Your Majesty, however unworthy it may be of you. My weakness has not stunned my ambition. I have thought that although the very name of Your Majesty seems to remove from you everything that is disproportionate to you, it will nevertheless not reject everything that is inferior to you; otherwise your greatness would be without homage, and your glory without eulogy. You will be content to receive a great effort of the mind, without demanding that it be the effort of a great mind like your own. Through this very condescension you deign to enter into communication with other men. All these considerations joined together lead me to assure you, with all the submission of which one of the greatest admirers of your heroic qualities is capable, that I desire nothing with more ardor, Madame, than to be acknowledged by Your Majesty as her very humble, very obedient and very faithful servant

BLAISE PASCAL

12. EXCERPT FROM A LETTER BY BLAISE PASCAL TO MONSIEUR PERIER

Paris, Friday, June 6, 1653.

I have just received your letter enclosing one from my sister which I have not yet found time to read; moreover, I believe it would be useless to do so.

My sister took her final vows yesterday, Thursday, June 5, 1653. It was impossible for me to postpone it. The gentlemen of Port Royal feared that a slight postponement would lead to a long one; they wanted to hasten it for the reason that they hoped soon to put her in a post of direction; therefore haste is necessary because it takes several years of profession for that. This is the way they have paid me off. After all, I was unable to . . . [sentence incomplete].

13. POTESTATUM NUMERICARUM SUMMA (SUMMATION OF POWERS OF NUMBERS)

[1654?]

Remark

HAVING GIVEN, BEGINNING WITH UNITY, SEVERAL CONSECUTIVE NUMBERS, SUCH AS 1, 2, 3, 4, WE KNOW HOW TO FIND, BY METHODS WHICH THE ANCIENTS HAVE TAUGHT US, THE SUM OF THEIR SQUARES, AND EVEN THE SUM OF THEIR CUBES. BUT THESE METHODS, WHICH ARE APPLICABLE ONLY TO THE SECOND AND THIRD POWERS, DO NOT EXTEND TO HIGHER POWERS. IN THIS TREATISE I SHALL TEACH THE CALCULATION NOT ONLY OF SQUARES AND CUBES, BUT ALSO THE SUM OF THE FOURTH POWERS AND THOSE OF HIGHER POWERS UP TO INFINITY. AND I SHALL DO THAT NOT ONLY BY A SUCCESSION OF CONSECUTIVE NUMBERS BEGINNING WITH UNITY, BUT FOR A SUCCESSION BEGINNING WITH ANY NUMBER, SUCH AS THE SEQUENCE 8, 9, 10 . . . AND I SHALL NOT LIMIT MYSELF TO THE NATURAL SEQUENCE OF

NUMBERS. MY METHOD WILL APPLY ALSO TO A PROGRESSION DEALING WITH 2, 3, 4 OR ANY OTHER NUMBER — THAT IS TO SAY, A SEQUENCE OF NUMBERS WITH A COMMON DIFFERENCE OF TWO UNITS, LIKE 1, 3, 5, 7 . . ., 2, 4, 6, 8 . . ., OR A COMMON DIFFERENCE OF THREE UNITS, LIKE 1, 4, 7, 10, 13 . . . AND WHAT IS MORE, NO MATTER WHAT THE FIRST TERM OF THE SEQUENCE IS; WHETHER THIS FIRST TERM BE 1, AS IN THE SUCCESSION WITH A COMMON DIFFERENCE OF THREE, 1, 4, 7, 10 . . . OR WHETHER IT BE ANOTHER TERM OF THE PROGRESSION, AS IN THE SEQUENCE 7, 10, 13, 16, 19; OR EVEN WHEN IT IS OUTSIDE OF THIS PROGRESSION, AS IN THE SEQUENCE 5, 8, 11, 14 . . . WITH A COMMON DIFFERENCE OF THREE, AND BEGINNING WITH 5. THE REMARKABLE THING IS THAT A UNIQUE AND GENERAL METHOD WILL SUFFICE TO TREAT ALL THESE DIFFERENT CASES. THIS METHOD IS SO SIMPLE, THAT IT WILL BE SET FORTH IN A FEW LINES, AND WITHOUT THAT APPARATUS OF ALGEBRAIC NOTATIONS TO WHICH DIFFICULT DEMONSTRATIONS MUST HAVE RECOURSE. PEOPLE WILL JUDGE IT AFTER HAVING READ THE PROBLEM WHICH FOLLOWS.

Definition

Let there be a binomial $A + 3$ whose first term is the letter A, and whose second is a number. Let us raise this binomial to any power, for example to the fourth, which will give
$$A^4 + 12 \cdot A^3 + 54 \cdot A^2 + 108 \cdot A + 81;$$
the numbers 12, 54, 108 which multiply the various powers of A and are formed by the combination of numbers figured with the second term, 3, of the binomial, will be called *coefficients* of A.

Thus, in the example cited, 12 will be the coefficient of the cube of A; *54 that of the square, and 108 that of the first power.*

As for the number 81, we shall call it an absolute number.

Lemma

Let there be some number such as 14, and a binomial $14 + 3$, whose first term is 14, and the second any number such as 3, so that the difference between the numbers 14 and 14 + 3 shall equal 3. Let us raise these numbers to the same power, the fourth, for example. The fourth power of 14 is 14^4; that of the binomial 14 + 3 is

$$14^4 + 12 \cdot 14^3 + 54 \cdot 14^2 + 108 \cdot 14 + 81.$$

In this expression, the powers of the first term, 14, of the binomial are clearly affected by the same coefficients as the powers of A in the development of $(A + 3)^4$. This being granted, the difference between the two fourth powers 14^4 and

$$14^4 + 12 \cdot 14^3 + 54 \cdot 14^2 + 108 \cdot 14 + 81$$

is $12 \cdot 14^3 + 54 \cdot 14^2 + 108 \cdot 14 + 81$; this difference includes, on the one hand, the powers of 14 whose degree is less than the proposed fourth degree, these powers being affected by the coefficients which the same powers of A have in the development of $(A + 3)^4$. On the other hand, this difference includes the number 3 (*the difference between the proposed numbers*) raised to the *fourth* power [*for* the absolute number 3]. From this we deduce the *following Rule:*

THE DIFFERENCE BETWEEN LIKE POWERS OF NUMBERS INCLUDES: THE DIFFERENCE BETWEEN THOSE NUMBERS RAISED TO THE PROPOSED POWER; PLUS THE SUM OF ALL THE POWERS OF LOWER DEGREE OF THE SMALLER OF THESE TWO NUMBERS — THESE POWERS BEING MULTIPLIED RESPECTIVELY BY THE COEFFICIENTS WHICH THE SAME POWERS OF *A* HAVE IN THE DEVELOPMENT OF A BINOMIAL RAISED TO THE PROPOSED POWER — THE BINOMIAL HAVING *A* FOR ITS FIRST TERM, AND HAVING THE DIFFERENCE BETWEEN THE GIVEN NUMBERS FOR ITS SECOND TERM.

Thus the difference between $14^4 + 11^4$ will be

$$12 \cdot 11^3 + 54 \cdot 11^2 + 108 \cdot 11 + 81$$

since the difference between the first powers is 3. And so on.

Unique and General Method for Finding the Sum of the Same Powers of Terms in Any Progression

HAVING GIVEN, BEGINNING WITH ANY TERM, ANY SEQUENCE OF NUMBERS IN AN ARBITRARY PROGRESSION, TO FIND THE SUM OF LIKE POWERS OF THESE TERMS RAISED TO ANY DEGREE.

LET ANY NUMBER SUCH AS 5 BE TAKEN AS THE FIRST TERM OF A PROGRESSION OF NUMBERS WITH THE COMMON DIFFERENCE OF three, *CHOSEN ARBITRARILY. IN THIS PROGRESSION LET AS MANY TERMS BE CONSIDERED AS WE WISH, AS FOR EXAMPLE THE TERMS* 5, 8, 11, 14, *AND LET THESE TERMS BE RAISED TO ANY ARBITRARY POWER SUCH AS THE CUBE. THE QUESTION IS TO FIND THE SUM OF THE CUBES* $5^3 + 8^3 + 11^3 + 14^3$.

THESE CUBES ARE 125, 512, 1331, 2744; THEIR SUM IS 4712. THIS IS HOW THE SUM IS FOUND.

LET US CONSIDER THE BINOMIAL $A + 3$ WHICH HAS A FOR THE FIRST TERM, AND HAS THE DIFFERENCE IN THE PROGRESSION FOR ITS SECOND TERM.

LET US RAISE THIS BINOMIAL TO THE FOURTH POWER; A POWER GREATER BY ONE THAN THE PROPOSED DEGREE OF three; WE OBTAIN THE EXPRESSION

$$A^4 + 12 \cdot A^3 + 54 \cdot A^2 + 108 \cdot A + 81.$$

THIS BEING GRANTED, LET US CONSIDER THE NUMBER 17, *WHICH IN THE PROPOSED PROGRESSION FOLLOWS IMMEDIATELY UPON* 14, *THE LAST TERM CONSIDERED. LET US TAKE THE* fourth *POWER OF* 17, *WHICH IS* 83521, *AND LET US SUBTRACT FROM IT:*

Firstly: *THE SUM* 38 *OF THE TERMS CONSIDERED,* 5 + 8 + 11 + 14, *MULTIPLIED BY THE NUMBER* 108, *WHICH IS THE COEFFICIENT OF A;*

Secondly: *THE SUM OF THE SQUARES OF THE SAME TERMS* 5, 8, 11, 14, *MULTIPLIED BY THE NUMBER* 54, *WHICH IS THE COEFFICIENT OF A^2.*

AND SO ON, IN CASE THERE ARE OTHER POWERS OF A OF A LOWER DEGREE THAN THE PROPOSED third *DEGREE.*

THESE SUBTRACTIONS HAVING BEEN MADE, WE SUBTRACT ALSO THE fourth *POWER OF* 5, *THE FIRST TERM PROPOSED.*

FINALLY WE SUBTRACT THE NUMBER 3 (*THE COMMON DIFFERENCE*) *ITSELF RAISED TO THE* fourth *POWER AND TAKEN AS MANY TIMES AS THERE ARE TERMS IN THE PROGRESSION; IN THIS INSTANCE* four *TIMES.*

THE REMAINDER DERIVED FROM SUBTRACTION WILL BE A MULTIPLE OF THE SUM SOUGHT; THIS WILL BE THE

PRODUCT OF THIS SUM BY THE NUMBER 12 WHICH IS THE COEFFICIENT OF A^3, THAT IS TO SAY, THE COEFFICIENT OF THE TERM A RAISED TO THE PROPOSED POWER OF three.

Thus in practice we must find the fourth power of 17, which is 83521, then subtract from it successively:

Firstly, the sum of the proposed terms $5 + 8 + 11 + 14$, or 38, then multiplied by 108, — the product being 4104;

Then the sum of the squares of the same terms, $5^2 + 8^2 + 11^2 + 14^2$, or $25 + 64 + 121 + 196$, or 406, which multiplied by 54, gives 21924;

Then the number 5 raised to the *fourth* power, or 625;

Finally the number 3 to the *fourth* power, or 81, then multiplied by *four*, which gives 324. Summing up, we must subtract the numbers 4104, 21924, 625, 324, whose sum is 26977. When we subtract this sum from 83521, the remainder is 56544.

The remainder thus obtained is equal to 4712, the sum sought, multiplied by 12; and in fact, 4712 multiplied by 12 equals 56544.

As can be seen, the application of the rule is easy. Now this is how it is demonstrated.

The number 17 raised to the *fourth* power, which we write 17^4, is equal to

$$17^4 - 14^4 + 14^4 - 11^4 + 11^4 - 8^4 + 8^4 - 5^4 + 5^4.$$

In this expression *only the term 17^4 appears with the + sign alone; the other terms are added and subtracted in turn.*

But the difference between the terms 17 and 14 is 3; similarly the difference between the terms 14 and 11, and the terms 11 and 8, and the terms 8 and 5. Since, then, according to our preliminary lemma:

$17^4 - 14^4$ equals $12 \cdot 14^3 + 54 \cdot 14^2 + 108 \cdot 14 + 81$.

Similarly

$14^4 - 11^4$ equals $12 \cdot 11^3 + 54 \cdot 11^2 + 108 \cdot 11 + 81$.

Similarly

$11^4 - 8^4$ equals $12 \cdot 8^3 + 54 \cdot 8^2 + 108 \cdot 8 + 81$.

Similarly

$8^4 - 5^4$ equals $12 \cdot 5^3 + 54 \cdot 5^2 + 108 \cdot 5 + 81$.

The term 5^4 does not need to be transformed.

Then as the value of 17^4 we find:

$12 \cdot 14^3 + 54 \cdot 14^2 + 108 \cdot 14 + 81$
$+ 12 \cdot 11^3 + 54 \cdot 11^2 + 108 \cdot 11 + 81$
$+ 12 \cdot 8^3 + 54 \cdot 8^2 + 108 \cdot 8 + 81$

$+ 12 \cdot 5^3 + 54 \cdot 5^2 + 108 \cdot 5 + 81$
$+ 5,^4$

or, *by inverting the order of the terms:*

$5 + 8 + 11 + 14$ multiplied by 108,
$+ 5^2 + 8^2 + 11^2 + 14^2$ multiplied by 54,
$+ 5^3 + 8^3 + 11^3 + 14^3$ multiplied by 12,
$+ 81 + 81 + 81 + 81$
$+ 5.^4$

If then we subtract from either side the sum:

$5 + 8 + 11 + 14$ multiplied by 108,
$+ 5^2 + 8^2 + 11^2 + 14^2$ multiplied by 54,
$+ 81 + 81 + 81 + 81$
$+ 5^4$;

There remains 17^4 diminished by the preceding quantities, or:

$- 5 - 8 - 11 - 14$ multiplied by 108,
$- 5^2 - 8^2 - 11^2 - 14^2$ multiplied by 54,
$- 81 - 81 - 81 - 81$
$- 5^4$;

which is found to equal the sum $5^3 + 8^3 + 11^3 + 14^3$ multiplied by 12. Q.E.D.

The statement and the general solution of the proposed problem can therefore be presented as follows.

Sum of Powers

HAVING GIVEN, BEGINNING WITH ANY TERM, ANY SEQUENCE OF TERMS OF ARBITRARY PROGRESSION, TO FIND THE SUM OF LIKE POWERS OF THESE SUPPOSED TERMS RAISED TO AN ARBITRARY DEGREE.

LET US MAKE UP A BINOMIAL WHICH HAS A FOR ITS FIRST TERM AND THE COMMON DIFFERENCE OF THE GIVEN PROGRESSION FOR ITS SECOND TERM. LET US RAISE THIS BINOMIAL TO A DEGREE WHICH IS ONE HIGHER THAN THE PROPOSED DEGREE, AND LET US CONSIDER IN THE DEVELOPMENT OBTAINED THE COEFFICIENTS OF THE VARIOUS POWERS OF A.

NOW LET US RAISE TO THE SAME DEGREE THE TERM WHICH, IN THE GIVEN PROGRESSION, IMMEDIATELY FOLLOWS THE LAST TERM TO BE CONSIDERED. THEN LET US

SUBTRACT FROM THE NUMBER OBTAINED THE FOLLOWING QUANTITIES:

First: *THE FIRST TERM GIVEN IN THE PROGRESSION — THAT IS TO SAY, THE SMALLEST OF THE GIVEN TERMS — RAISED LIKEWISE TO THE SAME POWER (JUST ABOVE THE PROPOSED DEGREE).*

Secondly: *THE COMMON DIFFERENCE IN THE PROGRESSION, RAISED TO THE SAME POWER, AND TAKEN AS MANY TIMES AS THERE ARE TERMS IN THE PROGRESSION.*

Thirdly: *THE SUMS OF THE GIVEN TERMS, RAISED TO THE VARIOUS DEGREES LESS THAN THE PROPOSED DEGREE, THESE SUMS BEING MULTIPLIED RESPECTIVELY BY THE COEFFICIENTS OF THE SAME POWERS OF* A *IN THE DEVELOPMENT OF THE BINOMIAL FORMED ABOVE.*

THE remainder *FROM THE SUBTRACTION THUS MADE IS A MULTIPLE OF THE NUMBER SOUGHT. IT CONTAINS THIS NUMBER AS MANY TIMES AS THERE ARE UNITS IN THE COEFFICIENT OF THE POWER OF* A *WHOSE DEGREE IS EQUAL TO THE PROPOSED DEGREE.*

Notice

The reader himself will deduce the practical rules which are applicable to each particular case. Suppose, for example, that we wish to find the sum of a certain number of terms of natural sequence beginning with an arbitrary number. Here is the rule we shall deduce from our general method:

IN A NATURAL PROGRESSION BEGINNING WITH ANY NUMBER, THE SEQUENCE OF THE NUMBER JUST HIGHER THAN THE LAST TERM, DIMINISHED BY THE SQUARE OF THE FIRST TERM AND OF THE NUMBER OF THE GIVEN TERMS, IS EQUAL TO DOUBLE THE SUM OF THE AFORESAID TERMS.

Let any succession of consecutive numbers be given whose first number is arbitrary, such as the *four* numbers 5, 6, 7, 8. I say that $9^2 - 5^2 - 4$ equals the double of $5 + 6 + 7 + 8$.

One can easily obtain analogous rules giving the sums of powers of higher degrees and applying to all progressions.

Conclusion

Those who are at all familiar with the doctrine of *indivisibles* will not fail to see what conclusion can be drawn from the preceding results for the determination of curvilineal areas. These results will permit immediate squaring of all kinds of parabolas and of an infinity of other curves.

If then we extend to continuous quantities the results found for numbers by the method presented above, we shall be able to state the following rule:

RULES RELATING TO NATURAL PROGRESSION WHICH BEGINS WITH UNITY.

THE SUM OF A CERTAIN NUMBER OF LINES IS TO THE SQUARE OF THE LONGEST, AS 1 IS TO 2.

THE SUM OF THE SQUARES OF THE SAME LINES IS TO THE CUBE OF THE LONGEST, AS 1 IS TO 3.

THE SUM OF THEIR CUBES IS TO THE FOURTH POWER OF THE LONGEST, AS 1 IS TO 4.

GENERAL RULE RELATIVE TO NATURAL PROGRESSION WHICH BEGINS WITH UNITY.

THE SUM OF THE SAME POWERS OF A CERTAIN NUMBER OF LINES IS TO THE POWER JUST HIGHER THAN THE LONGEST OF THEM AS UNITY IS TO THE EXPONENT OF THIS SAME POWER.

I shall not stop to give other cases because this is not the place to study them. It will suffice for me to have stated the preceding rules in passing. One can discover the others without difficulty by relying on this principle that *we do not increase a continuous magnitude when we add to it, in any desired number, magnitudes of an order of higher infinitude.* Thus points add nothing to lines; lines add nothing to surfaces; surfaces add nothing to solids. Or — to speak of numbers as is proper in a treatise on arithmetic — roots do not count in relation to squares, squares do not count in relation to cubes, and cubes do not count in relation to squared squares. So that we may neglect as void all quantities of a lower order.

I desired to add these few remarks, which are familiar to those who work with indivisibles, in order to bring out the ever admirable relationship which nature, charmed with unity, establishes between things which outwardly are far apart. The relationship appears in this example where we see the calculation of *dimensions of continuous magnitudes linked with the summation of powers of numbers.*

14. LETTER FROM MONSIEUR PASCAL TO MONSIEUR DE FERMAT

July 29, 1654.

Sir:

I have become just as impatient as you, and although I am still in bed I cannot refrain from telling you that last evening I received through Monsieur de Carcavi your letter on division of stakes which I admire more than I can say. I lack time to expatiate on it, but, in a word, you have found the two divisions in the games of dice and of points perfectly accurate. I am very well satisfied with this, for after the admirable agreement in which I find myself with you I no longer doubt that I am right.

I admire the method of the points much more than that of the dice. I have seen several persons find that of the dice, among them Monsieur le Chevalier de Méré who is the one who proposed these questions to me. Also Monsieur de Roberval, but Monsieur de Méré had never been able to find the exact value of the points, nor any way of arriving at it, so that I found that I was the only one who had known this proportion.

Your method is very certain and is the one which came to my mind first in this investigation. But since the labor in the combinations is excessive I found a short cut and, properly speaking, another shorter and more concise method which I should like to try to tell you briefly. For I should like subsequently to pour out my heart to you, if possible, so great is my joy at our meeting. I see very well that the truth is the same in Toulouse and in Paris.

This is approximately how I determine the share of each player when, for example, there are two players engaged in a game of three points, and each player has staked 32 pistoles on the match.

Let us suppose that the first player has won two points and the second has one point; they now play for a point on condition that if the first player wins it, he takes all the money at stake, namely 64 pistoles; if the other wins it, the games are two and two, and consequently if they wish to quit, each one ought to take out his original stake, namely 32 pistoles apiece.

Now consider, Sir, that if the first one wins, 64 belong to him; if he loses, 32 belong to him. Hence if he does not wish to risk this point and wants to quit without it, the first player must say: "I am sure of 32 pistoles, for even if I lose this point, I shall have them; but as for the 32 others, perhaps I shall have them, and perhaps you will have them; the chances are even. So let us divide these 32 pistoles equally, and in addition you give me the 32 of which I am sure. Then he will have 48 pistoles and the other will have 16.

Next let us assume that the first one has won two points and the other none, and they begin to play for a point. The stipulation now is that if the first wins, he will get all the money, 64 pistoles; if the other wins, they are back where they were in the preceding case, in which the first has *two* points and the other has *one*.

Now we have already shown that in this case 48 pistoles belong to the one who has the *two* points; then if they do not want to play further he must say as follows: "If I win, I shall win all or 64; if I lose, 48 will legitimately belong to me; so give me the 48 of which I am sure even if I lose, and let us divide the 16 others equally, since you have as good a chance to win them as I." Thus he will have 48 and 8, or 56 pistoles.

Finally, let us assume that the first one has only *one* point and the other has *none*. You see, Sir, if they begin to play for a new point, the stipulation is that if the first one wins it, he will have *two* points and the other will have *none*; and consequently as in the preceding case, 56 will belong to him; if he loses, they are even and so 32 pistoles belong to him. Therefore he must say: "If you do not want to play it, give me the 32 pistoles of which I am sure, and let us divide the rest of the 56 equally. Fifty-six minus 32 leaves 24; therefore divide the 24 equally, take 12 of them, and I take 12, which, plus my 32, makes 44."

Now in this way you see by simple subtractions that for the first point 12 pistoles of the other player belong to him; another 12 for the second; and 8 for the last.

Now, in order to end the mystery, since you also see everything in the open, and since I was doing this only to see if I was not mistaken, the value (by value I mean merely the amount of the other man's money due him) of the last two points is twice that of the last of three points, and four times that of the last of four points, and eight times that of the last of five points, etc.

But the proportion of the first points is not so easy to find. However, it is as follows, for I wish to conceal nothing; here is the problem by which I set great store, for it really pleases me very much.

Given any number of points we may wish, to find the value of the first one.

For example, let the number of points given be 8. Take the first eight even numbers and the first eight odd numbers, namely: 2, 4, 6, 8, 10, 12, 14, 16, and 1, 3, 5, 7, 9, 11, 13, 15.

Multiply the even numbers as follows: the first by the second, the product by the third, the product by the fourth, the product by the fifth, etc.; multiply the odd numbers as follows: the first by the second, the product by the third, etc.

The last product of the even numbers is the denominator, and the last product of the odd numbers is the numerator of the fraction which expresses the value of the first of *eight* points; that is to say, if each one stakes the number of pistoles expressed by the product of the even numbers, the number expressed by the product of the odd numbers will be the amount of money due from the other player.

This can be proved, though with much effort, by combinations such as you have imagined. I have been unable to demonstrate it by this other way of which I have just spoken; I have done it only by the combinations. Here are the propositions which lead to it; they are really propositions of arithmetic dealing with combinations. I am really quite pleased with their neat qualities.

If of any number of letters, let us say 8, such as A, B, C, D, E, F, G, H, you make all possible combinations of 4 letters, and then all possible combinations of 5 letters, and then of 6, of 7, and of 8, etc., and you take all possible combinations from half their total number up to their total, then I say this: If you join together half of the combinations of 4 with each one of the higher combinations, the sum will be the required number of the quaternary progression beginning with the binary, which is half of the total number.

For example, and I shall say it to you in Latin, because the French is of no help here:

Si quotlibet litterarum, verbi gratia octo:

A, B, C, D, E, F, G, H,

sumantur omnes combinationes quaternarii, quinquenarii, senarii, etc., usque ad octonarium, dico, si jungas dimidium combinationis quaternarii, nempe 35 (dimidium 70) cum omnibus combinationibus quinquenarii, nempe 56, plus omnibus combinationibus senarii, nempe 28, plus omnibus combinationibus septenarii, nempe 8, plus omnibus combinationibus octonarii, nempe 1, factum esse quartum numerum progressionis quaternarii cujus origo est 2: dico quartum numerum, quia 4 octonarii dimidium est.

Sunt enim numeri progressionis quaternarii cujus origo est 2, isti:

2, 8, 32, 128, 512, etc.,

Quorum 2 primus est, 8 secundus, 32 tertius, et 128 quartus, cui 128 aequantur:

+ 35 dimidium combinationis 4 litterarum
+ 56 combinationis 5 litterarum
+ 28 combinationis 6 litterarum
+ 8 combinationis 7 litterarum
+ 1 combinationis 8 litterarum.

That is the first proposition which is purely arithmetical; the other concerns the doctrine of the divisions of stakes and is as follows:

It should be said beforehand that if we have a game of 5, for example, and 4 are still to be played, the match will infallibly be decided in 8 which is the double of 4.

The value of the first point of the 5 on the money of the other is the fraction whose numerator is half of the combination of 4 over 8 (I am taking 4 because it equals the number of unplayed points, and 8 because it is the double of 4) and whose denominator is this same numerator plus all the higher combinations.

Thus, if I have one of 5 points, I will have $\frac{35}{128}$ on the money of my opponent. That is to say, if he has 128 pistoles I take 35 of them, and leave him 93, the remainder.

Now this fraction is the same as $\frac{105}{384}$, which is derived from the multiplication of the even numbers as the denominator and from the multiplication of the odd numbers as the numerator.

You will doubtless see all that well, if you take ever so little trouble to do so. That is why I consider it useless to speak further about it to you. Nevertheless I am sending you one of my old Tables; I lack the time to copy it. I shall reconstruct it. You will see there that the value of the first point is always equal to that of the second which is easily found by the combinations.

You will also see that the numbers in the first line constantly increase; so do those in the second; so do those in the third.

But then those in the fourth decrease; those in the fifth, etc. Which is strange.

I lack the time to send you the demonstration of a difficulty which astonished M . . . [onsieur Méré] very much, for he has a good mind, but he is not a geometrician (this, as you know, is a great shortcoming); he does not even understand that a mathematical line is infinitely divisible and thinks he understands very well that it is composed of a finite number of points. I have never been able to persuade him to the contrary. If you could do it, that would make him perfect.

Now he told me that he had found an error in the numbers for this reason:

If one undertakes to throw a six with one die, the odds in favor of doing it in 4 trials are as 671 to 625.

If one undertakes to throw a pair of sixes with two dice, the odds against it are 24 to 1.

Nevertheless 24 is to 36 (which is the number of the faces of the two dice), as 4 is to 6 (which is the number of faces of one die).

How great was his horror which made him say loudly that the propositions were not constant and that arithmetic was contradictory. But on the basis of the principles at which you have arrived you will easily see the reason for this.

I shall arrange in orderly fashion all that I have done with this when I have finished the Treatises on Geometry on which I have already been working for some time.

I have also made arithmetical calculations, and I am requesting you to give me your opinion of them on the following demonstration.

I refer to the lemma which everybody knows; that the sum of any given group of numbers in continued progression from unity such as

1, 2, 3, 4,

when multiplied by two is equal to the last number, 4, multiplied by the next higher number, 5. This is to say, that the sum of the numbers contained in A, when multiplied by two, is equal to the product of $A(A + 1)$.

Now I am coming to my proposition:

Duorum quorumlibet cuborum proximorum differentia, unitate dempta, sextupla est omnium numerorum in minoris radice contentorum,

Sint duae radices R, S unitate differentes: dico

$R^3 - S^3 - 1$.

aequari summae numerorum in S contentorum sexies sumptae.

Etenim S vocetur A; ergo R est

$A + 1$.

Igitur cubus radicis R, seu $A + 1$, est

$A^3 + 3A^2 + 3A + 1^3$.

Cubus vero S, seu A, est

A^3;

et horum differentia est
$$3A^2 + 3A + 1^3$$
id est
$$R^3 - S^3;$$
igitur si auferatur unitas,
$$3A^2 + 3A \text{ aeq. } R^3 - S^3 - 1.$$
Sed duplum summae numerorum in A seu S contentorum aequatur, ex lemmate,
$$A \text{ in } A + 1, \text{ hoc est } A^2 + A:$$
igitur sextuplum summae numerorum in A contentorum aequatur
$$3A^2 + 3A.$$
Sed
$$3A^2 + 3A \text{ aeq. } R^3 - S^3 - 1; \text{ igitur}$$
$R^3 - S^3 - 1$ aeq. sextuplo summae numerorum in A seu S contentorum. Quod erat demonstrandum.

People have raised no objections to this, but I was told that none were raised for the reason that everybody is today accustomed to this method. I claim that, without doing me a favor, people must admit the excellence of this sort of demonstration. Nevertheless I am very humbly awaiting your judgment.

Everything that I have demonstrated in arithmetic is of this nature; here are two more difficulties:

I have demonstrated a plane proposition by using the cube of one line compared with the cube of another. I claim that that is purely geometric and in the strictest manner.

Similarly I have solved this problem: Having given any four of four planes, four points and four spheres, find a Sphere which, touching the given Spheres, passes through the given points, and leaves on the planes portions of spheres containing given angles; *and this one:*

Having given any [three] of three circles, three points, and three lines, find a circle which, touching the circles and the points, leaves on the lines an arc containing a given angle.

I have fully solved these problems by using only circles and straight lines in the construction; but in the demonstration I made use of solid loci, of parabolas or hyperbolas. Nevertheless, I claim that, inasmuch as the construction is plane, my solution is plane, and must pass for such.

To importune you so long is to show but little appreciation of the honor you do me in permitting these conversations. My intention is always to say only a few words. What is closest to my heart is that the more I know you, the more I admire and honor you. If I do not say this to you, and if you saw the extent of this, you would award a place in your friendship to him who remains, etc.

PASCAL

PASCAL TO FERMAT
TABLE
MENTIONED IN THE PRECEDING LETTER

If each one stakes 256, in

		6 Trials	5 Trials	4 Trials	3 Trials	2 Trials	1 Trial
Of the 256 pistoles of my opponent there will belong to me for the	1st Trial	63	70	80	96	128	256
	2d Trial	63	70	80	96	128	
	3d Trial	56	60	64	64		
	4th Trial	42	40	32			
	5th Trial	24	16				
	6th Trial	8					

If each one stakes 256, in

		6 Trials	5 Trials	4 Trials	3 Trials	2 Trials	1 Trial
Of the 256 pistoles of my opponent there will belong to me for	The first trial	63	70	80	96	128	256
	The first 2 trials	126	140	160	192	256	
	The first 3 trials	182	200	224	256		
	The first 4 trials	224	240	256			
	The first 5 trials	248	256				
	The first 6 trials	256					

15. LETTER FROM PASCAL TO FERMAT

August 24, 1654.

Sir:

I am unable to disclose to you in full my thoughts on the division of stakes among several players in ordinary practice; moreover I have some hesitance about doing so, for fear that our admirable agreement which was so dear to me, might begin to be strained, for I am afraid that our opinions on this subject differ. I wish to disclose to you all my reasons, and you will do me the favor of correcting me, if I am in error, or of confirming me, if I have guessed right. I ask this of you earnestly and sincerely, for I shall feel certain only when you side with me.

When there are only two players, your method, which deals with combinations, is very reliable. But when there are three players I believe to have demonstrated that it is not quite accurate unless you are proceeding in some other way which I do not understand. But the method that I have disclosed to you and which I use everywhere applies to every imaginable condition in all sorts of divisions of stakes, whereas the method of combinations (which I use only in special cases where it is shorter than the general one) is good only in these very circumstances and not in others.

I am sure that I shall make myself understood, but it will require a bit of presentation on my part and a bit of patience on yours.

This is how you proceed when there are two players:

Suppose there are two players, playing for several points, and that one of them lacks two points to win, and the second lacks three; (as you say) we must determine in how many trials the match will be definitely decided.

It is easy to compute that this will be in four trials. From this you conclude that it is necessary to determine how these four trials are combined between the two players and how many combinations there will be for the first to win, and how many for the second, and how to divide the money proportionately. I should have had difficulty in understanding this discourse, if I had not known it beforehand; but then you had written with that thought in mind. Hence, to see how four trials are divided between two players, we must imagine that they are playing with a die having two faces, such as in heads and tails (since there are only two players) and that they are throwing four of these dice (because they are making four trials); now we must see how many different positions these dice may have. This is easy to compute. They may have sixteen, which is the second power of four, or its square. For let us imagine that one of the faces is marked a, favorable to the second. Then these four dice may fall in one of these sixteen positions: aaaa ... bbbb.

And because the first player lacks two points, every face which has two a's will make him win; hence he has 11 in his favor. And because the second lacks two points, all the faces with three b's can make him win: hence there are 5. Consequently they must share the sum 11 to 5.

That is your method when there are two players. On this you say that if there are more players, it will not be difficult to determine the shares by the same method.

On this, Sir, I must say to you that this division for two players, based on the combinations is good and accurate. But if there are more than two players, it will not always be accurate and I shall tell you the reason for this difference.

I have told our gentlemen about your method, to which Monsieur de Roberval raised this objection:

a	a	a	a	1
a	a	a	b	1
a	a	b	a	1
a	a	b	b	1
a	b	a	a	1
a	b	a	b	1
a	b	b	a	1
a	b	b	b	2
b	a	a	a	1
b	a	a	b	1
b	a	b	a	1
b	a	b	b	2
b	b	a	a	1
b	b	a	b	2
b	b	b	a	2
b	b	b	b	2

That it is wrong to base the mode of division on the supposition that we make four trials, since when one player has two to make and the other three, it is not necessary to make four trials. For it may happen that only two or three trials are made, or in fact perhaps four.

And so he did not see why we claimed to make the fair division on the feigned supposition that four trials were to be made, since the natural stipulation of the game is that the play ends as soon as one of the players has won. At least, if that were not wrong, that would not be demonstrated; consequently he had some suspicion that we had made a paralogism.

I replied to him that I was not relying so much on this method of combinations, which really is out of place here, as on my other universal method, which overlooks nothing and which carries its demonstration with it; this method finds precisely the same division as that of the combinations. Moreover I demonstrated the correctness of the division between two players by combinations in the following way:

Suppose that one of two players lacks two points and the other lacks three. They now agree to make four complete trials, that is to say, they will throw the four dice of two faces each all at the same time. I ask, is it not true that if they have resolved to play for the four points, the division must be such as we have said, following the number of positions favorable to each one?

He remained in agreement with this, and in fact this is demonstrable. But he denied that the same thing holds when the playing is not limited to the four trials. Hence I say this to him:

Is it not clear that the same players, not obliged to make four trials, but wishing to stop playing as soon as one has reached his number, may without loss nor advantage, limit themselves to making four complete trials and that this agreement does not change their situation at all? For if the first one wins the first two out of four, he will refuse to play two more, since if he wins them, he gets no more, and if he loses them, he gets no less; for these two which the other has won are not enough, since he needs three, and thus four trials are not enough for both of them to achieve the number they lack.

Certainly it is easy to see that it is all the same to both and a matter of indifference to them to play according to the natural rules of their game, which is to finish as soon as one had his score, or to make all four trials. Therefore, since these two conditions are alike and immaterial, the division must be the same in both. Now it is fair when they are obliged to make the four trials, as I have shown; therefore it is fair also in the other case.

That is how I demonstrate it, and if you observe carefully, this demonstration is based on the equality of the two situations, real and hypothetical of the two players, and that the same player will always win in both; and if he wins or loses in the one, he will win or lose in the other, and never will both have their due.

Let us follow in the same vein for three players, and assume that the first lacks one point, the second lacks two, and the third lacks two. In order to make the division, in accordance with the same method of combinations, it is necessary first to see in how many trials the game will be decided, just as we did when there were two players. This will be in three, for they could not make three trials without necessarily arriving at a decision.

Now we must see how three trials are combined among three players, and how many of them are favorable to the one, how many to the other, and how many to the third, and according to this proposition, we must distribute the money just as was done in the case of two players.

It is easy to see how many combinations there will be in all; it is the third power of 3, that is to say, its cube or 27. For if we throw three dice at a time (since we must make three trials), with dice of three faces each (since there are three players), the one marked a being favorable to the first, the one marked b being favorable to the second, the other marked c for the third, then it is manifest that these three dice when thrown together may have 27 different positions:

Now the first player lacks only one point: then all the positions in which there is an a are in his favor; hence there are 19.

The second player lacks two points: then all the positions in which there are two b's are in his favor; hence there are 7.

The third player lacks two points: then all the positions in which there are two c's are for him; hence there are 7.

If we concluded from this that it would be necessary to give to each player in the proportion of 19, 7, 7, we would be greatly mistaken, and I am sure you would not do so, for there are some faces favorable to the first and to the second at the same time, such as abb, since the first will find there an a which he needs; similarly acc is favorable to the first and to the third.

Consequently we must not count these faces which are common to two players as worth the whole amount to each one, but merely as a half. For if the position acc occurred, the first and the third player would have the same right to the amount, each one receiving his due share; hence they would divide the money in half; but if the position aab occurred, only the first one gains. Therefore the reckoning must be made as follows:

a a a	1		
a a b	1		
a a c	1		
a b a	1		
a b b	1	2	
a b c	1		
a c a	1		
a c b	1		
a c c	1		3
b a a	1		
b a b	1	2	
b a c	1		
b b a	1	2	
b b b		2	
b b c		2	
b c a	1		
b c b		2	
b c c			3
c a a	1		
c a b	1		
c a c	1		3
c b a	1		
c b b		2	
c b c			3
c c a	1		3
c c b			3
c c c			3

There are 13 positions which give the whole to the first, and 6 positions which give him half, and 8 which give him nothing. Therefore, if the whole sum is one pistole, there will be 13 faces, each of which is worth one pistole to him, there will be 6 faces each worth ½ pistole to him, and 8 which are worth nothing.

Consequently if we wish to share, we must multiply

              13 by one pistole, which makes   13
               6 by one half, which makes   3
               8 by zero, which makes   0
Sum   27   Sum   16

And we must divide the sum of the positions, 16, by the sum of the positions, 27, which gives the fraction $\frac{16}{27}$; this is what belongs to the first in case they share, that is to say 16 pistoles out of 27.

The shares of the second and of the third player are found in the same way.

There are 4 positions which are worth 1 pistole to him:

multiply 4

There are 3 positions which are worth $\frac{1}{2}$ pistole to him:

multiply . . . . $1\frac{1}{2}$

And 20 positions which are worth nothing to him

. . . . 0

Sum 27   Sum $5\frac{1}{2}$

Hence $5\frac{1}{2}$ pistoles out of the 27 belong to the second player, and, as many to the third, and these three sums, $5\frac{1}{2}$, $5\frac{1}{2}$ and 16, when added, make the 27.

This, it seems to me, is the way in which the division should be made on the basis of the combinations in your method, unless you have something else on this subject of which I am not aware. But if I am not mistaken, this division is inaccurate.

The reason is that it rests on a false supposition. This is the assumption that three trials will infallibly be made whereas the common practice in that sort of game is that the play continues only until one of the players has obtained the number of points he still needs, in which case the game ends.

Not that it may not happen that 3 trials are made, but it may happen also that only one or two are made, and there is nothing compulsory about it.

But people will say, Why is it not permissible in this situation to make the same hypothesis as when there are only two players? Here is the reason:

In the actual situation of these three players, only one can win, for the stipulation is that the game ends as soon as one has won. But in the hypothetical situation two may obtain the number of their points, namely, if the first one wins the one which he still needs, and if one of the others wins the two which he still needs. For they will have had only three trials, whereas when there were only two players the hypothetical situation and the actual situation agreed in every particular. That is what makes the extreme difference between the hypothetical and the actual situation.

Now let us assume that the first player lacks one point, the second player lacks two, and the third player lacks two. They then agree on three complete trials; furthermore they agree that anyone who reaches the number he still lacks may take the entire sum, if he alone achieves the number, or that if two have achieved it they will share equally. In this case the division must be made as I have just indicated, so that the first has 16, the second $5\frac{1}{2}$, and the third has $5\frac{1}{2}$ of the 27 pistoles. The demonstration is self-evident, if we make the above assumption.

But if they play simply on the stipulation, not that they take three trials, but that they play only until one of them gets his points, and that then the game ends without giving any other player the chance to obtain his points, then 17 pistoles of the 27 will belong to the first player, 5 to the second player, and 5 to the third.

And this is found by my general method which determines also that under the preceding condition 16 of them belong to the first, $5\frac{1}{2}$ to the second, and $5\frac{1}{2}$ to the third, without using the combinations, for it applies everywhere and without any obstacle.

These, Sir, are my thoughts on this subject, on which I have no other advantage than that of having meditated on it much more. But that is a trifle as far as you are concerned, since your views are more penetrating than my protracted efforts.

I shall not fail to present to you my reasons for expecting your judgment of this. I believe that herein I have indicated to you that the method of combinations happens to be valid for two players, and that it is valid also at times for three players when one of them lacks one point, the second lacks one point, and the third lacks two points, because in this case the number of trials in which the game will be finished does not suffice for two to win. But the method is not general, and is valid generally only when the playing is limited exactly to a certain number of trials.

Therefore, since you did not have my method when you proposed to me the division among several players, but had merely the method of combinations, I fear that we have different opinions on this subject.

I am requesting you to tell me how you proceed in the search for this division. I shall receive your reply with respect and with pleasure even if your opinion runs contrary to mine.

I am, etc. PASCAL

16. LETTER FROM PASCAL TO FERMAT

October 27, 1654.

Sir:

Your last letter has satisfied me perfectly. I admire your method for the division of stakes, and all the more so because I understand it very well; it is entirely yours, it has nothing in common with mine, and it achieves the same end easily. Now our understanding is re-established.

But, Sir, if I have vied with you in this, seek elsewhere for someone who will follow you in your numerical inventions, a statement of which you graciously sent me. As for me, I confess that it is quite beyond me; I can only admire it, and request you very humbly to use your earliest leisure to complete it. All our gentlemen saw it last Saturday and esteemed it most heartily; it is not at all easy to endure waiting for such beautiful and such desirable things. Please bear this in mind, and be assured that I am, etc.

PASCAL

17. LETTER FROM BLAISE PASCAL TO HIS SISTER, MADAME PERIER

[October-November, 1654?]

My dear sister:

I do not believe that you are earnestly displeased, for if you are so merely because we have forgotten you, you should not be displeased at all. I have no news for you, because general things are too general, and special things must always be new. I could tell you much that is going on very secretly, but I consider it useless to inform you of it. All I ask of you is to unite thanksgiving with the prayers you are uttering for me, and I ask you to multiply them in these days. With God's help I myself carried your letter so that it might be forwarded to Madame de Maubuisson. They gave me a little book in which I found that sentence written by hand. I don't know whether it is in the little book of sentences, but it is beautiful. I am so busy that I can say no more. Do not miss your Thursdays. Good-by, my dear.

To Mademoiselle Perier at Clermont (in Auvergne)

18. PASCAL'S MEMORIAL

☩

In the year of Grace, 1654,
On Monday, 23d of November, Feast of St. Clement, Pope and Martyr, and of others in the Martyrology,
Vigil of Saint Chrysogonus, Martyr, and others,
From about half past ten in the evening until about half past twelve,

FIRE

God of Abraham, God of Isaac, God of Jacob, not of the philosophers and scholars.
Certitude. Certitude. Feeling. Joy. Peace.
God of Jesus Christ
Deum meum et Deum vestrum.
"Thy God shall be my God."
Forgetfulness of the world and of everything, except God.
He is to be found only by the ways taught in the Gospel.
Greatness of the human soul.
"Righteous Father, the world hath not known Thee, but I have known Thee."
Joy, joy, joy, tears of joy.
I have separated myself from Him
Derelinquerunt me fontem aquae vivae.
"My God, wilt Thou leave me?"
Let me not be separated from Him eternally.
"This is the eternal life, that they might know Thee, the only true God, and the one whom Thou has sent, Jesus Christ."
Jesus Christ.
Jesus Christ.
I have separated myself from Him: I have fled from Him, denied Him, crucified Him.
Let me never be separated from Him.
We keep hold of Him only by the ways taught in the Gospel.
Renunciation, total and sweet.
Total submission to Jesus Christ and to my director.
Eternally in joy for a day's training on earth.
Non obliviscar sermones tuos. Amen.

19. WRITING ON THE CONVERSION OF THE SINNER

[November-December, 1654?]

The first thing which God inspires in the soul which He truly deigns to touch is an understanding and a quite extraordinary insight by means of which the soul considers things and itself in an entirely new manner.

This new light brings fear to the soul and an agitation which disturbs the repose which it found in the things that delighted it.

The soul can no longer tranquilly enjoy the things which charmed it. Constant scruples assail it in this enjoyment and because of this introspection it no longer finds the accustomed sweetness in the things to which it abandoned itself freely with an overflowing heart.

But the soul finds even more bitterness in the practice of holiness than in the vanities of the world. On the one hand, the presence of visible things touches it more than the hope of things unseen; on the other hand the stability of things unseen touches it more than does the vanity of visible things. And thus the presence of the one and the stability of the other contend for its affection; the vanity of the one and the absence of the other arouse its aversion. Consequently discord and confusion are born in it which . . . [two lines missing].

The soul considers perishable things as perishing and even as already perished. In the definite prospect of the annihilation of all that it loves, it is frightened by this consideration, when it sees every moment snatch away the enjoyment of its endowment; when that which is dearest to it slips away every moment, and when finally a certain day will come when it will find itself destitute of all the things on which it had set its hopes. And so it understands perfectly that since its heart is attached only to fragile and vain things, the soul must find itself alone and abandoned on leaving this life, since it has not taken care to unite itself with a good which is genuine, which exists independently, and which may sustain it during and after this life.

As a result, the soul begins to regard as nothing all that must return to nothingness, the sky, the earth, its mind, its body, its relatives, its friends, its enemies, its goods, its poverty, disgrace, prosperity, honor, ignominy, esteem, scorn, authority, indigence, health, illness, and life itself; in short, everything which is less enduring than the soul is incapable of satisfying the design of this soul which seriously seeks to establish itself in a felicity as enduring as it is itself.

It begins to wonder at the blindness in which it has lived; and when it considers on the one hand how long it has lived without such reflections and how many people live in this manner, and on the other hand how certain it is that the soul, being immortal, can never find its happiness among perishable things which are taken from it at least in death, it then enters into a holy state of confusion and of wonder which bring to it a wholly salutary agitation.

For it considers that no matter how great may be the number of those who grow old in the maxims of this world, and no matter what authority may reside in this multitude of examples of those who see their happiness in the world, nevertheless this is certain: If the things of this world afforded substantial pleasure — which is recognized as false through an infinite number of deadening and continual experiences, it is inevitable that the loss of these things or that death will ultimately deprive us of these things. As a result, since the soul has amassed treasures of temporal goods of whatever kind they may be, either gold or science or reputation, it is inevitable that it will ultimately find itself denuded of all the objects of its happiness. And so, even if they were capable of satisfying it, they will be unable to satisfy it forever; moreover, if this means producing genuine happiness, it does not offer a very enduring happiness, since it must be limited by the course of this life.

Thus through a holy humility which again elevates God above vainglory the soul begins to rise above the generality of men, it condemns their conduct, it detests their maxims, it mourns their blindness, it inclines to seek the true good; it understands that it must have these two qualities, the one, which endures as long as it does and which can be taken from it only by its consent, and the other, than which there is nothing more lovable.

It sees that in the love which it had for the world it found this second quality in its blindness, for it recognized nothing more lovable; but since it does not see the first, it knows that it is not the sovereign good. Hence the soul seeks this elsewhere, and knowing by an utterly pure light that this is not in the things which are in it, nor outside of it, nor in front of it (hence nothing in it, nothing at its sides), it begins to seek this above it.

This elevation is so eminent and so transcendent that it does not stop at the sky (this has nothing that would satisfy it), nor above the sky, nor with the angels, nor with the most perfect beings. It penetrates all creatures, and the heart can stop beating only when it has surrendered itself at the very throne of God where it begins to find its repose and this good which is such that there is nothing more lovable, and which can be taken from it only by its own consent.

For although it does not feel these charms with which God rewards habitual piety, it nevertheless understands that creatures cannot be more lovable than their Creator; its reason, aided by the light of grace, teaches it that there is nothing more lovable than God and that He can be taken only from those who reject Him, since to possess Him is to desire Him, and to refuse Him is to lose Him.

Thus it rejoices at having found a good which cannot be taken from it so long as it desires this good, and which is transcended by nothing. And amid these new reflections it comes to see the greatness of its Creator both in humiliations and in deep adoration. In consequence it annihilates itself, and, unable to form a low enough idea of itself, nor to conceive one high enough of its sovereign, it makes new efforts to humble itself to the very depth of nothingness, while considering God in the boundlessness which it multiplies incessantly. Finally, in this conception which exhausts its powers, it adores Him in silence, it considers itself as His vile and useless creature, and by this reiterated respect it adores Him and blesses Him and would like to bless and adore Him forever. Then it recognizes the grace He has bestowed upon it by manifesting His infinite majesty to so feeble a worm; and, after a firm resolve to be eternally grateful for this, it blushes at having preferred so much vanity to this divine Master; in a spirit of contrition and of penitence it has recourse to His pity so as to stop His wrath whose effect upon it seems appalling. At the sight of this boundlessness . . . [*five lines missing*].

It raises ardent prayers to God to obtain from His mercy that, having deigned to reveal Himself, He may be pleased to guide the soul and make known the means of coming to God. For since it is to God that the soul aspires, it aspires also to come to Him only by the means which come from God Himself, because it desires God alone to be its path, its object, and its ultimate end. As a result of these prayers, it begins to act and seeks among those . . . [*five lines missing*].

It is resolved to conform to His will for the rest of its life; but since its natural weakness, together with the habit it has of sinning wherever it has lived, have reduced it to the impossibility of attaining such happiness, it implores of His mercy the means of coming to Him, of attaching itself to Him and of adhering to Him eternally . . . [*seven lines missing*].

Thus the soul recognizes that as a creature it must adore God, as a debtor it must render Him thanks, being culpable it must make amends, and being needy it must implore Him.

20. PASCAL'S CONVERSATION WITH MONSIEUR DE SACI ON EPICTETUS AND MONTAIGNE. (EXCERPT FROM FONTAINE'S MEMOIRES, A CONTRIBUTION TO THE HISTORY OF PORT ROYAL)

[*January, 1655?*]

At this time, Monsieur Pascal went to live at Port Royal des Champs. I shall not take time to say who this man was, this man who was admired not merely in all of France but in all of Europe. His mind, which was ever alert and ever active, had an almost incredible range, profundity, clarity, penetration, and precision. No man was his equal in mathematics, as is demonstrated by the story of the famous *roulette* which at that time was the talk of all scholars. It is well known that he seemed to give life even to copper, and to endow brass with thought. He caused little wheels, devoid of reason, each of which bore the first ten numbers, to convey reason to reasoning beings, and somehow he made mute machines speak so as to solve without effort the difficulties inherent in numbers which had baffled the most learned scholars. This cost him so much concentration and mental effort that his mind was quite upset by it for more than three years. During this time he was perfecting the machine, which I have seen with my own eyes, to the point where everybody admired it. This admirable man, who was finally reached by God, yielded his highly trained intellect to the gentle yoke of Jesus Christ, and this great heart embraced penitence with humility. He went to Paris to throw himself into the arms of Monsieur Singlin, resolved to do whatever the latter should command.

On seeing this great genius, Monsieur Singlin believed that he would do well to send him to Port Royal des Champs, where Monsieur Arnauld might cope with him in the natural sciences, and where Monsieur de Saci would teach him to scorn them. And so he went to live at Port Royal. In all courtesy Monsieur de Saci could not decline to see him, especially since he had been requested to do so by Monsieur Singlin, but the holy understanding which he found in the Scriptures and in the Church Fathers gave him the hope that he would not be at all dazzled by the brilliance of Monsieur Pascal who nevertheless charmed and captivated everyone.

In fact, he found everything Pascal said quite pertinent. He acknowledged with pleasure the vigor of the latter's intellect and speech. But there was nothing novel about it. All the great things that Monsieur

Pascal told him, he had already read in Saint Augustine, and to do justice to everybody, he said: "Monsieur Pascal is to be highly esteemed, for although he has not read the Church Fathers, he has, without any aid, and merely by dint of his own penetrating mind, discovered the same truths which they had found. He considers them surprising, said he, because he has seen them nowhere, but, as for us, we are accustomed to seeing them on all sides in our books." And so, finding that the ancients had no less insight than the new interpreters, this wise ecclesiastic remained content, and esteemed Monsier Pascal highly for agreeing in all things with Saint Augustine.

In talking with people, the usual procedure of Monsieur de Saci was to adjust his conversation to those with whom he was speaking. If, for example, he saw Monsieur Champaigne, he would talk with him about painting. If he saw Monsieur Hamon, he would discuss medicine with him. If he saw the local surgeon, he would ask him about surgery. Those who cultivated grapevines or trees or grain would tell him all there was to be observed. Everything served him as an approach to God, and to lead others to Him. Consequently he thought he ought to meet him on his own ground and to talk with him about those readings in philosophy with which he was busying himself most. He brought up this subject at the first conversation which they had. Monsieur Pascal told him that the books he read most were by Epictetus and Montaigne, and he praised these two intellects highly. Monsieur de Saci, who had always deemed it his duty to read but little by these authors, requested Monsieur Pascal to discuss them thoroughly.

"Epictetus," said the latter, "is one of the world's philosophers who knew men's duties best. Above all, he wants man to consider God as his principal end; he is to be persuaded that God rules with justice; man is to submit to Him willingly and to obey Him voluntarily in everything as one whose great wisdom is manifest in all that he does. Such a frame of mind will put an end to all complaints and to all murmurs of protest, and will prepare man's spirit to endure the most trying experiences with calmness. He says: 'Never say, "I lost that," but rather, "I have given that up. My son is dead, I have surrendered him. My wife is dead, I have surrendered her."' Similarly with possessions and everything else. But you say: 'Whoever has taken them from me is an evil man.' Why be troubled when someone who has given things to you wants them returned? While he permits you to use them, watch over them as over a possession that belongs to someone else, just as a man who is traveling looks upon himself as a mere guest in an inn. You ought not, said he, desire to have things done as you wish, but rather you should wish them to be done as they are done. Remember, says he elsewhere, that you are here as an actor, and that you are playing a role in a play which he is pleased to assign to you. If he gives you a minor role, play it as such; if he gives you a major part, play it accordingly, if he wishes you to imitate a vagabond, you ought to do it with all the naïveté of which you are capable, and so on. It is your task to play well the role assigned to you, but it devolves upon someone else to choose your role for you. Ever be mindful of death and those evils which seem most unbearable; then you will never think ignobly, and you will never desire anything to excess."

"In a thousand ways he points out what man should do. He desires man to be humble, to conceal his good resolutions, above all at first, and to carry them out in secret; nothing is more disastrous to them than to make a display of them. He never grows weary of repeating that the whole study and the desire of man must be to recognize God's will and to follow it."

"These, Sir," said Monsieur Pascal to Monsieur de Saci, "are the illuminating thoughts of this great intellect that was so well versed in man's duties. I dare say he would deserve to be worshiped, if he had known his impotence, since one would have to be God to be able to teach both to men. But although he understood man's duties so well, he was, after all, a creature of clay and ashes, and consequently he was carried away by presumptuousness with regard to man's powers. He says that God has given to man the means of fulfilling all his obligations, that these means are within our power; that man must seek bliss through the things in his power, since God has given them to us to that end; that we must determine the extent of our freedom; that possessions, life, and esteem are not within our power and consequently do not lead to God. Furthermore, he says that the mind cannot be compelled to believe what it knows to be false, nor can the will be compelled to love that which it knows will render it unhappy: hence these two powers are free and by means of them we can perfect ourselves. He adds that by these powers man can know God perfectly, love, obey, and please Him, free himself from all his vices, acquire all virtues, and make himself holy and a companion of God. These superbly diabolical principles lead him into other errors: namely, that the soul is a portion of the divine substance; that pain and death are not evils; that man may take his life when he is so persecuted that he is forced to believe that God is calling him, and other errors as well."

"As for Montaigne, Sir, of whom you wish me to speak also, since he was born in a Christian state, he professed the Catholic faith, and there is nothing unusual about that. But since he wished to determine what moral reason should dictate without the light of faith, he based his principles on that supposition, and so, considering man devoid of all revelation, he discoursed in that vein. He places all things in universal doubt and in such general doubt that this doubt is carried away by itself. That is to say, [*he doubts*] whether he doubts, and since he doubts even this last supposition, his uncertainty constantly revolves about itself in a perpetual circle. This doubt is opposed equally to those who assert that everything is uncertain and to those who maintain that everything is not uncertain, for he wishes to assert nothing. It is in this doubt which doubts itself, and in this ignorance which is ignorant of itself, and which he calls his sovereign form, that the essence of his opinion lies. This he was unable to designate by a positive term. For, if he says that he doubts, he betrays himself in asserting that at least he doubts. Since this runs strictly counter to his intention, he was unable to explain it to himself except by interrogation, so that not wishing to say, 'I don't know,' he said, 'What do I know?' This he made his motto. Then he placed it under a picture of scales, which were found to be in perfect equilibrium, for they weighed contradictions. In other words, he is an out and out Pyrrhonist. All his discourses and all his *Essays* center around this principle. It is the only thing he pretends to establish although he does not always point out his intention. Thereby he imperceptibly destroys everything that men regard as most certain, not in order to establish the contrary with a certainty to which he is hostile, but merely in order to reveal that, appearances being equal on both sides, one does not know on what to base one's belief."

"In this frame of mind he derides all certainty. For example, he attacks those who were thinking of establishing in France a great remedy for lawsuits by the multitudinousness and the alleged justice of laws. As if one could cut the roots of doubts from which lawsuits arise, and as if there were dikes able to block the torrent of uncertainty and to restrain conjectures! Yet, when he says that one might as well submit his cause to the first passerby as to judges armed with quantities of statutes, he does not maintain that the order of things in the State should be changed; his ambition does not rise so high. Neither does he claim that his judgment is better, for he does not regard any opinion as good. He is concerned solely with proving the vanity of most widely accepted opinions. This he does by pointing out that the abolition of all laws would more likely diminish the number of disputes which this multitudinousness merely serves to increase, because disputes grow as one dwells upon them, obscurities are multiplied by commentaries, and the surest way of understanding the meaning of a discourse is not to examine it, but to take it at once at its face value, for as soon as one begins to reflect on it all its clarity is dissipated. Thus at random he judges all of man's acts and all matters of history, now from one point of view and now from another, freely following his first impulse, and without subjecting his thinking to the laws of reason whose standards are all false. And so he takes great delight in revealing the mind's contradictions through his own example. In this free disporting of his own genius it is quite immaterial to him whether he wins in the argument or not, for, by one example or another, he always contrives to show the weakness of opinions, since he is so inclined to universal doubt that he is fortified in it as much by his triumph as by his defeat."

"In this mood, which is quite *vacillating* and *wavering*, he combats the heretics of his time with relentless vigor for asserting that they alone know the true meaning of the Scriptures; similarly, he thunders most vigorously at the horrible impiety of those who dare to assert that there is no God. He takes them to task particularly in *Apologie de Raymond de Sebonde;* finding them voluntarily stripped of all revelation, abandoned to their own understanding, and waiving all consideration of faith, he asks them by what authority they undertake to judge the sovereign being that is infinite by his own definition, whereas they have no true knowledge of even the minutest things in nature. He asks them on what principles they base their views; he urges them to point them out. He examines all those that they are able to advance, and with the talent in which he excels, he probes into them so profoundly that he exposes the vanity of all those that are commonly regarded as the most natural and the most substantial. He asks whether the soul knows anything, whether it knows itself, whether it is substance or accident, whether it is body or spirit. Then he asks what each of these things is, and whether there is anything that does not fall into one of these categories, whether the soul knows its own body, what matter is, whether the soul can distinguish between innumerable varieties of opinions when good opinions have been advanced, how it is able to reason if it is made of matter, and how it can be linked with a particular body and feel its passions if it is spirit? He asks further when the soul came into being, whether or not it ends with the death of the body, whether it knows when it is in error, since the essence of error consists in not being aware of error;

whether amid all this obscurity it does not believe as firmly that two and three make six as it subsequently knows that they make five; whether animals reason, think and speak; who can determine what time, space and extension, motion and unity are, all of which are things that surround us and are quite inexplicable; what are health, sickness, life, death, good, evil, justice, and sin, of which we are constantly speaking; whether we have within us the principles of truth, and whether those in which we believe and which we call axioms or common notions, because they are held by all men, are in conformity with truth itself. Since we know only by faith alone that a thoroughly good Being has given these ideas to us as true, by creating us to know truth, who can know without the light of faith whether they are not uncertain because they may have come into being by chance, or whether they were not fashioned by a false, evil being which gave them to us to lead us astray. This would indicate that God and truth are inseparable, and that if the one exists or does not exist, or is uncertain or certain, then the same necessarily holds for the other. Who after all can know whether common sense, which we assume to be the judge of truth, partakes of the nature of him who created it? Moreover, who knows what truth is, and how can one be sure of being in possession of truth without knowing what it is? Who can even know what being is, which cannot be defined since there is nothing more general, and since to explain it one would have to use the same word by saying: It is . . .? And since we do not know what soul, body, time, space, motion, truth, good, and even being are, and since we do not know how to explain the idea which we have of them, how can we assure ourselves that this idea is the same for all men? After all, we have no criterion other than the uniformity of consequences which is not always a sign of the uniformity of principles, for these may be very different and yet lead to the same conclusions, inasmuch as everyone knows that we often reach the truth from false premises."

"With equal thoroughness he finally scrutinizes all sciences and geometry; he points out the lack of certainty in geometric axioms and the inexactness of undefined terms such as extent, motion, etc. He does the same with physics in many more ways, with medicine in an infinite number of ways, with history, politics, morals, jurisprudence and the rest. He does this in such a manner as to leave us convinced that at present we merely think in some sort of dream from which we shall awaken only at death, a dream during which we have as few principles of truth as during natural sleep. So he takes reason devoid of faith to task so vigorously and so unsparingly that he causes reason to doubt its reasonableness, and to doubt whether animals are reasonable or not, or merely more or less so. Thereby he forces reason to step down from the lofty height of excellence which it has arrogated to itself, and he charitably puts it on a par with beasts without permitting it to rise above that station until it is informed by its very Creator of its rank which is unknown to it. If reason complains, he threatens to assign the lowest rank to it, which is just as easy to do as the contrary, and to grant it no power to act except to observe its weakness with sincere humility rather than to exalt itself by stupid insolence."

Monsieur de Saci, who felt as if he were living in a new country and hearing a new language, repeated to himself the words of Saint Augustine: "O God of truth! Are those who are schooled in the subtleties of reason more agreeable to Thee because of that?" He pitied this philosopher who pricked and tore himself on every side with thorns of his own making, as Saint Augustine had said of himself when in a similar state. After a prolonged pause he said to Monsieur Pascal:

"I am indebted to you, Sir; I am sure that if I had read Montaigne for a long time I should not know him as well as I do after this conversation that I have just had with you. The man ought to wish to be known only by the recitals you make of his writings; then he might say with Saint Augustine: *Ibi me, vide, attende.* I do indeed believe that he had a keen intellect, but I am not sure that with your careful linking up of his principles you are not attributing to him a somewhat better one than he had. You may well believe that, having spent my life as I did, I have not often been advised to read this author, none of whose works contain what we must seek primarily in our readings as prescribed by Saint Augustine, for the words of this author do not seem to proceed from great humility and piety. One may well pardon the philosophers of old, who are known as academicians, for doubting everything. But what need did Montaigne have of entertaining his own mind by renewing a doctrine which Christians now regard as folly? This is Saint Augustine's opinion of such people. For the benefit of youth one may well say with him of Montaigne: "He brushes faith aside from everything that he says; consequently we who have faith must brush aside everything he says." I do not condemn the author's intellect which is a great gift of God, but he might have made better use of it and have offered it as a sacrifice to God rather than to the devil. Of what benefit is a good thing, when one makes bad use of it? *Quid proderat*, etc.? the saintly doctor said of himself after his conversion. You are fortunate, Sir, in having risen above these people called doctors who are engulfed in the intoxication of science, but whose hearts are devoid of truth. God has put into your heart other delights and other charms than those that you find in Montaigne. He has called you home from this dangerous pleasure, *a jucunditate pestifera*, says Saint Augustine, who thanks God for having pardoned the sins he committed in too great enjoyment of these vanities. One can place all the more reliance on Saint Augustine because at one time he had these same sentiments. You say that Montaigne combated the heretics of his time by this universal doubt; similarly, it was by this same doubt of the academicians that Saint Augustine renounced the Manichaean heresy. After he had turned to God, he renounced this vanity which he terms a sacrilege, and he did what he said of some others. He recognized with what wisdom Saint Paul warns us not to let ourselves be seduced by such discourses. For he admits that they have a certain captivating charm; we sometimes believe things are true merely because they are said eloquently. They are dangerous foods, says he, but they are served on beautiful dishes; yet instead of nourishing the heart, they empty it. Then we resemble people who are asleep and who believe they are eating in their sleep; these imaginary foods leave them as empty as they were to begin with."

Monsieur de Saci said a number of similar things to Monsieur Pascal. To these the latter replied that if he were complimented on knowing Montaigne and on being able to interpret him in charming fashion, he might say without being complimentary at all that Monsieur de Saci knew Saint Augustine far better, and that he could interpret the Saint with even greater charm, though hardly to the advantage of poor Montaigne. He agreed that he was highly edified by the soundness of all that had just been presented to him. Nevertheless, since he was still engrossed in his author, he could not refrain from saying:

"I admit, Sir, that I take no pleasure in seeing this author's superb reason so utterly routed by its own weapons, nor do I rejoice in this bloody revolt of man against man who, from his association with God, to which he had raised himself through the maxims of his feeble reason, is now cast down to the level of a beast. With all my heart I should have liked the man who was the instrument of this great revenge, if, being a disciple of the Church by faith, he had adhered to the rules of ethics. In that case he would not have led men, whom he had humiliated so unnecessarily, into angering by new crimes the One who can free them from these crimes which Montaigne convinced them they cannot even recognize."

"But, contrary to all this, he acts like a pagan. From the premise that without faith everything is uncertain, and that so many search for the true and the good without achieving any degree of tranquility, he concludes that one ought to leave the matter to others. Meanwhile, says he, one should remain calm and touch lightly on these problems for fear of being engulfed by too great insistence; one should accept the true and the false for what they seem and without pressing the matter, because they are so lacking in solid substance that at the slightest pressure they slip out of hand and leave a void. That is why he turns to the evidence of the senses and to common notions, for he would do himself violence by denying them, and, being ignorant of the truth, he does not know whether he would gain by doing so. And so he flees from grief and death, because his instincts prompt him to do so; for the same reason he does not wish to resist them. However, he does not conclude that they really are evils, since he has no great confidence in the natural emotions of fear, and, although nature tells us the contrary, we do derive pleasure from other emotions which are said to be evil. Thus there is nothing extravagant in his conduct, and he acts like others. Everything they do in the stupid belief that they are pursuing the truth, he does by proceeding from another principle: since the probabilities on both sides are equal, precedent and convenience overcome the balance and determine his conduct."

"Hence he conforms to the customs of his country because it is easy; he mounts his horse, like those who are not philosophers, simply because his horse permits him to do so. Yet he mounts it without believing that he has a right to do so, since he does not know whether, after all, the animal may not have a right to *his* services. Moreover, he is at great pains to avoid certain vices, and he even remains faithful in marriage because of the difficulties which follow upon irregularities. Yet if the difficulty he chooses is greater than the one he avoids, he remains calm, for the rule which determines his conduct is always convenience and tranquility. Hence he refuses to accept this stoic virtue which is pictured with a severe mien, a fierce look, bristling hair, a furrowed, perspiring brow, in a painful, tense posture, far removed from man in mournful silence, and isolated on the summit of a crag. This, he says, is a phantom fit to frighten children, but which with unremitting effort merely seeks the repose which it never acquires. His virtue is naïve, intimate, amusing, playful, and sportive, so to speak; it pursues whatever charms it; it toys casually with fortunate or unfortunate incidents; it reclines comfortably on the bosom of idle ease, from where it points out to men who struggle so hard for happiness, that this is the only place where happiness is to be found, and that ignorance and lack of curiosity are two downy pillows for a discerning head. These are his words."

"I cannot conceal from you, Sir, that while reading this author and comparing him with Epictetus I found that they were assuredly the two greatest champions of the two most celebrated sects in the world, and the only sects which are in accord with reason. After all, one can choose only one of these courses, either there is a God who is Montaigne's highest good, or there can be no certainty about God, in which case the true good is also uncertain because then Montaigne is incapable of knowing the truth."

"I took extreme delight in pointing out in these diverse arguments how both arrive at a certain conformity with the genuine wisdom which they were seeking. For if it is pleasing to note nature's desire to reveal God in all His works, in which we see some trait of His because they are in His image, how much more reasonable is it to see in the products of intellects the efforts which they make to imitate genuine virtue, even when they flee from it, and to observe how they arrive at virtue and how they stray away from it. That is what I have tried to do in this study."

"It is true, Sir, that you have just revealed to me admirably what little benefit Christians may derive from such studies in philosophy. Nevertheless, with your permission I shall take the liberty of telling you what I think of them, although I am ready to renounce all the light that does not come from you. In so doing, I shall have the advantage of having encountered truth by chance or of receiving it from you as a certainty. It seems to me that the source of errors of these two sects lies in their failure to recognize that the present state of man differs from that at the time of his creation. Now one of these sects sees some traces of man's former greatness, ignores his depravity, and views nature as healthy and in no need of a Saviour; all this carries man to the very pinnacle of pride. On the other hand, the other sect, conscious of man's present misery and unaware of his original dignity, regards nature as necessarily infirm and beyond repair: this causes man to despair of achieving real goodness, and so he descends to extreme baseness. Hence these two states, which ought to be combined, if one were to see the whole truth, necessarily lead, when separated, to one of two vices, to pride or to idleness in which all men assuredly are before receiving grace. For if they do not continue their disorderly ways out of baseness, they are prompted to rise above them by vanity. I say this because what you have just told me of Saint Augustine is so true and of such great significance. Indeed, people pay homage to the two [sects] in many ways."

"The consequence of these vague insights is that some, aware of man's duty and ignorant of his importance, are lost in presumptuousness; others, knowing man's impotence but not his duty, become utterly debased. From this, one may conclude the possibility of developing a perfect morality by combining the two, inasmuch as the one is true where the other is in error. But instead of a peaceful union, nothing but strife and general destruction would result, for since the one establishes certainty and man's greatness, and the other establishes doubt and man's weakness, they undermine each other's truth as well as each other's falsity. And so they cannot endure separately because of their shortcomings; neither can they be united, for they are opposed to each other. Thus they crush and annihilate each other to make way for the truth of the Gospel. It is the truth of the Gospel which reconciles these contradictions through a skill which is truly divine; by uniting everything which is true and dispelling everything false, it makes of them a veritably celestial wisdom in which the opposites, that were incompatible in human doctrines, are reconciled. Now the reason for this is that the wise men of this world place these opposites in a single entity; for some would attribute greatness to human nature, and others would attribute weakness to this same human nature. Yet that is impossible. On the other hand, faith teaches us to attribute them to different entities: all that is infirm belongs to human nature, but all that is powerful derives from grace. This is the astounding and novel union which God alone was able to teach, and which He alone is able to achieve. This union is but an image and but an effect of the ineffable union of the two natures in the single person of a Man-God."

"I beg your pardon, Sir," said Monsieur Pascal to Monsieur de Saci, "for being carried away in your presence into theology instead of adhering to philosophy which is my only field, but I was unaware of it. It is difficult not to touch upon theology, no matter what truth one is discussing, since it is at the heart of all truth. This seems quite obvious because theology so visibly embraces all truths which are to be found in these opinions. Moreover, I do not see how men could refuse to follow the lead of theology. For if they are imbued with the thought of man's greatness, what greatness have they conceived that is not inferior to the promises of the Gospel, promises which were redeemed only at the price of God's exalted sacrifice of Himself in death. And if they take pleasure in contemplating the infirmity of human nature, their idea falls short of the real weakness of sin which was expiated by this same sacrifice. Thus all find in the Gospel more than they had hoped for; and, what is admirable, those who were unable to unite on an infinitely lower plane, now find themselves in agreement."

Monsieur de Saci could not refrain from expressing to Monsieur Pascal his surprise at the subtle manner with which he had presented things, but at the same time he agreed that everybody did not have the latter's flair for making wise and lofty comments on his readings. He said that Monsieur Pascal resembled those skillful physicians who are able to prepare the greatest remedies from the greatest poisons. He added that although he could well see from what Monsieur Pascal had just told him that these readings were useful to him, nevertheless he could not believe that they were advantageous to many people whose intellect was a bit slow and not lofty enough to read and judge these authors and to be able to extract pearls from a heap of rubbish, *aurum ex stercore Tertulliani*, as one of the Fathers said. One may well say this of these philosophers who are quite likely to obscure the wavering faith of their readers by the black smoke which arises from their rubbish. For this reason he would always advise such people not to expose themselves lightly to such reading, for fear that they might lose themselves, become a prey to demons, and food for worms, as, in the words of the Scriptures, had happened to these philosophers.

"I shall tell you very briefly my thoughts about the usefulness of these readings," said Monsieur Pascal. "I find that Epictetus has an incomparable art of disturbing the calm of those who seek it in external things, and of compelling them to recognize that they are veritable slaves and miserable blind men; it is impossible for them to find anything but the error and the grief from which they are trying to escape, if they do not yield themselves completely to God alone. Montaigne is incomparable in his ability to confound the pride of those who boast of real justice without faith, to disabuse those who cling to their opinions, and who believe they can find unshakable truth in the sciences. He is unparalleled in his ability to convince reason so thoroughly of its limitations and its vagaries that one is not inclined to regard mysteries as repugnant while making good use of its principles. For the intellect is so worsted by these errors that it is not at all desirous of judging whether the Incarnation or the mystery of the Eucharist are possible, all of which does not often trouble the common run of men."

"But, if Epictetus combats laziness, he leads to pride in such a way that it may be very harmful to those who are not convinced of the corruption of the most perfect justice that is not rooted in faith. And Montaigne is absolutely pernicious to those who are inclined to impiety and to vice. For this reason his works should be read with great caution, with discretion, and with an eye to the condition and the morals of those to whom they are recommended. It seems to me that only when read together will their effect be not altogether injurious, because the one offsets the evil of the other. Not that these readings may lead to virtue but merely that they may disturb vice. Then the soul is troubled by these contradictions, one of which drives out pride, and the other of which drives out idleness, and so the soul cannot find rest in any of these vices by such reasoning nor can it flee from all of them."

Thus these two men of such splendid intellect finally reached agreement on the reading of these philosophers, and they met on common ground which, however, they had reached by different routes, Monsieur de Saci having arrived there at once thanks to the clarity of his Christian insight, and Monsieur Pascal only on a circuitous course by following the reasoning of these two philosophers.

Monsieur de Saci and all the members of Port Royal des Champs were thus overjoyed by the conversion and the sight of Monsieur Pascal. They admired the omnipotence of grace which, by its unparalleled mercy, had so profoundly humbled this intellect that had risen by itself to such lofty heights. And at about this same time they rejoiced even more over the almost miraculous change in another person [Monsieur Richer, lawyer] who crowned this whole desert with joy.

21. THE MYSTERY OF JESUS

[*1655?*]

Jesus wills to suffer in His passions the torments which men cause Him; but in His agony He suffers the torments which He inflicts upon Himself; *turbare semetipsum;* a torture that comes not from a human hand, but from an almighty hand, for one must be almighty to endure it.

Jesus seeks at least a small measure of comfort from His three dearest friends, and they are asleep. He entreats them to bear with Him for a little, and they leave Him with utter neglect, for they have so little compassion that it could not keep them from sleeping for one moment. And so Jesus was left alone to the wrath of God.

Jesus is alone on the earth; He has no one to feel and share or even to know His suffering; heaven and He alone are aware of it.

Jesus is in a garden, not of delight as was the first Adam where he lost himself and all mankind, but in a garden of torture in which He saved himself and all mankind.

He suffers this grief and this loneliness in the horror of the night.

I believe that Jesus complained only this one time, but then He complained as if He could no longer bear His extreme pain: "My soul is sorrowful, even unto death."

Jesus seeks the companionship and the comforting of men. This, so it seems to me, is unique in His whole life. But they are denied Him, for His disciples are asleep.

Jesus will be in agony even to the end of the world; we must not sleep during all that time.

Jesus, in the midst of this universal abandonment and in the abandonment of those friends who were chosen to watch with Him, when He finds them asleep, is angered because of the peril to which they expose, not Him, but themselves. He warns them for their own safety and their own good with a warm tenderness for them even in their ingratitude, and warns them that the spirit is willing and the flesh is weak.

Jesus, finding them still asleep, unrestrained either by regard for Him or for themselves, has the kindness not to waken them, and He leaves them to their repose.

Jesus prays, not knowing the will of God and fearing death; but when He knows God's will, He proceeds to offer Himself to death: *Eamus. Processit* (Joannes).

Jesus has besought mankind and was not heard by them.

Jesus, while His disciples slept, wrought their salvation. He has done this for all righteous men while they slept, both in the void before their birth and in their sins after birth.

Only once does He ask that the cup may pass away from Him, and even then with submission; twice He asks that it come if need be.

Jesus in weariness.

Jesus, seeing all His friends asleep and all His enemies watchful, yields Himself utterly to His Father.

Jesus does not behold enmity in Judas, but the will of God whom He loves and whom He acknowledges, since He calls him friend.

Jesus wrests Himself away from His disciples to enter into agony; man must wrest himself away from those nearest and dearest to imitate Him.

Jesus being in agony and in the greatest woe, let us pray longer.

We implore the mercy of God, not that He may leave us at peace in our vices, but that He may deliver us from them.

If God gave us masters with His own hand, oh, how willingly we should have to obey them. Infallibly necessity and events are such masters. Console thyself, thou wouldst not be seeking Me, if thou hadst not found Me.

I thought of thee in My agony, I have shed such drops of blood for thee.

It is tempting Me rather then to test thee, to think that if thou wouldst do such and such a thing on a fancied occasion, I shall do it in thee when the occasion arrives.

Be thou guided by My rules; behold how well I have guided the Virgin and the saints who have let Me work in them.

The Father loves all that I do.

Dost thou wish that I always pay with the blood of My humanity, without their shedding tears?

Thy conversion, 'tis my concern; fear not and pray with confidence as if for Me.

I am present with thee by My Word in the Scriptures, by My spirit in the Church and by inspiration, by My power in the priests, by My prayer in the faithful.

The physicians will not heal thee, for in the end thou shalt die. But it is I who will heal, and make the body immortal.

Suffer physical bondage and servitude; I deliver thee at present only from spiritual servitude.

I am thy friend more than these and those can be; for I have done more for thee than they, and they would not suffer what I have suffered for thee, and they would not have died for thee in the days of thine infidelities and cruelties, as I have done, and as I am ready to do, and am doing among those whom I have chosen and in the Holy Sacrament.

If thou knewest thy sins, thou wouldst lose heart.

I shall lose it then, Lord, for on Thy assurance I believe their malice.

No, for I, by whom thou learnest it, can heal thee of them, and what I say unto thee is a sign that I desire to heal thee. In proportion as thou dost expiate them, thou wilt know them, and it will be said unto thee: Behold the sins which are forgiven thee. Do penance then for thy hidden sins and for the secret malice of those that thou knowest.

Lord, I give Thee all.

I love thee more ardently than thou hast loved thy depravity, *ut immundus pro luto*.

Let the glory be Mine and not thine, worm of clay and earth.

Ask thy confessor when My own words are the occasion of thy evil, thy vanity, or thy curiosity.

I see within me an abyss of pride, lust of the eyes, and lust of the flesh. There is nothing in common in me with God, or Jesus Christ the righteous. But He has been made sin for me; all Thy scourges have fallen upon Him. He is more to be abominated than I, and, far from abhorring me, He feels honored that I should go to Him and succor Him.

But He has healed Himself, and all the more will He heal me.

I must add my wounds to His and join myself to Him, and He will save me as He saves Himself. But in the time to come I must add no more.

Eritis sicut Dei scientes bonum et malum. Everyone likens himself unto God when judging that this is good, that this is evil, and in grieving or rejoicing too much over whatever happens.

Do ye therefore the little things as if they were great things, because of the majesty of Jesus Christ who does them in us and who lives our life. And do ye the great things as if they were little and easy because of His omnipotence.

22. [A SHORT EXPOSITION OF THE PROBLEM OF GRACE]

[*1656?*]

It is an established fact that some men are damned and some are saved. Moreover, it is an established fact that those who are saved have willed to be so, and that God also has willed it. For if God had not willed it, they would not have been saved, and if they themselves had not willed it, it would not have come to pass. He who made us without our intervention, cannot save us unless we so will. It is also true that those who are damned have of their own volition committed the sins which brought about their deserved condemnation, and that God also willed their damnation.

Therefore, it is clear that the will of God and man's will work together for the salvation and the damnation of those who are saved or damned. And there is no question about all these matters.

If then people ask why men are saved or lost, we may say in a certain sense that it is because God so wills, and, in another sense, that it is because men will it.

But it is a question of knowing which of these two wills, the will of

God or the will of man is master, is dominant, is the source, the beginning, and the cause of the other.

We wish to know whether the will of man is the cause of the will of God, or whether the will of God is the cause of the will of man. The one which will be shown to be dominant and master of the other will be regarded as somewhat unique, not because of its dominance but because it implies the co-operation of the will which follows its lead. Besides, any act will be related to this first will, and not to the other. This does not mean that the act cannot somehow be related to the will which yields, but it is essentially related to the master will. For the will which follows the lead of the other is such that one may say in a certain sense that the act proceeds from it, since it concurs in it; in another sense the act does not proceed from it, since it is not its source. But the primary will is such that we may rightly say of it that the act springs from it, but we can by no means say of it that the act does not spring from it.

Thus Saint Paul says: "*I live, yet not I, but Christ liveth in me.*" Surely his first word, "*I live,*" is not untrue, for he was alive, not merely physically, but spiritually as well. He was in a state of grace, and he himself said elsewhere repeatedly: "*We were dead, and we are made alive,*" etc. But though it was quite true that he was alive, he disavows this straightway, saying: "*I live not, non ego vivo.*"

The apostle is not uttering a falsehood. It is therefore true that he is alive, since he says: "*I live.*" Nevertheless, it is equally true that he is not living, since he says: "*Jam non ego, I live not.*" Hence these two truths exist together because his life, although his own, does not originally come from Him. He lives only in Jesus Christ. Christ's life is the source of his life. Thus it is true in one sense that he lives, since he has life. In another sense it is true also that he is not alive, since he lives only through the life of Another. But it is true that Christ lives, and one cannot say that he, Paul, does not.

Therefore, Christ Himself says: "*It is not I who work, but the Father that worketh in me.*" Nevertheless, He says elsewhere: "*The works that I have done.*" Jesus Christ is not a deceiver, and His humility does not belie His truthfulness. We may then say, since He said it, that He has done works, and likewise that He has not done them. But it is certain that divinity did them in Him, and we cannot assert that divinity did not do them.

Thus the prophet says: "*Thou, O Lord, hast wrought all our works in us.*" And it follows that these works are of God, since He did them, and yet they are of us, since they are ours.

And so Saint Paul says: "*I have labored, yet not I, but the grace of Jesus Christ which is with me.*" How did he work, and yet not work — but for the grace which was with him that worked — unless it be that his work can be called his, inasmuch as his will took part therein, and that it cannot be called his because his will was not the source of his own desires? Yet of the grace of God we can say that it is that which labored, for it prepared his will, and determined desire and deed in him; and we cannot say of it, that it did not labor, for it was the origin and the source of his work.

Therefore he says elsewhere: "*Non ego, sed quod inhabitat in me peccatum,*" in speaking of the unpremeditated stirrings of his will.

In the Scriptures there are a great number of examples of this kind of commentary which indicate that, when two wills work together to an end while one is the supreme master and infallible cause of the other, then the act can be both attributed and denied to the secondary will; it can be attributed to the dominant one, and, moreover, it must not fail to be attributed to it.

We are, therefore, considering the dominant will as the only one, although [in reality] it is not so, for it is the only one to which we can attribute the act and to which we cannot refuse to assign it. According to this mode of expression we must determine: Whether the number of men saved and damned is due to the will of God or to the will of men.

That is to say:

We seek to know whether God, in placing Himself in submission to the will of men had the absolute intention to save some and to damn others; and whether, as a consequence of this decree, He inclines the will of the elect to the good and the will of the condemned to evil, in order thus to make both conform to his absolute purpose of saving some and destroying others.

Or whether, by submitting the use of His grace to the free will of men, He foresaw how each would react, and whether in conformity with their own volition, He created the will to salvation or to condemnation.

That is the question which is today being debated among men and which is being decided differently by three schools of thought.

The first are the Calvinists, the second are the Molinists, and the third are the disciples of Saint Augustine.

Calvinists

The opinion of the Calvinists is:

That God, in creating men, created some to be damned and some to be saved by His absolute will and without foreknowledge of merit [whatever on their part].

That, in order to carry out this absolute will, God caused Adam to sin, and not only permitted, but caused his fall.

That, as regards God, there is no difference between *doing* and *permitting*.

That God, having caused Adam to sin and having caused all men to sin through him, sent Jesus Christ for the redemption of those whom He wanted to save when He created them, and that He unquestionably gives them love and salvation.

That God abandons and deprives of love throughout the whole course of their lives those whom He resolved to condemn when He created them.

That is the terrible doctrine of these heretics, a doctrine which is slanderous to God and unbearable to men. Those are the blasphemies by which they establish in God an absolute will without any provision for merit or for sin in the damning or saving of his creatures.

Molinists

Because of their hatred of this abominable doctrine and of the excesses which it involves, the Molinists did not content themselves merely with adopting an attitude opposed to it — which would have sufficed; they chose one which is absolutely contrary to it. This is that God has a provisional intent to save all men as a whole, and that to this end Jesus Christ became flesh to redeem all mankind without exception. Since His grace is given to every man, the good or ill use of that grace depends upon the will of man, and not on God's will. They assert that, since God has from all eternity foreseen the good or evil use to which His grace would be put by free will alone without the aid of a discriminating grace, He willed to save those who would properly use it, and to damn those who made wrong use of it; they hold that, in doing this, He had no absolute intention either to save or to damn any man.

This doctrine, which runs contrary to that of the Calvinists, produces an effect that is decidedly contrary. It flatters common sense whereas the other offends it. It flatters common sense by making it the master of its own salvation or perdition. It denies to God all absolute purpose, and makes salvation or damnation proceed from the human will, whereas in the doctrine of Calvin both come from divine will.

These are errors which run contrary to each other. The disciples of Saint Augustine, who tread more carefully and thoughtfully among such errors, hold the following beliefs:

[*Disciples of Saint Augustine*]

They believe in two estates in human nature. The first is the one in which nature was created in Adam, pure, stainless, just and upright, coming from the hands of God, from whom nothing can come which is not pure, holy, and perfect.

The other is the state to which human nature was reduced by sin and the rebellion of the first man by whom that nature became sullied, abominable, and detestable in the eyes of God.

In the state of innocence, God could justly condemn no man. God could not even refuse him grace sufficient unto salvation.

In the state of corruption, God could justly damn the whole mass [of men]; those who are being born even today without being redeemed through baptism, are damned and forever deprived of blessed vision, which deprivation is the greatest of evils.

On the basis of these two states, which differ so greatly, the disciples of Saint Augustine establish two different views concerning the purpose of God with regard to the salvation of men.

They claim, as regards the state of innocence, that God had a general and conditional intention to save all men provided that they themselves wanted it of their own free will, supported by sufficient grace which He offered them for their salvation; this, however, did not infallibly cause them to persevere in what is right.

They assert, however, that Adam, having by his free will made evil use of that grace, and having rebelled against God by the impulse of his will and without any impulsion from God (which would be horrible to contemplate), corrupted and infected the whole race of men so that that race has been the just object of God's wrath and indignation. They hold that God has divided this mass [of men], all of whom are equally guilty and fully worthy of condemnation; that He has willed to save part of them by an absolute act of will founded upon His mercy which is wholly pure and wholly free; that, leaving the other part in damnation where it was and where He might justly have left the whole mass, He foresaw either the particular sins that each would commit, or, in any case, the original sin of which they all are guilty; and that, as a consequence of that foreknowledge, He resolved to condemn them.

They [the disciples of Saint Augustine] hold that to that end God sent J. C. to save absolutely and by the most effective means those among them whom He chose and predestined; He willed absolutely that only they should merit salvation through His death; that He did not have the same purpose toward the rest who have not been delivered from that universal and just perdition.

They believe, nevertheless, that some of those who are not predestined are yet called for the good of the elect and thus to share in the redemption through Jesus Christ; that it is the fault of these persons that they do not persevere, and that they could do so, if they wanted. But, since they are not numbered among the elect, God does not give them those efficacious graces without which they never truly desire to persevere. Consequently, there are three kinds of men. First, those who never come to faith. Then, those who come to it, but die in mortal sin because they do not persevere; lastly, those who come to faith and continue in it in charity until death. Jesus Christ did not have the absolute intention that the first of these should receive any grace through His death, since in fact they received none from it.

He willed to redeem those of the second group. He gave them graces which would have brought them to salvation if they had used them well. But He willed not to give them that special grace of perseverance without which grace is never employed unto good.

But, as for the last of the three, J. C. willed their salvation absolutely, and He brought them thereto by sure and infallible means.

The disciples of Saint Augustine hold that all men are forced to believe, but by a belief mingled with fear and unaccompanied by certainty, and that they are of the small number of the elect whom Jesus Christ wills to save. They are never to judge of any man living on this earth — so long as he has a moment of life left to him — no matter how wicked and impious he may be, that he is not numbered among the predestined; for they leave the separation of the elect from those who are rejected to the impenetrable secret of God. This obliges them to do for the latter whatever may contribute to their salvation.

That is their opinion from which it is seen that God has willed absolutely to save those who are saved and has willed conditionally and through foreknowledge to damn those who are damned. And this salvation springs from the will of God, and damnation from the will of men.

This is the opinion of the disciples of Saint Augustine, or, rather, that of the Fathers and of the whole tradition, and consequently of the Church. The other opinions should be considered only as aberrations of the human mind. Now, although it is a very deep sorrow to the Church to see herself rent by opposing errors which combat the most holy truths, and although she has reason to complain of the Molinists and the Calvinists, nevertheless she recognizes that she is harmed less by those, who, misled by error, remain in her bosom than by those who have left her to build altar against altar, and who no longer have any affection for her motherly voice which calls them, nor any deference for her decisions which condemn them. If the error of the Molinists afflicts her, nevertheless their submission consoles her; but the error of the Calvinists joined with their rebellion makes her cry to God: "*I have nourished children, and they have scorned me.*" She knows that, in the case of the Molinists it suffices for her to speak through her Popes and councils; she knows that they venerate the tradition of the Church, that they do not undertake to make private interpretations of the words of Scripture, and that they intend to follow the interpretations which the hosts and the succession of those holy doctors and of her Popes and councils have given.

But as regards the Calvinists, their rebellion leaves her disconsolate. She is forced to act toward them as toward an equal, and to use reason as she waives her authority. Nevertheless, she calls them all to her, and prepares to convince them, each according to his own principles.

She is consoled by the fact that those errors, which combat each other, confirm her truth, that all that is needed to destroy them is to abandon them to themselves, and that the weapons which these diverse enemies employ against her cannot harm her and can only ruin them.

This is not the only case in which she has suffered from enemies who themselves oppose each other. She has almost never been free from this twofold combat. And just as she has experienced this conflict in the person of Jesus Christ, her Head, whom some have pronounced man only and others God only, so she has experienced conflict on almost all the other matters of faith. But, as she imitates her Head in this, too, she holds out her arms to both to call them all and subsequently to embrace them all to form a happy union.

23. EXCERPT FROM A LETTER BY BLAISE PASCAL TO MONSIEUR AND MLLE DE ROUANNEZ

[September, 1656]

Your letter has filled me with the utmost joy. I admit to you that I was beginning to be apprehensive or at least to wonder. I do not know what the affliction is to which you refer, but I know that such things are bound to come. A little while ago I was reading the thirteenth chapter of Saint Mark, and so I shall tell you what I found there. In it Jesus Christ pronounced a sublime discourse to His apostles on His last coming. And since everything that happens to the Church happens also to every Christian as an individual, it is certain that this whole chapter also foretells the state of each and every person who by his conversion destroys the old man within him. It likewise foretells the state of the entire universe which, as the Scriptures say, shall be destroyed to make way for a new heaven and a new earth. Accordingly I thought that this prediction of the ruin of the rejected Temple indicates that no passion of the old man shall be permitted to remain. For it is said that no stone of the Temple shall remain upon another; this, then, symbolizes the ruin of the rejected man in each one of us. And these dreadful civil and domestic wars represent so well the inward turmoil felt by those who give themselves to God that no better picture of it can be drawn.

But here is an astounding word: When ye see abomination where it should not be, then let everyone flee without re-entering his house to take anything at all. It seems to me that this word foretells perfectly the present time when corruption of morals is to be found in houses of holiness and in the books of theologians and monks where it should not be. One is in need of fresh air after such foulness, and woe to them who are with child and that give suck in those days; that is to say, woe to those who have ties with the world that hold them back. The words of a saint are pertinent to this theme: We should not ponder whether we are called to leave the world, but rather whether we are called to remain in it, just as one would not take counsel about leaving a pestilent or burning house.

This chapter of the Gospel, which I should like to read with you in its entirety, concludes with an exhortation to watch and to pray that we may avoid all these misfortunes; moreover, it is meet that prayer be unceasing, for the peril is unceasing.

To this end I am sending prayers which have been requested of me; they are to be offered at the three o'clock afternoon service. After your departure a miracle happened to a nun of Pontoise who, without leaving her convent, was cured of an extraordinary headache by a special consecration to the Holy Thorn. I shall let you know more about it some day, but I want to tell you a beautiful quotation from Saint Augustine that applies to it, one that is very consoling for certain people. He says that those who are benefited by miracles truly see them, for we do not see them if they do not benefit us.

I can't tell you how greatly I am indebted to you for the present you have given me. I did not know what it might be, for I had opened it before reading your letter, and then I deeply regretted that I had not treated it at first with the respect I owed it. It is a truth that, until it appears visibly in the resurrection, the Holy Spirit dwells invisibly in the relics of those who died in the grace of God. For God never abandons His own, and not even in the grave where their bodies, although dead in the eyes of men, are more living before God. For sin is no longer in them, whereas it always resides in them during life; at least its root does so, for the fruits of sin are not always there. And this unfortunate root, which is inseparable from the body during life, does not permit us to honor the body while it is alive, for then it is worthy of hate.

Consequently death becomes necessary so that this unfortunate root may be fully mortified, and it is this that makes death desirable. But it is idle to tell you what you know so well. It would be better to tell it to those other people of whom you speak, but they would not listen.

24. EXCERPT FROM A LETTER BY BLAISE PASCAL TO MONSIEUR AND MLLE DE ROUANNEZ

[September 24, 1656]

It is undeniable that we never break ties without pain. We are unaware of a bond when we voluntarily follow him who leads us on, as Saint Augustine says. But when we begin to resist and to withdraw, we suffer greatly; the bond is stretched and undergoes heavy strain, and this strain is our own body which is broken only in death. Our Lord said that since the coming of John the Baptist, that is to say since His own advent into the world, and consequently since His advent in all the faithful, the Kingdom of God has been suffering violence, and that the violent take it by force. Before being reached [by the message of election], we have but the weight of our lust which bears us down to earth. When God draws us upward, the two opposing forces cause this violence which God alone can overcome. But we can do all things, says Saint Leo, with Him, without whose aid we can do nothing. Therefore we must resolve to suffer this warfare all our life, for there is no peace here below. Jesus Christ came to send not peace but a sword. Nevertheless, one must admit with the Scriptures that the wisdom of this world is but folly before God. Moreover, we may say that this struggle, which seems so hard to mankind, is peace with God, for it is this peace also which Jesus Christ has brought. Yet it will be perfect peace only when the body shall be destroyed. It is this that makes us long for death, while nevertheless we willingly suffer life for the love of Him who suffered life and death for us, and who is able to do exceeding abundantly above all that we ask or think. Thus says Saint Paul in the epistle of the Mass for today . . . [sentence incomplete].

25. EXCERPT FROM A LETTER BY BLAISE PASCAL TO MONSIEUR AND MLLE DE ROUANNEZ

[October, 1656](?)

Thanks to God, I no longer have any fears for you, and I have an admirable hope. There is great consolation in a word of Jesus Christ: "For whosoever hath, to him shall be given." By this promise those who have received much have a right to hope for more, and so those who have received extraordinarily much, may well hope for extraordinarily much. I try as much as possible to let nothing trouble me and to make the best of everything that happens. I believe this to be a duty, and that we sin in doing otherwise. For, after all, the reason why sins are sins is that they are contrary to the will of God; and so, since the essence of sin consists in having a will which is opposed to what we know to be God's will, it seems obvious to me that when He discloses His will to us through events, it would be a sin not to adjust oneself to them. I have learned that there is something admirable about that which happens, since it bears the stamp of God's will. With all my heart I praise Him for the perfect continuation of His mercies, for I see that they do not decrease.

The affair of . . . is hardly going well; it is a thing which makes those who are truly committed to God tremble when they see the impending persecution not only of persons (that would be little) but of the truth. Indeed, God has been much abandoned. It seems to me that this is an age when the service we render Him is very easy indeed. He desires us to judge of grace through nature; and so He allows us to consider that just as a prince driven from his country by his subjects has extreme affection for those who remain faithful to him during a public revolt, so it seems that with particular kindness God considers those who today are defending the purity of religion and of morals which are so strongly attacked. But there is this difference between the kings of the earth and the King of Kings: princes do not make their subjects faithful, but they find them so; on the other hand, God never finds men anything but faithless, and He makes them faithful when they are so. Hence, instead of kings having unique obligation toward those who remain in their fealty to them, it happens, on the contrary, that those who remain in the service of God are themselves under infinite obligation to Him. Let us then continue to praise Him for this grace if He has bestowed it upon us, for which we shall praise Him in eternity; let us pray that He continue to do so, and that He may have pity on us and on the whole Church outside of which there is nothing but malediction.

I sympathize deeply with . . . who was persecuted, and of whom you speak. I see well that God has reserved unto Himself hidden servants, as He said to Elijah. I pray to Him that we may be good servants, as we should, in spirit and in truth and in sincerity.

26. EXCERPT FROM A LETTER BY BLAISE PASCAL TO MONSIEUR AND MLLE DE ROUANNEZ

[October 27(?), 1656]

. . . It seems to me that you are sufficiently interested in the miracle for me to send a special word to you that its verification was completed by the Church, as you will see from this sentence of the Grand Vicar. There are so few people to whom God reveals Himself through these extraordinary interventions. For He departs from the secrets of nature, which hide Him, only in order to stimulate our faith to serve Him with all the more ardor when we know Him with greater certainty. If God revealed Himself continually to men, there would be no merit at all in believing in Him; if He never revealed Himself, there would be no faith. But ordinarily He conceals Himself, and He reveals Himself but rarely to those whom He wishes to engage in His service. This strange secrecy, into which God has withdrawn and which is impenetrable to the eyes of man, is a great lesson to lead us into solitude far from the eyes of man. He has remained hidden under the veil of nature which hid Him from us until the Incarnation; and when He finally appeared in the fullness of time under the veil of human flesh, He was hidden even more than before. He was far more recognizable when He was invisible than when He had rendered Himself visible. And finally when He wanted to fulfill the promise which He had made to His apostles to remain with mankind until His final coming, He chose to remain there in the strangest and most hidden mystery of all, namely, in the Eucharistic species. This is the Sacrament which in the Apocalypse Saint John calls a hidden manna. And I believe that Isaiah saw it in this state when he said in the spirit of prophecy: "Verily, Thou art a hidden God." That is the final secret in which He may be. The veil of nature which hides God has been penetrated by several infidels who, as Saint Paul said, have recognized an invisible God through visible nature. Heretical Christians have known Him through His humanity, and they adore Jesus Christ, God and man. But to recognize Him through the species of bread is the attribute of Catholics alone: we alone have been enlightened thus far by God. To these considerations may be added the secret of the Spirit of God which is still hidden in Scripture. For there are two perfect meanings, the literal and the mystical; the Jews who stop at the one do not even think there is another, and do not think of seeking it. Just so the impious, on seeing natural effects, attribute them to nature without thinking that there is another author. And just as the Jews, on seeing a perfect man in Jesus Christ, did not think of seeking another nature in Him, so we did not think it was He, as Isaiah again says. Similarly the heretics, on seeing the perfect appearance of the bread, do not think of seeking another substance in it. All things hide some mystery; all things are veils which hide God. Christians should recognize Him in everything. Temporal afflictions hide the eternal good to which they lead. Temporal joys hide the eternal ills which they cause. Let us pray God that we may recognize Him and serve Him in all things. Let us return infinite thanks, that inasmuch as He has hidden Himself from others in all things, He has revealed Himself to us in all things and in so many ways . . . [sentence incomplete].

27. EXCERPT FROM A LETTER BY BLAISE PASCAL TO MONSIEUR AND MLLE DE ROUANNEZ

[Sunday, November 5, 1656]

I do not know how the loss of your letters has affected you. I hope very much that you have taken it well. It is time to begin to judge what is good or evil by the will of God, who can be neither unjust nor blind, rather than by our own will which is always full of malice and error. If these have been your sentiments, I shall be quite content, so that you may find consolation on more solid grounds than those I have to advance, namely, that I hope the letters may be found. The letter of the fifth has already been brought to me, and although it is not the most important one, for the one of Monsieur du Gas is more so, nevertheless that gives me hope of having the other again.

I do not know why you complain that I have written nothing for you; in my thoughts I never separate you, and I always join you in my thoughts. You see very well that my other letters and this one concern you very much indeed. In truth, I cannot refrain from telling you that I should like to be infallible in my judgments; you would not fare badly if that were the case, for I am quite content with you, but my judgment is nothing. I say that about the way in which I see you speak of this good persecuted friar and of what is being done by. . . . I am not surprised to see Monsieur N. [Monsieur Singlin?] take an interest in it, for I am accustomed to his zeal, but yours is quite new to me; it is the language which a new heart produces. In the Gospel Jesus Christ gave this sign by which we recognize those that have faith. This sign is that they shall speak a new language, and, indeed, the renewal of thoughts and of desires causes the renewal of discourses.

What you say about the days when you [Mlle de Rouannez] found yourself alone and about the consolation which reading gave you, are things which Monsieur N. will be very glad to know when I point them out to him; so will my sister. They are assuredly new things which, however, must be renewed without ceasing, for this newness which cannot displease God, just as the old man cannot please Him, is different from the novelties of this earth. For the things of the world, however new they may be, grow old as they continue, whereas the new spirit is renewed in proportion as it endures. The old man perishes, says Saint Paul, and is renewed from day to day, and will be perfectly new only in eternity, where he will sing unceasingly this new song of which David speaks in the psalms of praise, that is to say, this song which comes from the new spirit of love.

The news which I shall tell you concerning these two persons is this: I see very well that their zeal does not abate; that amazes me, for it is far more rare to see people continue in their piety than to see them enter into piety. I always have them in mind, and particularly so the one concerned in the miracle, because it is a most extraordinary thing, although the other person is likewise very much so and almost unparalleled. It is certain that the mercies which God performs in this life are the measure of the glory which He prepares in the life beyond. Consequently, when I foresee the end and the crowning of His work in their beginnings as they appear in persons of piety, I enter into a veneration which overwhelms me with awe for those whom He seems to have chosen as His elect. I confess to you that I already seem to see them on one of those thrones where those who have forsaken all will judge the world with Jesus Christ, in accordance with the promise He has given. But when I begin to think that these same persons may fall and be, on the contrary, among the unhappy number who are judged, and that there will be many who shall fall from their glory, and who by their negligence will let others take the crown which God has offered them, I cannot bear this thought. The terror I should have at seeing them in this eternal state of misery, after having had such good reason to imagine them in the other state, makes me shrink from this idea, and return to God to pray Him not to abandon the feeble creatures He has acquired, and to say to Him for the two persons whom you know what the Church says today with Saint Paul: Lord, achieve Thou the work which Thou hast begun. Saint Paul often thought of himself in these two estates, and that is what led him to say elsewhere: But I chastise my body, for fear that I myself, who have converted so many people, might become a castaway. I shall conclude then with the words of Job: I have always feared the Lord as I do the billows of a sea that grows furious to engulf me. And elsewhere: Blessed is the man who lives in everlasting fear . . . [incomplete sentence].

28. EXCERPT FROM A LETTER BY BLAISE PASCAL TO MONSIEUR AND MLLE DE ROUANNEZ

[November, 1656](?)

. . . to reply to all your articles and to write clearly in spite of my limited time.

I am delighted that you have enjoyed the book by Monsieur de Laval and the *Meditations on grace*. I am drawing important inferences from this for what I desire.

I am writing the details about this condemnation which had frightened you; thanks to God, it is nothing at all, and it is a wonder that they have done nothing worse about it, since the enemies of truth have the power and the will to oppress it. Perhaps you [Mlle de R.] are one of those who deserve that God should not abandon her and not withdraw her from the earth which has rendered itself so unworthy of her. It is certain that you are serving the Church by your prayers if the Church has served you by hers. For it is the Church which merits with Jesus Christ, who is inseparable from her, the conversion of all those who are not [living] in the truth; and then it is the converted persons who save the mother who has delivered them. With all my heart I praise the slight fervor that I have observed in your letter for union with the Pope. The body is no more living without a head than the head without the body. Whoever separates himself from the one or from the other no longer is part of the body, and no longer belongs to Jesus Christ. I do not know whether there are persons in the Church more attached to this unity of the body than are those whom you call ours. We know that all the virtues, martyrdom, austerities and all good works are useless outside of the Church and of the communion of the head of the Church who is the Pope.

I shall never separate myself from communion with him, at least I pray God to grant me that grace, without which I should be lost forever. I am making a kind of profession of faith to you, and I do not know why; but I shall not erase it nor begin anew with it.

This morning Monsieur du Gas [Singlin?] talked with me about your letter with all the astonishment and the joy that it can cause. He does not know the source of your words which he has reported to me; he has told me surprising things about them which no longer surprise me so much. I am beginning to grow accustomed to you and to the grace which God is giving you, and nevertheless I admit to you that this grace is ever new to me, as in fact it is always new.

For it is a continual flux of grace which the Scripture compares with a river and with the light which the sun incessantly sends out and which is ever new, so that if the sun ceased for one moment to send it forth, all the light which we have received would disappear, and we would remain in darkness.

He told me that he had begun a reply to you, and that he would transcribe it to make it more legible and that at the same time he would expand it. But he has just sent it to me with a little note in which he tells me that he has been unable either to copy or to expand it; this leads me to believe that it will be badly written. I am witness to his lack of leisure and to his desire to have leisure for you.

I share the joy which the affair of [the nuns] ... will give you, for I see very well that you are interested in the Church; you are greatly obligated to her. For sixteen hundred years she has been grieving for you. It is time to grieve for her and for all of us together, and to give to her all that remains of our lives, since Jesus Christ has taken His life only to lose it for her and for us ... [sentence incomplete].

29. EXCERPT FROM A LETTER BY BLAISE PASCAL TO MONSIEUR AND MLLE DE ROUANNEZ

[November or December, 1656](?)

... Whatever may happen in the affair of [the priests], thanks to God it has already gone far enough so that we can turn it to admirable account against those cursed maxims. Those who have had some part in this ought to render fervent thanks to God, and their relatives and friends should pray to God for them, so that they may not fall from such high happiness and from so great an honor which God has conferred upon them. All the honors of the world are but an image of it; it alone is substantial and real, and nevertheless it is useless without the proper inclination of one's heart. For it is neither austerity toward the flesh nor tribulation of the spirit but rather the good impulses of the heart which have merit and which relieve bodily and mental suffering. For, after all, these two, suffering and pleasures, are necessary to sanctification. Saint Paul said that those who would enter into the good life shall find sufferings and anxieties in great numbers. That should console those who feel them because, being warned that the road to heaven which they seek is full of them, they ought to rejoice on encountering signs that they are on the right road. But these afflictions are not devoid of pleasure, and they are surmounted only by pleasure. For those who abandon God to return to the world do so only because they find greater sweetness in the pleasures of the world than in those of a union with God, and because this victorious charm carries them away and makes them the Devil's penitents by causing them to repent their first choice, as Tertullian says. And similarly we would not abandon the pleasures of the world to embrace the cross of Jesus Christ if we did not find greater sweetness in the scorn, in the poverty, in the destitution and in the rebuffs of men than in the delights of sin. Therefore, as Tertullian says, we must not believe that the life of Christians is a life of sadness. We give up pleasures only for other greater pleasures. Pray without ceasing, says Saint Paul, in everything give thanks, rejoice evermore. It is the joy of having found God which is the principal source of sadness at having offended Him and of the complete change of one's life. He who has found a treasure in a field is so filled with joy that for joy thereof, according to Jesus Christ, he selleth all that he hath and buyeth that field. The people of the world do not have this joy *which the world can neither give nor take*, as Jesus Christ Himself said. The blessed have this joy without any sadness; the people of the world have their sadness without this joy, and the Christians have this joy mingled with the sadness of having followed other pleasures and with the fear of losing it by the attraction of those other pleasures which tempt us without any respite. And thus we must work ceaselessly to conserve for ourselves this joy which tempers our fear and to conserve this fear which conserves our joy; and when we feel too strongly carried away by the one we must incline toward the other to remain upright. Remember the good in the days of thine affliction, and remember thine affliction in the days of rejoicing, says the Scripture, until the promise be fulfilled which Jesus Christ made to us to make his joy full in us. Then let us not be cast down by sadness and let us not believe that piety consists only in bitterness without consolation. True piety, which is found perfect only in heaven, is so full of satisfactions that with them it fills the beginning, the progress, and the consummation of piety. It is so radiant a light that it streams over everything belonging to it. And if there is any sadness mingled with it, and above all at the beginning, it comes from us and not from virtue, for it is not the effect of the piety which is beginning to be in us, but rather the impiety which still dwells there. Let us remove the impiety, and the joy shall be unalloyed. Then let us not blame piety but rather ourselves and let us seek relief in it only by our correction ... [sentence incomplete].

30. EXCERPT FROM A LETTER BY BLAISE PASCAL TO MONSIEUR AND MLLE DE ROUANNEZ

[December, 1656(?)]

... I am delighted with the hope you give me for the success of the affair whose vanity you feared. There is much to be feared on every hand, for if it should not succeed, I should fear for it that evil sadness which, as Saint Paul says, worketh death, whereas there is another which gives life. It is certain that this was a thorny affair, and if the person involved is extricated from it, there will be cause for some degree of vanity, if it is not for the fact that we have prayed to God and must consequently believe that the good which will come from it will be His work. But if it is unsuccessful, we shall not be dejected, for the selfsame reason that we have prayed to God, and because there is a likelihood that He has taken charge of this affair. Moreover, He must be regarded as the author of all things good and of all ills excepting sin. In this connection I shall repeat what I have previously cited from Scripture. *In the day of prosperity be mindful of the adversities which you deserve, and when you are in adversity be mindful of the prosperity for which you hope.* Nevertheless, I shall say to you about the other person you know that I am quite vexed to see him in his state of mind, for he writes that he has many things which trouble him. His troubles cause me great grief and I should like very much to be able to comfort him; I am begging him not to prejudice the future, and to remember that Our Lord said, *sufficient unto the day is the evil thereof.*

The past should not embarrass us, since we need but regret our errors. But the future should concern us even less, since it is nonexistent as far as we are concerned, and since we may never live to see it. The present is the only time which is truly ours and which we must use according to God. It is the present with which our thoughts must reckon. Nevertheless, the world is so uneasy that we almost never think of life in the present and of the moment in which we are living, but rather of the moment in which we will be living. Hence we are always in readiness to live in the future, and never to live in the present. Our Lord did not desire our cares to extend beyond this present day. These are the bounds within which we must live both for our salvation and for our own repose. For in truth, Christian precepts carry most consolation; more, I say, than the maxims of the world.

I foresee troubles as well for that person as for others and for myself. But when I find myself involved in such cares I pray God to keep me within my bounds; I collect myself, and I find that I am failing to do various things to which I am obligated in the present. In doing so, I am dissipating myself in futile thoughts of the future; I am not at all obliged to attend to these; on the contrary, I am under obligation not to attend to them. It is only for want of knowing how to understand and study the present that we have made a pretense of studying the future. What I am saying here, I say for myself and not for this person who assuredly has far greater virtue and penetration than I, but I point out my shortcomings to him so that he may not succumb to them. We are often corrected better by the sight of evil than by good example; and it is well to accustom ourselves to profit from evil, since it is so common, whereas the good is so rare.

31. EXCERPT FROM A LETTER BY BLAISE PASCAL TO MONSIEUR AND MLLE DE ROUANNEZ

[December 24(?), 1656]

... I feel sorry for the person you know because of the anxiety in which I know her to be and in which I am not surprised to see her. It is a minor day of judgment which cannot come without sweeping emotion to the individual, just as the general judgment will cause general emotion in the world excepting for those who have already judged themselves as she claims to have done; this temporal suffering should protect us from eternal suffering through the infinite merits of Jesus Christ who endures it and makes it His own. That should console her. Our yoke is also His; otherwise it would be unbearable. *Take my yoke upon you*, He said. It is not our yoke; it is His, and so He bears it. *Know ye*, said He, *that my yoke is gentle and light*. It is light only for Him and for His divine strength. I should like to tell her to remember that these anxieties do not come from the good which is beginning to be in her, but from the evil which is still there and which must constantly be decreased; moreover, she must do as a child does that is taken from the arms of its mother by thieves, for it must not accuse the mother, who holds it back so lovingly, of the violence it is suffering, but rather the unjust ravishers. The whole worship of Advent is well suited to give courage to the weak, and in it this word of Scripture is often spoken: *Take courage, ye who are fearful and weak, behold your Redeemer cometh*. And in the vespers of today it is said: *Be strong, and fear not; behold, your God; He will come and save you* . . . [sentence incomplete].

32. EXCERPT FROM A LETTER BY BLAISE PASCAL TO A FRIEND IN CLERMONT [DOMAT(?) OR PERIER(?)]

[April–May, 1657](?)

You give me pleasure in writing all the details of your uprising, and especially so because you are interested in it. For I imagine that you are not imitating our Frondeurs in this region who are making such bad use, at least it seems so to me, of the advantage which God offers them of tolerating some things for the establishment of His truths. For even if it were for the establishment of their truths, they would not do otherwise; and it seems that they are ignorant of the fact that the same Providence which has given insight to some has refused it to others. It seems also that in endeavoring to persuade these they are serving a God other than the one who permits obstacles to oppose their progress. They believe they are rendering service to God when they grumble at obstacles as if there were one power who aroused their piety and another that gave strength to those who oppose their piety. This is the way our own mind is constituted. When we want something to succeed of our own accord, we are irritated by obstacles, because we feel in these hindrances something which our motive for action has not placed there, and we find things there which are not of our own making.

But when God truly causes us to act, we never feel anything outwardly which does not come from the same principle that causes us to act; there is no opposition to the motive which impels us. The same motive power which drives us to act, drives others to resist us, or at least permits them to do so. Consequently, since we find no difference there, and since it is not our mind which combats outside happenings, but the one same spirit which produces good and permits evil, this sameness does not trouble the peace of the soul, and it is one of the best signs that we are acting through the spirit of God. For it is much more certain that God permits evil, however great that may be, than that God (and not some other secret incentive) does the good in us, no matter how great that may seem to us. And so, in order to recognize well whether it is God who causes us to act, it would be far better to examine ourselves through our outward acts than through our inner motives; for if we examine only the interior, even though we find nothing but good there, we cannot be assured that this good really comes from God. But when we examine ourselves on the outside, that is to say when we consider whether we tolerate outward hindrances with patience, this means that there is a sameness of spirit between the motive force that inspires our passions and that which permits resistance to our passions. And since beyond doubt God permits the one, we have the right to hope humbly that it is God who brings forth the others.

But indeed! We act as if it were our mission to make truth triumph, whereas our mission is merely to fight for the truth. The desire to vanquish is so natural that when it is cloaked by the desire to make truth triumph, we often take the one for the other and we believe we are seeking the glory of God when in reality we are seeking our own. It seems to me that the manner in which we tolerate these obstacles is the surest sign of this. For if, after all, we want only the ways ordained of God, we shall doubtless desire the triumph of His justice as much as that of His mercy; and when there is no negligence on our part, we shall be in equanimity of spirit, whether the truth be known or whether it be challenged, since in the one case God's mercy and in the other case His justice will triumph.

Pater juste, mundus te non cognovit. O righteous Father, the world has not known Thee. Saint Augustine remarks on this that it is an outcome of His justice that He is not known by the world. Let us pray and labor and rejoice in all things, as Saint Paul says.

If you had reprimanded me at the time of my first errors, I should not have made this one, and I should have turned to moderation. But I shall blot out this one no more than the other; you will blot it out yourself if you wish. I have not been able to refrain from it, because I am so enraged with those who insist absolutely that we believe the truth which they demonstrate; Jesus Christ did not do this when He assumed our flesh. It is mockery and it seems to me to treat . . . [sentence incomplete].

I greatly regret the illness of Monsieur de Laporte. I assure you that I honor him with all my heart. I . . . [sentence incomplete].

33. [COMPARISON OF THE CHRISTIANS OF THE EARLIEST TIMES WITH THOSE OF TODAY]

[1657(?)]

[At the time of the birth of the Church] we saw only Christians perfected in all matters necessary to salvation.

Today, however, we see such crude ignorance that it causes all those to groan who have feelings of tenderness for the Church.

In those days people entered the Church only after great toil and long desire.

Today people find themselves there without any trouble, without any care and without toil.

People were admitted to the Church only after a very rigid examination.

People are received into it now before being ready to be examined.

At that time people were received into it only after having foresworn their past life, and only after having renounced the world and the flesh and the Devil.

People enter into it now before being able to do any of these things.

Finally, it was formerly necessary to leave the world in order to be received into the Church.

On the other hand, today people enter into the Church at the same time that they enter the world.

People then knew by this process an essential distinction between the world and the Church.

People considered these to be two opposites, two irreconcilable enemies, one of whom persecuted the other ceaselessly; the one who outwardly seemed the weaker was considered certain to triumph some day over the stronger. Consequently people left one of these two opposing parties in order to enter the other; they abandoned the maxims of the one to embrace the maxims of the other; people discarded the opinions of the one in order to adopt the opinions of the other.

Finally, people left, people renounced, people foreswore the world in which they had first been born in order to consecrate themselves entirely to the Church in which they had been born a second time. And thus they perceived an appalling difference between the one and the other, whereas now people find themselves in both almost at the same moment; the same moment in which we are born in the world sees us reborn in the Church. And so supervening reason no longer makes any distinction between these two worlds which are so opposed to each other. Reason is elevated in both of them together. People partake of the Sacraments and enjoy the pleasures of this world, etc.

And thus, whereas people formerly saw an essential distinction between the two, they now regard them as mingled and blended, so that they are now scarcely distinguishable.

As a result, only very well-informed people were to be seen among Christians.

On the contrary, they now are in an ignorance which inspires horror.

As a result, those who had formerly been regenerated by mistaken baptism and who had forsaken the vices of the world to enter into the godliness of the Church, so rarely fell back into the world from the Church; whereas now nothing is seen more commonly than the [vices] of the world in the hearts of Christians.

The Church of the saints is so defiled by being confounded with the wicked; and her children — whom she has conceived and borne in her bosom since infancy, that is to say, even unto participation in her most august mysteries — are the same ones who bear in their hearts the cruelest of her enemies, namely the spirit of the world, the spirit of ambition, the spirit of vengeance, the spirit of obscenity, the spirit of lust. And the love which she bears for her children obliges her to admit into her very inmost parts the cruelest of her persecutors.

But it is not to the Church that we must attribute the misfortunes which have followed a change in so salutary a discipline. For since she saw that delayed baptism left a large number of children in the curse of Adam, she desired to deliver them from this mass in perdition, by hastening the succor which she gives to them. And this good mother beholds only with extreme regret that what she had provided for the salvation of her children is becoming the occasion for the destruction of adults.

Her true disposition is that those whom she withdraws at so tender an age from the contagion of the world may be removed far from the opinions of the world. She anticipates the use of reason in order to anticipate the vices into which corrupted reason might drag them; and before their spirit may act, she fills them with her spirit, so that they may live in ignorance of the world and in a state all the farther removed from the vice which they would never have known.

This is manifest in the ceremonies of baptism, for she accords baptism to children only after they have declared through the voice of their godfathers that they desire, that they believe, and that they renounce the world and Satan. And since she desires them to retain this disposition in the whole course of their life, she commands them expressly to keep it inviolate, and by an indispensable commandment she orders godfathers to instruct children in all these things. For she does not wish that those whom she has nourished in her bosom from childhood shall today be less well instructed and less zealous than those whom she formerly admitted to her numbers. She desires no less perfection in those whom she nourishes than in those whom she receives.

Nevertheless, people are making use of this in a manner so contrary to the intention of the Church that we cannot think of it without horror. People are scarcely reflecting any more on so great a benefit, because they have never asked for it, and because they do not even remember having received it . . . [sentence incomplete].

But since it is evident that the Church asks no less zeal in those who have been brought up in the household of faith than in those who aspire to it, we must place before our eyes the example of the catechumens, we must consider their ardor, their devotion, their horror of the world, their generous renunciation of the world. And if we did not judge them worthy of receiving baptism without these dispositions, those who do not find these within them . . . [sentence incomplete].

They must therefore submit to receiving the instruction which they would have had if they were beginning to enter into the communion of the Church. In addition they must submit to a penitence such that they shall no longer desire to reject it [the communion] and such that they shall have less aversion for the austerity of the mortification [of the senses] than they find charm in the practice of the vicious delights of sin.

In order to dispose them to instructing themselves, it will be necessary to make them understand the difference in the customs that have prevailed in the Church in accordance with the diversity of the times.

They must understand that the newly born Church instructed her catechumens, that is to say, those who laid claim to baptism, before conferring it upon them; and that they were admitted to the Church only after full instruction in the mysteries of religion; after penance for their past life, after profound knowledge of the greatness and excellence of the profession of faith and of the Christian maxims into which they desired to enter forever; after conspicuous indications of a veritable conversion of their hearts, and after a fervent desire for baptism. When these things were known by the whole Church, the Sacrament of incorporation was conferred upon them, by which they became members of the Church.

Instead of having baptism accorded, for very important considerations, to children in those days before they could use their reason, it happens that the negligence of parents allows Christians to grow old without any knowledge of the greatness of our religion.

When instruction preceded baptism, all were instructed; but now that baptism precedes instruction, the teaching which was necessary for the Sacrament has become voluntary, and then neglected, and finally almost abolished.

The real reason is that people are persuaded of the necessity [*of baptism*, *and not of the necessity*] of instruction. Consequently when instruction preceded baptism, the necessity of the one caused people to have recourse necessarily to the other. Whereas, now that baptism precedes instruction, since people have been made Christians without being instructed, people believe they can remain Christians without receiving instruction. And whereas the first Christians manifested their gratitude [toward the Church for a grace which she accorded to them only after their long prayers], they today manifest so much ingratitude for this same grace which she accords them even before they have been in a state to ask it.

And if the Church so strongly detested the falling from grace of her first members, rare as that was, how great must be her abomination of the falling and continual falling anew of her last members, even though they are under far greater obligation to her, since she has drawn them much earlier and much more generously from the damnation to which they were consigned by their first birth.

She cannot, without grieving, behold abuse of the greatest of her graces and see that which she has done to assure their salvation become almost a certain occasion of their perdition, for she has not . . . [sentence incomplete].

34. LETTER FROM A LAWYER IN PARLIAMENT TO ONE OF HIS FRIENDS CONCERNING THE INQUISITION WHICH THEY WANT TO ESTABLISH IN FRANCE AS A RESULT OF A NEW BULL OF POPE ALEXANDER VII

Paris, June 1, 1657.

Sir:

You believe that all your affairs are going well, because your lawsuit is not going badly, but you are going to find out that you scarcely know what is happening. You are very fortunate in seeing matters from afar. We were about to see the establishment of an inquisition in France, and the danger is not yet over. The agents of the Court of Rome and some bishops who dominated the Assembly co-operated toward its establishment, and for its basis they chose the Bull of Pope Alexander VII on the five propositions. They forced the clergy to accept it, and with results that were in keeping with their design. For it was decreed in the Assembly that it should be subscribed to by all the clergy of the realm without any exception, and that all those who would refuse to sign it should be proceeded against with all the penalties directed against heretics, that is to say, by the loss of their benefices and by many other violent means, as everyone knows.

You can see very well what that means, and that the inquisition is established unless Parliament opposes it. However, there is talk about sending this Bull to Parliament so that if it is received there, the result will be that France will be bound and in subjection like other nations.

I often think of all this, and I find nothing good in it. People do not know to what this leads, nor what the consequences of it may be. This is not a matter of politics, but of religion. If I am not mistaken, Jansenism, which seems to be the cause of it, is in reality but an occasion and a pretext for it. For while they dangle before us the hope of abolishing Jansenism, they are imperceptibly bringing us under the sway of the inquisition which will oppress us before we are aware of what is taking place.

I grant that it is a laudable design to make people believe that those five propositions are Jansen's. But the means do not please me at all. I consider this manner of depriving people of their benefices to be a wicked innovation and one which will affect those who are not expecting it. Do you believe, Sir, that we have no interest in the matter because we do not belong to the clergy? Let us not deceive ourselves. It concerns all of us, no matter who we are, if not for ourselves, at least for our relatives, our friends, our children. Can your son, who is now studying at the Sorbonne, have the benefices of his uncle? And is not my son, the prior, personally affected? You will say that they need merely sign in order to protect themselves. Granted; but is it any concern of ours that their security depends upon that! What! If my son gets the notion that these propositions are not to be found in Jansen, as I fear he may do, for he often sees his cousin, the doctor, who says that he has never been able to find them there; if, not believing them to be there, my son cannot sign that he believes them to be there, because he would consider that a lie and because he would prefer to lose everything rather than to offend God; if then my son gets all these notions, it would be good-by to my benefices that I have taken so much trouble to secure.

You see clearly, therefore, that whoever has no interest in this matter today, may tomorrow, and that that is scarcely preferable. Why do they not seek other means to show that these propositions are in this book instead of disturbing a whole kingdom as they are doing? Is it important enough to create such an uproar about it? As long as they merely disputed in their books, I let them write without letting myself become embroiled. But it is a fine way of settling their differences, when they trouble so many families that have nothing to do with their disputes, and when they plant a new inquisition in France which would lead us a merry dance. For God knows, once it has taken root, how much the inquisition will grow in a very short time. We shall see in no time at all that no one will be safe in his own home. For you will merely need powerful enemies to denounce you and to accuse you of being a Jansenist, simply because you have Jansenist books in your study or because you have spoken somewhat freely about these new Bulls, as you know that we lawyers often do. Thereupon your property will be in jeopardy. And suppose that all they should do to you would be to start a lawsuit, would that not still be a great enough evil? Now, nothing is so easy as to start one, and even against those who least suspect it. We have already had examples of that. They have been meditating on such designs for some time. They have had training in harassing people about the Bull and the Apostolic Briefs of Innocent X. You know, for example, how uneasy the canons of Beauvais were when an attempt was made to compel them to subscribe to them under penalty of losing their benefices. Today they might well be dispossessed of them, were it not for an appeal by writ of error which they made to Parliament in the matter, and which defeated all such designs.

For there is nothing so effective against the inquisition as appeals by writ of error. Well they know it, and they do not fail to close that door when they wish to tyrannize someone unmolested. That is how they proceeded against the curé of Libourne in Guienne whom they had des Recollets accuse of Jansenism; they summoned him to appear before commissioners whom they had had appointed by the council of the Archbishop of Bordeaux. However, since they did not have jurisdiction over him and since, moreover, they appeared to be swayed by their passions, he appealed the case and demanded to be remanded to the grand vicars or to the official of the Archbishop of Bordeaux. His appeal was not granted. Therefore he appealed to the Archbishop of Bordeaux himself, and finally to the Pope. But those commissioners would not drop his case. He finally appealed by writ of error to Parliament. The latter gave him a decree to suspend the execution [of the act of the commissioners]. By dint of this decree he was about to escape from their clutches when they obtained a decree from the council which denied Parliament jurisdiction in the case, and sent it back to the former commissioners. Thus he was abused for more than six months, during which he was forced to leave his rectory and to come to Paris at much trouble and expense to ask justice of the king and of his archbishop. And so I have heard that only a few days ago he went back to his rectory after all that hardship which his accusers had the pleasure of causing him without exposing themselves to any danger.

Now don't you think that the inquisition is a very convenient way to dispose of one's enemies, no matter how innocent they may be? For the priest of Libourne could not be accused of any wrong any more than the priest of Pomyrol, likewise in Guienne, whom they first threw into jail and into a dungeon without any preliminary inquiry, and without telling him why — after the manner of the Roman Inquisition. Thereupon they sought evidence to convict him of Jansenism. But the judges who heard this case were greatly surprised to find as a result of their investigation that the man was innocent and that his parishioners were incredibly superstitious. One of the principal charges on which his accusers had insisted most was this: *That he had preached to them that Jesus Christ was in the Holy Sacrament, and not in their banner.* For he had rebuked them because, when the Host was elevated, they had turned toward their banner on which Jesus Christ was painted, and not toward the Holy Sacrament to worship it. This so overwhelmed his judges with shame that they immediately discharged him from prison where he had been for two months. Yet in spite of his insistence that they end the suit, and that they punish either him or his accusers, he could not obtain any amends for so much ill treatment.

Truly, Sir, that is not so bad for the inquisitors who, after all, are just beginning. If they have been guilty of such acts of violence on the basis of constitutions and briefs which have not been received in Parliament, what would they do in the case of a Bull which Parliament had received? They make me die of laughter when they tell me that the declaration of the king for the registry of the Bull will declare that the inquisition is not to be established and that our liberties are not to be jeopardized. They might as well say that they are putting us to death without jeopardizing our lives. It is not the word inquisition which frightens us, but the thing itself. Now, by whatever word they may call it, it is a very real matter and a real violation of our liberties when we are treated as the clergy seeks to do.

Do you not consider, too, that it is just as weak a consolation for us to be told that Parliament will always have jurisdiction in cases of writs of error? For, in receiving the Bull, it would take away one of the best means for appeal in cases of writs of error; this would have remained if the Bull had been rejected. But even if it were still possible to ask for a writ of error, how they would persecute those people in distant provinces who could not avail themselves of that remedy! What would not a poor priest of Lionnois or of Poitou suffer rather than go to Paris?

They are therefore powerful enough if this Bull is received, even though writs of error are still allowed. And so I feel that they were ill advised to pass the resolution which is to be found on page two of their last official report as printed by Vitré: *That the king shall be very humbly requested to send to all Parliaments a general decree denying them writs of error by virtue of these signatures.* What did they gain by that other than to testify that they themselves are well aware of the injustice of their designs, since they feared the Parliaments, and have tried to tie their hands in order to assure the success of their own designs? Could they have better demonstrated their passionate desire to act as high-handed masters and as sovereign inquisitors? But it was not very adroit of them to warn everyone so of their intention. To show thus in advance to what ends they wished to use it was not the way to secure the support for which they asked. And they recognized this, but all too late. For after having allowed that printed official report to be circulated, formal copies of which, signed by the agents of the clergy, were sent even to the bishops, they finally became aware that that was doing them harm; then it occurred to them to try to suppress it, which merely serves to reveal their trickery more and more clearly. Yet they imagine that because they are now requesting only a simple consent, which is seemingly of the slightest moment, Parliament will be caught in their snare, and will consider only this Bull which is presented to it, and will give no attention to the purpose it is to serve. And this they imagine, although they have disclosed their purpose so openly in authentic documents. Isn't it admirable to see them try to make Parliament their dupe? But I am much mistaken if they are not deceiving themselves. I can see very well the direction this matter is taking. Every morning I talk to some of the councilors as they leave the palace, and there is not one who does not see through the whole thing. Your special secretary was telling me just this morning that he did not regard this affair as an ordinary matter and that one should not consider this Bull as a simple Bull which is to decide some contested point that might be of little consequence, but rather as the basis for a new inquisition which they wish to establish, and whose establishment requires only the consent of Parliament.

I have been greatly pleased to see Parliament go to the root of the whole matter. And in fact, if there were nothing in the nature of this Bull to make it deserve rejection — although I shall show you that it is full of the most blatant illegalities — nevertheless Parliament could not receive it today simply in view of the conclusions which they are trying to draw from it. For are there not many things which may be acceptable at one time, but not at another? That is what the Sorbonne set forth very well when the attempt was made to force all the doctors to testify *that they would say nothing contrary to the decrees of the Popes, that they would do this without any restriction and without adding that the rights and liberties of the kingdom were to be excepted.* And an attempt was made to bring them to do this because of the example of some doctors of old who were alleged to have done so. But in an investigation of the matter which Monsieur Fillesac, the Dean of the Sorbonne, had printed in 1628, they [of the Sorbonne] declared, first, *that if some had sworn this oath in the past, it was a special case, and created no precedent;* moreover, *that it could have been done conscientiously at a former time, but that this did not mean that it could be done so today when things are new and different.* And these are the reasons they give in support on page 89: *For some centuries the Popes have issued a large number of decrees, decretals, bulls and constitutions, contrary to decrees of long standing and even to Holy Writ;* of the above they give many examples, both of those which are contrary to Scripture, and of those which run counter to the liberties of the Gallican Church and to the authority of our kings. Among others is that of Pope Boniface VIII who declares those to be heretics who will not believe that the King of France is subject to him even in temporal matters. In his Bull, UNAM SANCTAM, he defines: *That it is necessary to salvation to believe that the Pope is master of two swords, spiritual as well as temporal, and that every human creature is subject to him.* Therefore, according to that Pope, to say the opposite is to be a heretic. To this those doctors add the Bull, *Cum ex Apostolatus*, which declares *that persons of every estate and condition, kings and private individuals, who lapse into heresy, or who aid, shelter, or conceal heretics, are fallen and forfeit forever all honors, dignities and wealth; these become forfeit to the first comer who may be able to get hold of them.* Accordingly they point out that, in view of the present attitude of the Court of Rome, they cannot possibly be obliged to obey them without reservations. And they confirm this by reference to the state of mind at that time, when they say, to wit, on page 47: *We have arrived at a time when for fifty years we have seen many similar Bulls published which arrogate to themselves this imaginary right to dispose of kingdoms. During the same time we have seen many books of this same stamp which are highly prejudicial to the State and even to the life of our kings. Among others there is the execrable book entitled* Admonitio, *and that of Santarel, the Jesuit, written to sustain those maxims against the king and his states. Whence it is clearly to be seen,* they say on pages 53 and 95, *what the purpose is of those who seek these new oaths which they demand of us; their purpose is none other than craftily to overthrow the fundamental maxims of this state which are undone by the decrees of the Popes. It is only too evident and manifest that the practices and crafty dealings which they carry on to establish this innovation have no other aim and purpose than to lend authority to the bills against the authority of the king and to evade the censures of the books by the Jesuits Santarel and Mariana as well as the decrees of the council and Parliament which condemn the aforesaid doctrine as detestable.* From this they conclude what they had said on pages 46 and 47, namely, *that even though it were true that these oaths had been consented to for a long time — which is not the case — it would be necessary to reject them at present.*

I say the same concerning our affair. If it were true — which it is not — that this Bull could be received entirely on its own merits, nevertheless it ought not to be received now. That would mean favoring the obvious designs of those who ask for its acceptance only to misuse it, and to bring us into subjection to that villainous tribunal of the inquisition under which almost all Christianity is groaning. But I have more to say. It is so full of flaws in itself that it cannot be accepted without serious harm to every form of justice. I shall now mention some of these flaws, for I have not yet forgotten all my canon law.

Don't take it into your head to laugh at the first which is the crude solecism known to everybody under the word *imprimantur*. For that renders it void by the decrees of Pope Luce III: *c. ad audientiam* under the heading *de Rescriptis*, and so indubitably void that the gloss adds, *according to the opinion of all the writers on canon law no proof of the validity of a Bull is to be admitted against any such presumption of falsity: contra istam praesumptionem non est admittenda probatio.* This indicates with what fickleness and with what deceitfulness it was done. And so a great clamor was made about it in Flanders. For it is evident that that flaw is in the original; and so there was no point in correcting it as was done in the latest editions. For since the original was null and void, the copies are likewise null and void. Moreover it is stated in the law *that the slightest change, even of a period, renders a Bull void, and whoever made the change is excommunicated in Bul. Coenae c. licet, Rebuf. in praxi.*

Another flaw and one which concerns us more closely, is that in which the Pope threatens to invoke penalties against those who shall not obey his Bull. Whereupon I leave it to Parliament to judge whether it behooves the Pope to threaten the king's subjects with penalties: *sub poenis ipso facto incurrendis*.

Still another flaw is the harmful way in which it disparages the sacred and supreme order of the Episcopacy, by ranking it with the lesser orders in the clause in which the Pope, speaking of himself when he was a cardinal and a bishop, says that he then was *in minoribus*. This is an expression which makes the Bull void according to the chapter *Quam gravi*, under the heading *de crimini falsi*. There it is stated that if a Pope, in speaking of a bishop, calls him *his son* instead of calling him *his brother*, to the disparagement of the relation which exists between him and all the bishops of the Episcopacy the world over, then the act which contains that expression is to be considered null and void. What then will be said of this expression by which the Pope treats the bishops not as *sons* but as *minors?* This term is so shocking and so contemptuous that the Assembly of the clergy, which is not exactly overzealous as regards the interests of the Episcopacy, changed it in the version of the Bull which it made, by recasting that sentence as far as that was feasible. By so doing, however, they did nothing that would redound to the honor of their character which remained tarnished in the original as well as in the Latin which they quote. And so this correction merely indicates more clearly the outrage to their dignity and the weakness they manifested in permitting it.

Do you want other examples? What will you say about the Pope's no longer being satisfied with forbidding people to write, preach and say anything contrary to his decisions, which admittedly is within his power because of his supreme rank in the Church? But he wants to go beyond that, and to force us to believe what he alone has decided, *Teneant:* That is what we could not submit to without admitting that *we and our kings are his subjects even in temporal matters*, for their Bulls declare roundly *that it is a heresy to say the contrary*. *Aliter sentientes haereticos reputamus*, said Boniface VII to our King Philip the Handsome. And so, beyond all doubt, if we accept the Pope as infallible, we must necessarily acknowledge ourselves to be his slaves or else pass for heretics, since we would be resisting an infallible authority. Moreover, the Church has never recognized this infallibility in the Pope, but only in the universal council to which unjust decisions of the Popes have always been appealed. Although, to establish their sovereign control, they have often undertaken to treat as heretics those who might appeal from them to the councils — as did Pius II, Julius II, and Leo X — the Church on the contrary maintains, as was determined in full universal council, that the

Pope is subject to it. That is why our kings, their attorney generals, the whole universities, and private individuals have so often appealed from Bulls to the councils, as we see in the entire thirteenth chapter of the liberties of the Church. And so the principal basis of our liberties, the one upon which, according to Monsieur Pithou, they all depend is this old maxim *that although the Pope is suzerain in spiritual things, nevertheless in France sovereign power has no place, but it is limited by the canons and rules of erstwhile councils: Et in hoc maxime consistit libertas Ecclesiae Gallicanae*, according to the University of Paris. Whereupon Monsieur du Puy, in his commentaries on the liberties of the Church, dedicated to the late Monsieur Molé, the first President and Keeper of the Seals, printed by Cramoisy with permission to publish, states on page 30, that our theologians call that full power of the Pope *a perfect tempest and a diabolical statement: Plenam tempestatem, et verbum diabolicum.*

Those are the sentiments of our doctors, in accordance with whom we have always held *that the decision of the Pope does not require anyone to believe what he has decided even in matters of faith, because he is subject to error in matters of faith. Nevertheless, nothing to the contrary is to be maintained unless there are solid reasons for it. In causis fidei determinatio solius Papae ut Papae non ligat ad credentum, quia est deviabilis a fide*, as Gerson has said. The Pope, therefore, is encroaching on our liberties in this Bull in which he wants to force us to believe his decisions. Thus it is clearly void.

Another flaw which is of far greater significance than appears on the surface, is that the Pope says that, in looking into this matter, the greatest desirable diligence has been used: *qua major desiderari non possit*. For in this there is a hidden artifice which we must expose. It is, as I have already told you, that the Popes want us to believe that they alone can decide on matters of faith, so that subsequently there is nothing more to be desired. We, however, maintain that only the councils can require belief and leave nothing further to be desired. Thus, in accordance with his claim, the Pope does very well to try to make us acknowledge that *every desirable attention* has been given to this matter, even though he has done nothing more than consult with some regulars. But it would be a great error to consent to it. For that would be to recognize him as infallible, to do infinite harm to our liberties, to destroy appeals to the Council General, and even to render all councils useless. For the Pope alone would suffice, if he were infallible. And do not doubt that, if this Bull were passed, the partisans of the Court of Rome would some day make good use of it to get these results from it.

There are many other grave flaws that would take too long to recall. No Bull ever had so many. But what makes it quite impossible of acceptance by Parliament is that, having been made by the Pope alone, without a council, and even without the advice of the College of Cardinals, it can be regarded only as having been made at the instigation of the Pope alone, *motu proprio*, and therefore by no means to be recognized in France. For, in France, Bulls made *motu proprio* in matters of faith or anything which affects the whole Church have never been accepted, no matter what efforts the Popes made to that end, as Innocent X did in his Bull of the residence of the cardinals in 1646. In it he declares *that although it was made at his own instigation, it is his understanding that it shall carry the same weight as if made by the Council of Cardinals*. On that score Monsieur Talon, the late Solicitor General, says *that in this clause the Pope tried in vain to give support, by an assumption of power, to the essential point of an important act*. Consequently it was thrown out as an abuse of power. And as regards the last constitution of the same Pope on the five propositions — although it decided matters of faith which were recognized by all the theologians without exception — nevertheless, despite the general desire for its entry, no one dared to request it, and the sole reason for this was that it represented only the voice of the Pope. How then would it be possible for Alexander's [Bull] not to be rejected? For even if it did not present so many flaws, its essential defect of being made solely by the Pope would make it unacceptable.

Therefore, Sir, it is certain that there never was a less acceptable Bull than this one. It should be thrown out because of its flaws even though no ill use were to be made of it. Moreover, even if there were no flaws in it, it should be thrown out just because of the wrong use of it which they contemplate. Now what will it be, if we take into account both the flaws and the contemplated use? Is it not obvious that if this Bull is accepted, there is none that we shall not be forced to accept, and that thus we shall find ourselves exposed to all those that may come from Rome? And that is a matter of no little consequence. You can judge what may come of it by what has already happened. Do you not see that what they are trying to do is to multiply the Bulls so that they may be so many titles to infallibility which is in need of them, and so that people may gradually get accustomed to blind credence in them. Once they have thus made themselves masters of the mind of the people, Parliaments will vainly oppose Rome's encroachments on the temporal power of our kings. Their opposition will be looked upon only as politics and not as dictated by conscience. Whenever it pleases Rome, those in the opposition will be treated as heretics. For how is it possible to make anyone believe that an infallible authority has been mistaken? And so, according to the Bulls of Boniface VIII and those like him, there is no difference between saying that the Pope is infallible, and saying that we are his subjects.

You see, Sir, from all this both how dangerous this Bull is because of the end to which they wish to use it, and how badly it is drawn up. All that there is left for me to do is to point out to you how unimportant it is basically and in the matter it decides; since this is but a simple point of fact, it by no means merits all the clamor they are trying to make over it. For all the theologians in the world remain in firm agreement that this fact cannot make heretics of those who deny it; at most they may be considered rash. Now it is unreasonable to assume that a rash act should suffice to have people deprived of their property and their benefices, and punished as heretics. Why treat those as heretics who are not at all heretical, when the dispute is only over a point of fact which cannot give rise to heresy? Yet some bishops who resolved to dispossess the holders of benefices and whose only pretext for doing so rested upon that point of fact, decreed, in their circular letter of the seventeenth of last March *that those who will refuse to subscribe to the fact shall be treated as though they refused to subscribe to doctrine.* Nevertheless, their attempt is in vain. With all their power they cannot join those things that are by nature separate. A simple fact will always remain a simple fact, and it can never provide cause for depriving people of their benefices: I constantly come back to that.

After all, is it not clearer than day that in all this they have not been at all interested in instructing us in the faith, but only in making us subject to the inquisition? That is what I would show you in detail, if I had time, not only as regards the point which they have chosen for their objections, but also the way in which they go about it. Isn't it a fine article of faith to believe that propositions which everyone condemns are in a book? Is it conceivable that the signatures of the whole Church are demanded merely to create belief on that point? One would have to be very simple to believe that. If they had so greatly desired to bring about that belief, all they needed to do was to cite the pages. If their design had been really to enlighten us, they would have explained to us what Jansen meant; this they condemn without saying what it is, as the 18th [Provincial Letter], which my son showed me this morning, well says. Understand, then, Sir, they thought only of themselves, and not of us. They chose that point only because, in view of the prejudice against Jansen, it was favorable to their ends. They determined to make use of this opportunity, and, profiting by the desire people manifested for having this doctrine condemned, they thought we should be inflamed enough on the subject to buy their Bulls with the loss of our liberties.

Just as I was writing these last lines, I saw one of the ablest councilors who told me it is an accepted maxim of Parliaments that the Parliaments are the legitimate and natural judges of questions of fact on ecclesiastical matters; consequently, since it is a question here only of knowing whether the five condemned propositions are taken from Jansen, it is for them to examine this in case the Bull is brought before them. Likewise, in the famous conference at Fontainebleau, when Cardinal du Perron brought a charge of falsehood against 500 passages of the Fathers as cited by Du Plessis Mornay, King Henry IV appointed lay commissioners to judge the matter. There it was a question of determining whether the passages were really in the Fathers, just as it is a question here of finding out whether those propositions are in Jansen. And despite the protests which the Nuncio made at first because members of the clergy were not chosen to examine into an ecclesiastical matter, they remained the judges of the case, inasmuch as it was merely a question of taking up points of fact. He [the councilor] gave me other examples. But this one will suffice to put the matter beyond all doubt, and to show that if pressure is put upon Parliament on the subject of the Bull, we shall have the pleasure of seeing the question, whether those five propositions are in Jansen's book, investigated with due regularity and in a plenary assembly of the chambers. We shall find out whether it is temerity not to believe it. We shall see the judgment of the Pope scrutinized by Parliament.

And so, in view of the fact that it was in charge of such clever persons, I am utterly amazed to see how badly this design to establish the inquisition has worked out. For they could not have chosen a weaker and more ruinous basis than this Bull which, based only on a fact, could never be significant enough to uphold so great an enterprise. Would it not be a shameful and unbearable thing for the inquisition, which would not have been countenanced in France in matters of faith, to be introduced today on a point of fact? And would it not have been shameful and unbearable for everyone to contribute voluntarily to this end, the bishops by establishing it through their authority, and Parliament by allowing them to do so?

I do not believe that Parliament is ready for that. I am not speaking in jest. It affects *them*, as I said a little while ago, at least through their relatives and friends, for there is almost no one who can remain unaffected by a general issue. The less servitude we can have, the better. Wise people will never accept any of it lightly. Then let them seek other ways of making us believe that these propositions are in this book. Let them write as much as they wish, or rather, let them all be silent. People have spoken only too much of this. Let them let people alone, and let them leave our benefices secure.

If Parliament takes up this matter, I have good enough data to show how great a difference there is between the primacy which God has truly given to the Pope for the edification of the Church, and the infallibility which his flatterers would like to give him for the destruction of the Church and of our liberties.

35. [AN IMPORTANT DOCUMENT. EXCERPT FROM THE DECREE OF THE INDEX, CONDEMNING THE PROVINCIAL LETTERS (September 6, 1657)]

THE CONDEMNATION OF THE EIGHTEEN LETTERS AND OTHER WRITINGS OF THE JANSENISTS WITH THE FOLLOWING WORKS OF ANTOINE ARNAULD, DOCTOR OF THE SORBONNE BY OUR HOLY FATHER THE POPE. THE SIXTH DAY OF SEPTEMBER ONE THOUSAND SIX HUNDRED FIFTY-SEVEN.

The sixth day of September, one thousand six hundred fifty-seven.

In the general meeting of the holy and universal Roman Inquisition held in the Apostolic Palace of Saint Marie Majeur in the presence of Our Holy Father, Pope Alexander VII, and of the Most Eminent and Reverend Lords Cardinal of the Holy Roman Church, Inquisitors General through all Christian lands, and specially appointed by the Holy Apostolic See against Heresies,

Our Holy Father, Pope Alexander VII, by this present decree forbids and condemns the books hereinafter mentioned, and has resolved that they be considered condemned and forbidden under the penalties and the censures contained in the [decree of] the Holy Council of Trent, and in the index of forbidden books, with whatever other penalties it shall please his Holiness to exact.

List of Books Condemned

Eighteen letters written in the French language and having the following titles:

1. Letter written to a provincial by one of his friends on the subject of the present disputes at the Sorbonne, from Paris this 23 January, 1656, and beginning: Sir, We were very much mistaken . . . [thereupon follows the enumeration of the 18 letters].

Letter of a lawyer in Parliament to one of his friends regarding the inquisition. . . .

The following works of Antoine Arnauld, doctor of the Sorbonne Foundation. . . . [Thereupon follows the enumeration of Arnauld's works composed after the *Letter to a person of quality.*]

And because there have been *circulated certain writings printed in the year 1657 which bear the title "Tredecim Theologorum ad examinandas quinque propositiones ab Innocentio X. selectorum suffragia, seu, ut appellant, vota summo Pontifici scripto tradita,"* His Holiness by this present decree forbids them, and commands no belief be placed in them, any more than in apochryphal things, and declares that none may nor should cite them . . . [sentence incomplete].

36. FACTUM FOR THE PRIESTS OF PARIS AGAINST A BOOK ENTITLED APOLOGY FOR THE CASUISTS, AGAINST THE CALUMNIES OF THE JANSENISTS. PARIS, 1657. AND AGAINST THOSE WHO COMPOSED, PRINTED AND SOLD IT

[*January 25, 1658*]

Our cause is the cause of Christian morality. Our adversaries are the Casuists who corrupt it. The interest we have in it is that of the consciences that have been entrusted to us. The reason why we raise our voice with more vigor than ever before against this new libel is that in this case the ever growing boldness of the Casuists has soared to its ultimate excess. We are forced to resort to final remedies, and to carry our complaints before every tribunal which we deem it our duty to reach, so that without respite we may seek the condemnation and the censure of these pernicious ideas.

To make known to everyone the justice of the end we seek, we need merely set forth clearly the state of affairs and the manner in which the new Casuists have conducted themselves from the beginning of their undertakings to this last book which crowns them all. Having seen how pernicious to the Church has been the patience with which these have been tolerated, people will understand the necessity of having no more of them today. But, first of all, it is important to make clear of what the venom of their evil doctrines primarily consists, for too little attention has been given to this point.

What is most pernicious about these new moral codes is that they lead not merely to the corruption of moral standards, but also to the corruption of basic *mores*. And this is a matter of far greater importance. For it is a much less dangerous and less general evil to introduce irregularities, while leaving untouched the Laws which forbid them, than it is to pervert the Laws and to justify irregularities; for since man's nature always leans toward evil from the very time of his birth, and since it is ordinarily held in restraint only by fear of the law, his evil desire spreads unchecked as soon as this barrier is broken down. Consequently there is no difference between making vices permissible and making all men vicious.

For this reason the Church has always taken particular care to keep its rules of conduct inviolate in the very midst of the licentiousness of those whom it could not prevent from violating them. And so when people saw bad Christians, at the same time they saw holy laws which condemned them and recalled them to their duty; and, before these new Casuists, it had never happened that anyone in the Church undertook to overthrow the purity of her rules publicly.

This outrage was reserved for these latter days which the clergy of France calls the *dregs and the end of the centuries*. In them *instead of adjusting the life of men to the precepts of Jesus Christ*, these new theologians *have undertaken to adjust the precepts and rules of Jesus Christ to the interests, passions, and pleasures of men*. By this horrible reversal we have seen those who pass themselves off as doctors and theologians, substitute for true morality, which should have divine authority alone as its principle, and charity alone as its end and aim, a totally human morality, whose principle is reason alone, and whose aim is merely carnal desire and natural passions. This is what they declare with incredible boldness, as will be seen in these few maxims which are most current among them. *An act*, they say, *is probable and indisputably in accord with conscience if it is based upon a reasonable reason*, RATIONE RATIONABILI, *or on the authority of some serious authors, or even on that of a single one, or if it has an honest object as its aim.* What they call an honest object will be seen by the following examples which they give. *It is permissible, they say, to kill someone who has done us some wrong, provided that, in so doing, we have no desire to win the esteem of men,* AD CAPTANDAM HOMINUM AESTIMATIONEM. *One may go to the place assigned for a duel if his aim is that he shall not be regarded as chickenhearted but as a man of courage,* VIR ET NON GALLINA. *He may give money for a benefice, provided that his sole intent is the temporal advantage to be derived from it, and not to put a temporal matter on a spiritual level. A woman may adorn herself, no matter what evil results therefrom, provided that she does so solely through her natural inclination toward vanity,* OB NATURALEM FASTUS INCLINATIONEM. *One may eat and drink to one's heart's content without any necessity, provided that it is done purely out of voluptuousness and without endangering one's health, because natural appetite may without sin enjoy acts which are appropriate to it,* LICITE POTEST APPETITUS NATURALIS SUIS ACTIBUS FRUI.

These few words reveal the spirit of these Casuists. By destroying the rules of piety, they substitute for the precepts of Scripture, which requires us to refer all our acts to God, a frank and unrestrained permission to refer them all to ourselves. That is to say, that, instead of Jesus Christ having come to deaden in us the carnal desires of the old man and to make charity reign over the new man, these persons have come to give new birth to lust and to put an end to the love of God from which they absolve men, declaring that it is sufficient not to hate Him.

Such is the utterly carnal morality which they have brought forward. It is supported *on the arm of flesh,* as the Scripture puts it. And the only basis they offer for it is that Sanchez, Molina, Escobar, Azor, etc., consider it reasonable, whence they conclude *that it can be followed with a clear conscience and without any risk of damnation.*

It is an astonishing thing that the temerity of man should have reached such a point. But that has come about imperceptibly and by degrees in this way: These accommodating opinions did not begin with such excesses. They came into being less crudely, and were first advanced merely as doubts. They were gradually fortified by the large number of sectarians whose loose maxims are always with us. And so, when a rather large group of Casuists had developed in support of them, the ministers of the Church, who feared to offend so large a number and who hoped that gentleness and reason might succeed in reclaiming those gone astray, tolerated this confusion with a patience which subsequently proved to be not merely ineffectual but even harmful. For, seeing themselves at liberty to write, they wrote so much in so short a time that the Church today groans under the monstrous weight of volumes. The licentiousness of their opinions, which has grown as their books multiplied, has swept them along rapidly in the corruption of opinions and in the boldness with which these are set forth. Thus the maxims which they tossed off at first as casual thoughts were very soon set down as probable. They then proceeded to present them as definite matters of conscience, and finally they were asserted to be as definite as contrary opinions. And all this progressed so boldly that the powers of the Church finally began to be stirred up, and pronounced various censures of these doctrines. The General Assembly of France censured them in 1642 in the book of Father Bauny, a Jesuit, in which almost all of them are collected, for those books merely copy from each other. The Sorbonne, too, condemned them, and then the faculty of Louvain. The late Archbishop of Paris likewise condemned them in several censures. There was, therefore, some reason to hope that so many authorities in collaboration would check an evil that was constantly growing. But things were far from coming to a halt. Father Hereau at the College of Clermont gave very strange lectures on the permissibility of homicide. Fathers Flahaut and le Court at Caën, too, spoke so terribly in favor of authorizing duels that this forced the University of Paris to bring them to trial before Parliament and enter upon the long proceedings that are known to everyone. The ardor of the Casuists was cooled somewhat when on these charges Father Hereau was sentenced by the council to imprisonment in the College of the Jesuits and forbidden to teach thereafter. However, they were merely preparing new materials, all to be produced at the same time on a more favorable occasion.

In fact, shortly afterward, Escobar, Father Lamy, Mascaregnas, Caramuel, and several others appeared, so filled with ideas that had already been condemned and with many new ones even more horrible that we, who through our insight into consciences were able to see the evil caused by such irregularities, felt obliged to oppose them vigorously. That is why in recent years we appealed to the Assembly of the Clergy, which was sitting then, to request it to condemn the principal propositions of the aforementioned authors of whose works we had presented an extract.

It was then that the ardor of those who wished to defend them became manifest. They brought to bear the most powerful appeals and all sorts of means to prevent censure or at least to have it deferred, for they hoped that if it were postponed until the end of the Assembly there would no longer be time enough to go into the matter. In part they were successful. Despite all their scheming and all the matters the Assembly had on its hands toward the last, and though on our side we had but truth alone which counts for so little today, nevertheless, by the providence of God, all that did not prevent the Assembly from resolving not to adjourn without some marked indication of its indignation at such laxity and of its desire to have solemnly condemned it, if time had permitted.

To make that known to everyone, they drew up a circular letter to all our lord prelates of the kingdom and sent to them with this letter the book by S. Charles Borromeo which had been printed last year at their command. And to combat these evil maxims they here began with the doctrine of probability which is the basis for all of them. These are their words: *For a long time we have grieved with reason to see our dioceses in this respect not merely in the same state as the Province of S. Charles but in a much more deplorable state. For, even if our confessors are more enlightened than his, there is great danger that they may become imbued with certain modern ideas which have so altered Christian morality and the teachings of the Gospel that profound ignorance would be much more desirable than such knowledge which teaches the belief that all things are problematical; moreover, it teaches that we should seek means, not to destroy the evil habits of mankind, but to justify them and to provide men with scheming ways of gratifying such habits that will appease their conscience.*

Then they [the Casuists] proceed to the compromises which they have based on this doctrine of probabilism. *They do not say that J[esus] C[hrist] gave us his precepts and left us his example in order that those who believe in Him might obey them and adapt their lives to them. Instead, they say that the purpose of these authors seems to be to accommodate the precepts and rules of J[esus] C[hrist] to the interests, pleasures and passions of men; so ingenious do they show themselves in flattering their covetousness and their ambition by the opportunities they give them to avenge themselves on their enemies, to lend money usuriously, to become ecclesiastical dignitaries in all sorts of ways, and to maintain the false honor which the world has established by very bloody means.* After ridiculing the Casuists' method of careful direction of intention, they strongly condemn the abuse which the former make of the Sacraments.

Finally, to demonstrate to the whole Church that what they [the Casuists] did was little in comparison with what they would have liked to do if they had had the power, they conclude as follows: *By their complaints to us about these dissensions, with the permission of their high prelates and by their entreaties that we find some remedy for them, several priests of the city of Paris and of other important cities of this kingdom have heightened our zeal and have greatly increased our sorrow. If they had addressed our Assembly — which they did not — we should have scrutinized most carefully all the new propositions of the Casuists from which they gave us extracts, and we should have pronounced a solemn judgment which would have checked the course of this plague of consciences. But, not having had leisure to undertake this scrutiny with all the diligence and meticulousness which the importance of the subject required, we felt that for the time being we could offer no better remedy for such deplorable license than to have the instructions that were drawn up by S. Charles Borromeo printed at the expense of the clergy. This was for the purpose of instructing these Confessors in the way they should administer the Sacrament of penitence, and to send them all to the lord bishops of the kingdom.*

The attitude of our lord bishops was thus made clear and all the more evident because we cannot doubt that it was the power of truth alone which impelled them to speak in this manner. It now seemed to us that henceforth the authors of these innovations would be more discreet; that, having seen all the priests of the chief cities of France and their lord prelates unite in condemning their doctrine, they would thereafter keep quiet, and would consider themselves very fortunate to have escaped censure which was well deserved and which was as extraordinary as the excesses against the Church of which they had been guilty.

That was the state of affairs, and our only concern was the quiet instruction of our people in pious Christian doctrines without fear of being annoyed in so doing, when this new book appeared with which we are dealing today. As the Apology of all Casuists, it alone contains as much as all the others combined; it renews all the propositions which had been condemned, and it does this with a scandalous boldness which is all the more worthy of censure because they have presumed to bring forth this book in the wake of so many censures that they scorn. It deserves punishment all the more because one must recognize the futility of the remedies hitherto tried and the necessity of resorting to more vigorous remedies in order to halt so dangerous and rebellious an evil once and for all.

We come now to our special reasons for seeking the condemnation of this libel. There are several very important ones. The first of these is the utterly blatant effrontery with which the most abominable ideas of the Casuists are affirmed in this book. For they no longer make any attempt at disguise. They no longer take a defensive attitude as they formerly did in saying that these are propositions which are ascribed to them. They proceed more openly here. They acknowledge these propositions and at the same time they defend them as being definitely in accord with their conscience; *and just as surely so,* they say, *as contrary opinions. It is true,* says this book in a hundred places, *that the Casuists hold these doctrines, but it is also true that they are right in holding them.* At times the book even goes beyond the reproaches which have been directed at them. *Indeed,* it says, *we uphold this proposition which has been condemned so sharply, and the Casuists go even further.* Thus it no longer is a statement of fact. The book is in complete accord; it admits that according to the Casuists *there is no longer any such thing as usury* in the most usurious contracts, as set forth on pages 101, 107, 108, etc. Holders of Benefices are exonerated of *simony,* regardless of their traffickings if their intent is properly directed, page 62. Blasphemies, perjury, indecencies, *in short, all the crimes against the Decalogue are no longer sins if they are committed through ignorance or in anger or passion, pages 26, 28. Valets may rob their masters in order that their wages may be commensurate with their labors, according to Father Bauny who confirms this on page 81. Wives may take money from their husbands for gambling, page 152. Judges need not make restitution of what they have accepted for doing an injustice, page 123. People are not obliged to give up opportunities and to abandon professions in which they run risk of perdition, if it is not easy to do so. One may be granted absolution and worthily receive the Eucharist with no regret for his sins other than for the temporal loss he suffers from them, pages 162 and 163. Without committing a crime, we may slander those who say evil of us by charging them with crimes of which we know they are innocent, pages 127, 128, 129.*

In a word, anything will be permissible; the law of God will be annihilated, and our natural reason alone will become our light in all our acts, even to discern when individuals may be permitted to slay their neighbor, which is the most pernicious thing in the world and which has the most terrible consequences. *Let them show me,* says he, page 87, etc., *that we should not be guided by the natural light of reason to discern when it is permissible and when it is forbidden to kill one's neighbor.* And to confirm this statement: *Since monarchs have made use of natural reason alone to punish malefactors, the same natural reason should serve to judge whether a private individual may kill someone who attacks not merely his life but also his honor and his property.* And in reponse to the objection that the law of God forbids this, he says in the name of all Casuists: *We believe we are right in exempting from this commandment of God those who kill to protect their honor, their reputation and their property.*

If we consider the consequences of this teaching, namely *that it is natural reason which should discern when it is permissible or forbidden to kill one's neighbor,* and if we add to this the execrable teachings of very serious doctors who by their natural reason have decided that under certain circumstances it is permissible to commit strange acts of parricide against persons who should be most inviolable, then we shall see that if, after all this, we kept silent, we should be unworthy of our ministry; we should be the enemies and not the shepherds of our people, and God would rightly punish us for so criminal a silence. Therefore, we are but doing our duty in warning people and judges against such abominations. And we hope that people and judges will do their duty, the former by avoiding them, and the latter by punishing them in keeping with the seriousness of the matter.

But we are impelled all the more to take this action because those ideas cannot be considered as coming from a book which is anonymous and lacks authority. On the contrary, they come from a book which is supported and authorized by a body of considerable importance. It grieves us to say this. For, although we have never been in ignorance as to the primary advocates of these licentious ideas, nevertheless we were unwilling to expose them, and even now we should not have done so if they had not exposed themselves, and if they had not chosen to make themselves known to everyone. But since they want it known, it would be futile for us to hide it. Since it is among themselves that they have caused this libel to be disseminated, since this scandalous traffic has been carried on in the College of Clermont, since those who took their money there carried away as many Apologies for the Casuists as they wanted, since these Fathers took them to their friends in Paris and in the Provinces, since Father Brisacier, Rector of the House of Rouen, distributed them, since he had them right in the refectory as objects of edification and piety, since he asked permission of one of the principal magistrates for reprinting them, since the Jesuits of Paris have begged two doctors of the Sorbonne to give them their approval, since they asked the Lord Chancellor for a privilege, since, in a word, they have taken off their mask and are desirous of making themselves known in so many ways, it is time that we act, and since the Jesuits now publicly declare themselves the protectors of the *Apology for the Casuists*, it is time for the priests to come out as their denunciators. Everyone ought to know that, just as those pernicious doctrines are disseminated in the College of Clermont, so Christian doctrines in opposition to them are taught in our parishes. This shall be done so that, on hearing these errors proclaimed so loudly by so numerous a company and on seeing no one arise to oppose them, everyday people shall not take them for truths, and gradually be deceived by them. May the judgment of God be brought to bear on people and on their pastors according to the doctrine of the prophets who, in speaking against these new opinions, declare that both those who have not received the necessary instruction and those who have not given it shall perish.

Thus we are under an indispensable obligation to speak in this case. What heightens that obligation still more is the harmful way in which the authors of that *Apology* are undermining our ministry. For that book is, properly speaking, nothing more than a defamatory libel of the priests of Paris and of the provinces who have opposed their licentiousness. It is a strange thing to see how they speak in their book about the extracts from their most dangerous statements which we presented to the clergy, and how in this connection they have the audacity to call us *ignorant, seditious, heretical, wolves and false shepherds*, pages 2 and 176. *The company of the Jesuits*, they say (page 176), *is very sorry to see that the accusations against it are drawn up by ignorant persons who are not worthy to be counted among the dogs who watch over the flock of the Church, whom some take for true shepherds, and who are followed by the sheep who allow themselves to be led by those wolves.*

That is the height of insolence to which the Jesuits have raised the Casuists. After having taken advantage of the moderation of the ministers of the Church to introduce their ungodly doctrines, they have today arrived at the point of trying to drive from the ministry of the Church those who refuse to consent to such doctrines.

This seditious and schismatic undertaking, by which they are trying to sever the people from their legitimate pastors through inciting them to flee from the latter as from false shepherds and from wolves for the sole reason of their opposition to an utterly impure moral standard, is of such great importance within the Church that we should no longer be able to serve her if that insolence were not repressed. For in the end we should have to renounce our duties and abandon our Churches if, amidst all the Christian tribunals established to keep the rules of the Gospels alive we were not permitted, without being defamed as wolves and false shepherds, to say to those whom we are under obligation to instruct: That it is always a crime to slander one's neighbor; that it is more in keeping with one's conscience to offer the other cheek after having received a blow than to kill the man who flees after having delivered the blow; that duelling is always a crime and that it is a horrible falsehood to say *that it is for natural reason to discern when it is permissible or forbidden to kill one's neighbor*. If we are not at liberty to speak our minds without seeing books published at once and publicly upheld by the body of Jesuits who call us seditious, ignorant persons and false shepherds, then it is impossible for us to govern faithfully the flocks which are committed to us.

There is no place among infidels and savages in which it is not permissible to say that slander is a crime, and that one may not kill his neighbor merely to defend his honor. Only where the Jesuits are, one does not dare to say so. We must either permit slander, homicide, and profanation of the Sacraments or expose ourselves to the consequences of their vengeance. Yet God has ordered us to carry His commandments to His people; nevertheless we shall not dare to obey Him without feeling the fury of those Casuists of flesh and blood. To what condition, then, are we reduced today? Woe unto us, says the Scripture, if we preach not the Gospel. And woe unto us, say these men, if we preach the Gospel. On the one hand we are threatened by the wrath of God, and on the other hand the audacity of these men requires us either actually to become false shepherds and wolves, or to be torn to pieces by thirty thousand mouths which decry us.

Such is the subject of our complaint. This is what compels us to demand justice for ourselves and for Christian morality, our common cause. This is what makes us redouble our zeal to defend it as others increase their efforts to crush it. The more powerfully it is opposed, and the more we find ourselves alone in defending it, the dearer this cause becomes to us. In our joy that God deigns to use our feeble efforts to contribute to that end, we venture to say to Him with the Psalmist who was according to His heart: *It is time for Thee, Lord, to work: for they have made void Thy law. Therefore I esteem all Thy precepts concerning all things to be right, and I hate every false way.*

Nevertheless, it is a deplorable thing to see ourselves abandoned and treated so outrageously by those to whom we should rather look for help. And so we have to combat the passions of men which are not merely accompanied by all their natural impetuosity but which are swollen and supported by the approbation of so large a body of ecclesiastics. And so, instead of our being able to make use of their teachings to correct the errors of the people, we are compelled to make use of what remains of pious sentiments in the people in order to make them abhor the errings of these Fathers.

This is the situation in which we find ourselves today. But we hope that God will move the hearts of those who can render us justice so that they may aid in our defense, and that they may be all the more inclined to do so since they themselves are being made a party to such corruption. The Pope, the bishops, and Parliament are thus included in this extravagant claim which the authors of this libel advance on various pages as an established fact: *The Bulls of the Popes against the five propositions constitute general approbation of the doctrine of the Casuists.* Nothing could be more harmful to these Bulls; it is all the more impertinent in itself because there is no connection between these matters and the other. All that there is in common between these five propositions and those of the Casuists is that they are all heretical. For just as there are heresies in the faith, so, according to the Fathers and the councils, there are also heresies in morals, and these are all the more dangerous because they conform to natural passions and to the unhappy foundation of lust from which the most holy are not free. We believe, therefore, that those who have manifested so much zeal against the condemned propositions will have no less zeal in this encounter. For the welfare of the Church, which perforce was their only aim, is all the more at stake, whereas the heresy of the five propositions is understood by none but the theologians, and no one dares to support those propositions; on the contrary, the heresies of the Casuists are understood by everyone, and the Jesuits support them publicly.

37. [SUGGESTED PRONOUNCEMENT AGAINST THE APOLOGY FOR THE CASUISTS]

[1658]

Since the love we have for our peoples demands constant vigilance on our part, in order that we may anticipate everything which may harm them, we have felt obliged to redouble our vigilance when the pernicious book entitled *Apology for the Casuists* began to be circulated in this diocese. That is why in response to the request for censure of it which our priests immediately presented to us and because of the assurance that the importance of the matter warrants it, we have resolved to grant them so reasonable a request. At the same time we have resolved to labor in order to fortify the faithful not merely against the slackening which might be induced in them by these flattering opinions, but also against a far more serious temptation, one which would lead to the complete overthrowing of the faith, if we were not upheld and confirmed by the full knowledge of its principles. For there is no doubt that from these abuses the impious are drawing certain conclusions against the verity of our religion which are capable of shaking [the faith of] the feeble. For these conclusions are then represented as signs that God does not regulate the conduct of the Church, since after she had been assured of eternal possession of the truth, we see her abandoned to errors and to fearful aberrations.

This is the worst of the evils which these impieties produce. For all the enemies of the faith they serve as weapons with which to combat us, and they are equally useful to the Devil to corrupt the faithful and to fortify the unfaithful. But since people fall into these errors only through lack of understanding of the Scriptures, we feel obliged to explain them so clearly to those whom we owe Evangelical instructions, that devout persons will henceforth be out of danger and the impious will be without excuse in the conclusions which they draw from the aberrations of the Casuists. For these abuses which creep into the Church are so far from rendering the truth of Jesus Christ's promises suspect that nothing could better prove their truth; and, on the contrary, His promises would be false if these very abuses did not occur.

If, on promising the Church that his truth and his spirit would dwell in her eternally, J[esus] C[hrist] had at the same time assured her calm and tranquil continuation of truth and of peace, we should have cause for surprise on seeing lies and error make their appearance with such insolence. But what reason is there for surprise at this after He declared that some would make trouble [in the Church], though under the pretense of piety, and that they would come in His name in order to turn men from the true course; as a result, these disorders, which would always increase, would finally be so great at the end of centuries that the elect themselves would be seduced, if it were possible to seduce them. It was beyond doubt that these scandals were bound to come although they would bring destruction to those who caused them and to those who went astray. For God tolerates them, not that we may follow these disorders but that we may combat them, and so that in this test it may become evident who are truly faithful to Him.

And that is why, since it is important to avoid them, Saint Paul, who made the same prediction, at the same time gives us the description of these seducers, so that we may recognize them better. He said to Timothy: *That in the last days would come men having the appearance of piety, but who would reject its essence, who would be full of ambition and self-love, proud, false accusers, without the love of God, who would creep into the houses of individuals, and who would bring into subjection simple-minded women by flattering them in their sins and in the desires of their hearts, who would ceaselessly strive to become learned, and never arrive at the knowledge of the truth.* And he completed this picture by saying *that they shall not succeed in their design, and that in the end their feebleness and their impertinence shall be manifest unto all men.*

Who would not say that Saint Paul saw what is happening before our eyes today, where under the guise of piety men are presenting to the faithful a moral code that banishes the love of God, which is the essence of piety; men who are authorizing calumny, pride, and ambition by their precepts and by their example, men who are studying without ceasing and who cannot come to the first knowledge of Christianity, men who finally have fallen into excesses which have made them the laughing stock of all men.

Therefore we cannot doubt that all these things have come about through the command of the same Providence that foretold them and that permits them in order to test those who are truly faithful. But we learn from these same prophecies that these disorders must proceed much further.

Indeed, today we see a very powerful company which upholds these corruptions, but at the same time we see a very different, notable and authorized company which opposes them. And if we have reason to grieve at seeing some loose priests and some corrupt Casuists who introduce this laxity, we have reason to bless God because the parish priests of the Church resist them. And thus the body of the hierarchy, of which the Church properly consists, remains exempt from this laxity, in which only a few erring persons participate who are outside of the hierarchy and who have among us the rank which the false prophets held among the Jews; they are steeped in these impieties. In all this there is nothing which is not in conformity with what Saint Peter foretold as follows: *But just as there were false prophets among the Jews, even so shall false ones arise among you.*

That is the present state of things. Although this license is great, nevertheless it is not without powerful opposition. But a time must come of which it is written: *Woe unto them that are with child in those days; do you believe that then the Son of man shall find faith on the earth?* And it is in these days, when the priests themselves and the rest of the faithful have almost all consented to the impieties of false doctors, and when the measure has thus been filled, that the end of the Church and of the universe must come with the second coming of the Messiah. And this will happen even as the destruction of the former temple and of the synagogue came about in similar corruption when at the first coming of the Messiah the false prophets had drawn into their party the people and even the priests.

For, according to Saint Paul, just as all things happened to them as a type, and just as the synagogue was the image of the Church, so from what happened to it we may learn what must happen to us, and in their example we may see the source, the progress and the consummation of impiety. Thus Scripture teaches us that impiety had its origin in false prophets and that from them it spread to the rest of men, as Jeremiah says: *Abomination was born of the prophets, and from them it has gone forth into all the land.* It teaches us that they have formed an open conspiracy against the truth in the midst of the people of God, [*conjuratio prophetarum*] *in medio ejus;* that the great of the world were the first abettors of their flattering doctrines; that subsequently the people were infected by them. But so long as the priests of the Lord remained free therefrom, God withheld the effects of His wrath. But when the priests themselves plunged in, and when nothing remained to stop His divine anger, the scourges of God fell upon the people beyond all measure, and they have remained there until this day. *The prophets*, said Jeremiah, *have announced false doctrines as coming from God; the priests have lent themselves to these, and my people have taken pleasure in them; what punishment is then prepared for them?* Then there is no more mercy to expect, for there is no one left to ask it. *The priests*, said Ezekiel, *have themselves violated my law; the princes and the peoples have used oppression, and the prophets flattered them in their disorder. I sought for a man among them who would oppose his justice to my vengeance, and I found none. Therefore I shall pour out upon them the fire of my indignation, and I shall cause the fruit of their impieties to fall back upon their heads.*

That is the final misfortune which by the grace of God has not yet been visited upon the Church and into which she will not fall so long as it will please God to uphold His Shepherds against the corruption of the false doctors who combat them. And this is what must be made intelligible to those who are in our charge so that they may not cease to ask of God the continuation of a zeal which is so important and so necessary, and that they may themselves avoid the lax and flattering doctrines of those seducers who are laboring merely to destroy them. For just as the piety of the saints of the Old Testament consisted in opposing the innovations of the false Prophets who were the Casuists of their times, so the piety of the faithful must now aim to resist the laxity of the Casuists who are the false prophets of today. And we must not cease to make clear to our peoples what the true prophets incessantly cried to their peoples, namely, that the authority of these doctors will not make them pardonable before God if they follow their false doctrines; that the whole society of Casuists could not assure conscience contrary to eternal truth; that this abominable doctrine of probability which is the foundation of all their errors is the greatest of their errors; that only the truth and prayer can save them; and that it is a horrible falsehood to say that one can be saved as well by one of these two contrary opinions as by the other, of which one consequently is false. This is what they all maintain, and without it their whole doctrine falls. For they have no other foundation for these horrible maxims which they are renewing again in this new book. In it they say *that we can discern, by the sole light of reason when it is permitted or forbidden to kill our neighbor; that we may kill him in order to defend or repair our honor; that without committing a crime we may slander those who speak ill of us; that all our sins will be forgiven, provided we confess them even without desisting from them in the future, without doing penance in this life, and without any regret for having sinned excepting for the temporal evil which results from them, and with even that regret so feeble that the sinner and the penitent judge that he is ready to repeat it shortly.* When they are asked on what they base these horrible maxims, they have no reply other than, that since their Fathers and their doctors have judged them to be probable, they are definitely in accord with conscience and as certain as contrary opinions. In view of this we are announcing to all those over whom God has given us authority that these are diabolical falsehoods, and that all those who shall follow these maxims on the assurance of these false doctors shall perish with them. Similarly the Prophets of God in the past announced to their peoples who were thus relying on their false prophets, *that God shall exterminate them altogether, the masters, and the disciples, magistros et discipulos; and that those who thus lull men's consciences into a feeling of security, and those whose consciences are thus dulled shall together be hurled into the same destruction. Et qui beatificant, et qui beatificantur.* And thus probability of opinions and this authority of the doctors who teach them are so far from excusing their followers in the eyes of God that on the contrary this confidence is the object of God's greatest anger at them. For in reality it proceeds merely from a corrupted desire to seek repose in one's vices, and not from a pure and sincere search for the truth of God which would make it easy to discern the falsity of these opinions which horrify all those who have true opinions of God. And that is why this complacency about crimes swells them so that God has declared through prophets to the synagogue and by it to the Church that all the prayers of the most just would not save from His fury those who had thus followed the teachers of false doctrines. That is what we see in Jeremiah when he asked God's mercy for the Jews and when he pointed out that they had persisted in their crimes because of their faith in these false prophets. *Lord,* said he, *they have done this because their prophets assured them Thou wouldst approve of their conduct, and that far from punishing them Thou wouldst fill them with happiness and peace.* That is to say, they had followed the authority of several great doctors who were regarded as prophets. Nevertheless, how does God answer this holy man? *The prophets have spoken according to their own understanding and not according to mine,* said the Lord; *these are not my words but their own words that they have spoken, and that is why I shall destroy these doctors, but I shall likewise exterminate those who have heard and followed them. Therefore do not pray for these people. For even if Moses and Samuel appeared before me to stay my fury, I should not grant them mercy. And if they ask you: What then shall we do? say unto them: that those who are destined to die shall go to their death, and that those who are reserved for famine and murder shall hasten to the end to which they are destined.*

If God thus treated the Jewish people in the shadows and in the darkness where they dwelt; if He did not pardon their crimes even though they engaged in them on the authority of so many doctors who were of grave and eminent appearance; if He did not spare men of the earliest times, as Saint Peter said, how will He treat a people upon whom He has lavished such lights and so many marks of His love, if they have enough blindness and ingratitude to dispense with loving Him because of the faith of which they are assured by some modern Casuists?

We therefore declare solemnly that those who fall into these errors shall be absolutely unpardonable for accepting falsehood from these foreign hands that offer it to them at the expense of the truth which is presented to them by the paternal hands of their own shepherds; they shall be doubly guilty in these impieties and for having accepted these opinions which they should never admit, and for having accepted those to which they should not have listened.

For since these persons, who are outside of the hierarchy, have no power to exercise any function excepting under our orders and according to our laws, everything they say contrary to our pronouncement must be regarded as suspect and unacceptable, and thus the faithful must remain free from it and must ask of God the perseverance of the natural shepherds of His Church, so that this unfortunate slothfulness and this general consent to error which must call forth the last judgment of God may not arrive in our day as it arrived at the end of the synagogue when the prophets became lax. *The princes are in corruption, the priests accompany these, the prophets confirm them therein, and in this state they all still repose together on the Lord, saying: God is in the midst of us; no evil shall befall us. It is for this reason, said the Lord, that Jerusalem shall be totally destroyed and that the Temple of God shall be overthrown and annihilated.*

38. THE MIND OF THE GEOMETRICIAN

[*1658 or 1659*](?)

First Fragment

We may have three fundamental aims in the study of truth: first, to discover it as we search for it; secondly, to demonstrate it when we have it; lastly, to distinguish it from falsehood when we examine it.

I am not speaking of the first. I am dealing particularly with the second, and it includes the third. For, if we know the method for proving truth we shall at the same time have the method for discerning it, since, by examining whether the proof which we give for it conforms to known rules, we shall know whether it is demonstrated exactly.

Geometry, which excels in these three categories, has expounded the art of discovering unknown truths; it calls this *analysis*. It would be useless to discuss it after the many excellent works on the subject.

The art of demonstrating those truths that have already been discovered, and of clarifying them in such a manner that their proof is incontrovertible, is the only one with which I wish to deal. To that end I need merely explain the method which geometry follows, for geometry teaches it perfectly.

First, however, it is necessary for me to give an idea of a method which is even higher and more effective, but one which man can never achieve, for whatever transcends geometry transcends us. Nevertheless, it is necessary to say a word about it, even if it is impossible to make use of it.

This authentic method, which would achieve demonstrations of the highest excellence, if that could be attained, would consist of two fundamental things. One would be to use no term whose meaning had not previously been clearly explained. The other would be never to state any proposition that was not demonstrated by truths already known, that is to say briefly, to define all terms and to prove all propositions. But, to follow the very procedure which I am explaining, I must state what I mean by *definition*.

In geometry we recognize only those definitions which logicians call *definitions of name*, that is to say, giving a name only to those things which have been clearly designated in perfectly known terms. I am speaking only of those and of no others. They are useful and valuable in clarifying and condensing presentation by expressing in a single given word what otherwise would require several terms. However, this presupposes that, if it have other meanings, the name given shall be used in no other sense, so that it may retain only the one attribute assigned to it. Here is an example. In dealing with numbers, if we find it necessary to distinguish between those which are divisible by two without a remainder and those which are not, we give them a suitable name in order to avoid frequent restatement of this characteristic; we call every number which is divisible by two without a remainder an even number. That is a geometrical definition because, after having clearly designated a thing — for example, every number divisible by two without a remainder — we give this thing a name from which we exclude any other meaning it may have, in order to apply to it only the meaning of the thing indicated.

From this it will appear that definitions are very arbitrary and that they are never subject to contradiction, for nothing is more permissible than to give any name we may wish to a thing which we have clearly designated. We need merely be careful not to abuse the liberty we have of giving names by giving the same one to two different things. Not that this is not permitted, provided that it does not result in confusion, and that we do not extend their use from one thing to another. But if we fall into that vicious habit, there is one sure and infallible cure for it: mental substitution of the definition for the thing to be defined, and always having the definition so clearly in mind that when, for example, we are speaking of an even number we understand precisely that it is one which can be divided into two equal parts without a remainder, and that these two things are so joined together and so inseparable in one's thinking that as soon as a discourse refers to the one, the mind immediately associates the other with it. For geometricians and all those who proceed methodically give names to things only to shorten their presentation, and not to lessen nor change the meaning of the things which they are presenting. They maintain that the mind should always supply the full definition of the short terms which they are using merely to avoid the confusion that grows out of a multitude of words. Nothing more quickly and more vigorously dispels the captious artifices of the sophists than this method which must always be borne in mind and which alone suffices to banish all sorts of difficulties and equivocations.

With these things clearly understood, I now return to the explanation of correct procedure, which, as I have said, consists in defining everything and proving everything. Certainly this method would be splendid, but it is absolutely impossible. For it is evident that the very first terms we might try to define would presuppose other prior terms to aid in explaining them, and that similarly the very first propositions we might want to prove would presuppose others that precede them. And thus it is obvious that we could never arrive at the first ones. Moreover, as we carry our search farther and farther, we necessarily arrive at primitive words which permit of no further definition, and at principles which are so clear that no clearer ones can be discovered to aid in proving them. Hence it becomes evident that men are naturally and invariably incapable of dealing with any field of knowledge by an absolutely perfected procedure.

But it does not follow from this that we should abandon orderly procedure altogether. For there is one, that of geometry, which, to be sure, is inferior in that it is less convincing, but not because it is less certain. It does not define everything, and it does not prove everything, and in that respect it is inferior. But it posits only those things which are clear and constant to natural insight, and that is why it is perfectly true, inasmuch as nature supports it when other explanation fails.

This orderly procedure, the most perfect known to men, consists not in defining everything and demonstrating everything, nor in defining or demonstrating nothing, but rather in maintaining proper balance, by not defining those things that are clear and known to all men, and by defining all others; by not proving those things that are known to all men and by proving all others. This order is sinned against equally by those who undertake to define and prove everything and by those who neglect doing so in matters that are not self-evident.

This is what geometry teaches perfectly. It does not define any such things as *space, time, motion, number, equality*, nor very numerous similar things, because these terms designate the things which they denote so naturally to those who understand the language, that any explanation which we might want to make would bring more obscurity than clarification. For nothing is feebler than the explanation of those who try to define primitive words. For example, what need is there of explaining what we mean by the word *men?* Do we not know well enough what the thing is that we want to designate by that term? What advantage did Plato think it would be to us for him to say that man is a two-legged creature without feathers? As if the idea which I naturally have of man and which I cannot express were not clearer and more certain than the one he gives by his useless and even ridiculous explanation. After all, a man does not lose his human character by losing his two legs, nor does a capon become a man by losing his feathers.

There are some people who go to such absurd lengths as to explain a word by the same word. I know of some who have defined light as follows: *Light is a luminary motion of luminous bodies,* as if we could understand the words *luminary* and *luminous* without the word *light.* We cannot undertake to define being without involving ourselves in this absurdity, for we cannot define a word without beginning with the words *it is,* whether expressed or understood. Therefore, to define being we should have to say *it is,* and thus we should use the word to be defined in the definition.

From the above we see clearly enough that there are words which cannot be defined. If nature had not made up for this shortcoming by giving all men the same idea, all our expressions would be confused. As it is, we use them with the same assurance and the same certainty as if they were perfectly explained and free from ambiguity. For nature herself has given us, without words, a clearer comprehension of them than the art of definition provides for us through our explanations.

It is not because all men have the same idea of the essence of things that I say it is impossible and useless to define. For example, time comes under this category. Who can define it? And why undertake this, since all men comprehend without further designation what we mean when we speak of *time?* Nevertheless there are many different ideas about the essence of time. Some say that it is the motion of a created thing; others say it is measurement of the motion, etc. Therefore, I do not say that it is the nature of these things which is known to all; it is merely the relation between the name and the thing. Thus when we encounter the expression *time,* we all have the same object in mind, and that suffices to make definition of the term unnecessary, even though subsequently our feeling about it differs as we examine it and when we have begun to think about it. For definitions are made only to designate the things named, and not to set forth their nature.

This does not mean that it is not permissible to give the name *time* to the motion of a created thing. For, as I have just said, nothing has greater freedom than definitions. But, as a result of this definition, there are two things to which we may give the name *time*. One is that which everyone naturally understands by this word, and which all those who speak our language so designate. The other is the motion of a created thing, for people will also call it by that name in consequence of this new definition. It therefore becomes necessary to avoid ambiguities and not to confuse conclusions. For it does not follow from the above that the thing which we understand naturally by the word *time* is in fact the motion of a created body. We are free to give the same name to these two things, but we are not free to make them conform in essence as well as in name.

Hence, if we propose the explanation that *time is the motion of a created thing*, we must ask what is understood by this word *time;* that is to say, whether we give it its ordinary meaning, as accepted by everybody, or whether we strip it of that meaning in order to give it for the time being that of *motion of a created thing*. Now if we take every other meaning away from it, no contradiction is possible, and this will be a free definition as a result of which, as I have said, there will be two things which have the same name. But if we leave it its ordinary meaning and yet maintain that what is to be understood by that word is the motion of a created thing, we may be in contradiction. It is no longer a free definition; it is a proposition which must be proved unless it is perfectly self-evident. In that case, it is a principle or an axiom but never a definition, because by this statement we do not understand that the word *time* signifies the same as *the motion of a created thing*. What we understand by the term *time* is conceived as implied motion.

If I did not know how necessary it is to understand this perfectly and how often, both in ordinary speech as well as in scientific discourse, occasions arise like the one of which I have just given an example, I should not have dwelt upon it. But in view of the confusion arising from disputes in my experience, it seems to me that we cannot penetrate too deeply into this matter of clarity. And I am developing this whole treatise with that interest in mind rather than for the sake of the subject which I am treating.

How many people there are who think they have defined time when they say it is the measure of motion, even though they allow it to retain its ordinary meaning! Yet they have set forth a proposition and not a definition. How many there are likewise who think they have defined motion when they say: *Motus nec simpliciter actus nec mera potentia est, sed actus entis in potentia*. And yet, if they allow the word *motion* to retain its ordinary meaning, as they do, that is not a definition but a proposition. And when they thus confuse definitions that they call definitions of names, which are true, free, permissible and geometric definitions, with those that they call definitions of things, which properly speaking are by no means free but subject to contradiction, then they are taking the liberty of doing the one as well as the other. In defining the same things after his own fashion with a freedom which is forbidden as much in this kind of definition as it is permissible in the first kind, everyone is confusing everything and is losing sight of all order and of all clarity; he is losing himself and going astray in an inexplicable maze.

No one who follows the order of geometry will get into this difficulty. This discreet branch of knowledge carefully refrains from defining such primitive words as *space, time, motion, equality, majority, diminution, whole*, and all others which people understand as self-evident. But apart from these, the rest of the terms which geometry uses are so clarified and defined that no dictionary is needed for the understanding of a single one of them. And so, to put it briefly, these terms are perfectly intelligible either through natural insight or through the definitions which geometry gives of them. This is how geometry avoids all the errors that may be encountered on the first count, which consists in defining only those things that need definition. Geometry proceeds in the same way on the other count which consists in proving propositions which are not self-evident. For, when geometry has arrived at known primary truths, it stops there and asks that they be conceded, since it has nothing clearer by which to prove them. Thus everything which geometry proposes is demonstrated perfectly either through natural insight or by proofs.

It follows that if this science does not define and demonstrate everything it is for the sole reason that that is impossible for us. It may perhaps be considered strange that geometry cannot define any of the things with which it is principally concerned, for it can define neither motion, nor numbers, nor space. And yet these three things are the ones with which it deals particularly, and on the basis of their study it assumes the three different names of *mechanics, arithmetic*, and *geometry*, the last of which applies to form and space. But we should not be surprised if we observe that this admirable science, in dealing only with the simplest things, makes them incapable of definition because of this very quality of simplicity which makes them worthy of being the objects of that science. Thus the lack of definition is a mark of excellence rather than a defect, because it is not due to any obscurity of these things but rather to their extreme clarity which is such that, although it does not carry the conviction of demonstrations, nevertheless it does afford the same full certainty. It therefore supposes that we know what is understood by such words as *motion, number*, and *space;* and without spending time in useless definition, it discerns their nature and discovers their marvelous properties.

These three things, which, according to the words *Deus fecit omnia in pondere, in numero, et mensura,* include the whole universe, and have a reciprocal and necessary connection. For we cannot imagine motion without something which moves; and since this thing is one, this unity is the source of all numbers. Finally, since motion cannot exist without space, we see these three things included in the first. Even time is likewise included, for motion and time are relative to each other inasmuch as speed and slowness, which are differences of motion, have a necessary relation to time.

Thus there are properties common to all things, and the knowledge of them opens the mind to the greatest wonders of nature. The principal one includes the two infinities which are to be found in all things, infinite largeness and infinite smallness. For no matter how fast a motion may be, it is always possible to conceive one that is faster, and then to accelerate this one even more, and so on infinitely without ever attaining any motion so rapid that it cannot become more so. On the other hand, no matter how slow a motion may be, it can still be retarded, and this retarded motion can again be retarded, and so on infinitely without ever attaining such a degree of slowness that we cannot decrease the speed by an infinite number of gradations without reaching the point of rest. Likewise, no matter how large a number may be, we can always conceive a greater number, and then another to surpass this one, and so on infinitely without ever reaching one which cannot be increased. And conversely, no matter how small a number is, as for example, a hundredth or a ten-thousandth, we can still conceive of a smaller one, and so on infinitely, without arriving at zero or nothing. No matter how large a space is, we can imagine a larger one, and still a larger one than this, and so on infinitely, without ever arriving at one which could no longer be increased. And conversely, no matter how small a space may be, we can still think of a smaller one, and so on infinitely, without ever reaching one which is indivisible because it no longer has any extent.

The same applies to time. We can always conceive of a greater duration of time without final limit, and of a lesser duration without arriving at one moment and at an absolute cessation of duration. In short, this is the same as saying that no matter what motion, number, space, or time there may be, there is always one which is greater or less, so that they all are in progression between nothingness and infinity, always infinitely distant from these extremes.

All these truths cannot be proved, yet they are the foundation and the principles of geometry. However, since the quality which makes them incapable of proof is not their obscurity, but rather their extreme obviousness, that lack of proof is not a defect but rather a mark of excellence. From this we see that geometry cannot define objects nor prove principles, but the one and very weighty reason for it is that both possess an extreme inherent clarity which convinces reason more strongly than does argumentation. For what is more obvious than this truth that a number, no matter what it may be, can be increased? Can we not double it? Or that the speed of motion can be doubled, or that a space may likewise be doubled? And who furthermore can doubt that any number whatever can be halved, and the half halved again? For could that half amount to nothing? And if the two halves were two zeros, would they make a number? And similarly, cannot any motion, however slow it may be, be retarded to half that speed, so that it traverses the same space in twice the time, and so on with the resulting speed? Can it become absolute rest? And how could those two halves of a speed, each being absolute rest, add up to the original speed? Finally, no matter how small a space is, can it not be divided in two, and cannot these halves again be halved? And how could those two halves, if they were indivisible and without extent, equal the former extent when added together?

Man has no natural knowledge which takes precedence over the above, and which has greater clarity. Nevertheless, there should be examples of every kind. And so we find minds which are excellent at all other things, but which are shocked by these infinities and who find it impossible to agree to them at all. I have never known anyone who did not think that space can be increased. But I have seen some, who moreover were very able, who asserted that a given space could be divided into two indivisible parts, no matter to what absurdity that might lead. I endeavored to ascertain what in them could be the cause of this obscure way of thinking, and I found only one fundamental reason for it, namely, that they could not conceive of a continuous whole that is infinitely divisible. From this they concluded that it is not so divisible.

It is a natural weakness of man to believe that he possesses truth directly. For that reason he is always ready to deny anything which is incomprehensible to him. Yet, in fact, by nature he knows delusions only, and he ought to regard as genuine only the opposite of those things that seem to him to be false. That is why, whenever a proposition is inconceivable, we should suspend judgment and not deny it because of that; we should, however, examine the opposite. Then if we find this manifestly false, we boldly affirm the first proposition, however incomprehensible it may be. Let us apply this rule to our subject.

There is no geometrician who does not believe that space is infinitely divisible. One can no more be a geometrician without accepting that principle than be a man without a soul. Nevertheless there is no one who understands an infinite division. But people are convinced of this truth for but one reason — certainly a sufficient one. They understand perfectly that it is not true that by dividing a given space they can arrive at a part which is *indivisible;* that is to say, at a part which has no extent whatsoever.

What is more absurd than to claim, that by continually dividing a space, we shall finally arrive at a division such that, when we divide it in half, each of these halves will remain indivisible and without any extent whatever, and that thus two "nothings of extent" will together make an actual extent of space? For I should like to ask those who harbor this notion whether they can clearly conceive of two indivisibles which touch each other; and whether, if they touch everywhere they are not one and the same thing and consequently the two together are *indivisible;* if they do not touch everywhere, then they touch only in part. In that case they have parts, hence they are not *indivisible.* But if they confess, as in fact they do when pressed, that their proposition is as inconceivable as the other, let them acknowledge that it is *not* by our ability to conceive them that we should judge the truth of these things; for if these two opposites are both inconceivable, it is nevertheless necessarily certain that one of them is true.

However, let them compare these fancied difficulties, which *seem* great only in proportion to our weakness, with natural insight and on the basis of the following substantial truths. If it were true that space is composed of a certain finite number of *indivisibles*, then it would follow that in the case of two spaces, each of which is a square — that is to say equal and the same on all sides — and one of which is double the other, the one would contain twice as many of these *indivisibles* as the other. Let them bear this conclusion in mind carefully, and then let them try to arrange points in squares until they find two squares, one of which has double the points of the other. When they succeed in doing that, I shall declare them superior to all the geometricians in the world. But if that is impossible in the very nature of the thing, that is to say, if it is utterly impossible to arrange these points in squares so that one of them is double the other, as I would demonstrate right here if the matter were worth the time it took, then let them stand by their conclusion.

And, to relieve them in the troubles they will have with certain particulars, such as when they conceive of a given space as having an infinity of *divisibles* — since these can be traversed in so short a time, during which one would be supposed to have traversed that infinity of *divisibles* — we must warn them that they should not compare things as disproportionate as an infinity of *divisibles* is to the short time in which they can be traversed. We must advise them to compare space as a whole with time as a whole, and the infinite *divisibles* of space with the infinite instants of that time. And so they will find that one can traverse an infinity of *divisibles* in an infinity of instants, and a short space in a short time. In doing this, they will no longer encounter the disproportion which astounded them.

Finally, if they find it strange that a small space may have as many parts as a large one, let them realize also that the parts are small in proportion. Let them look at the firmament through a small glass in order to familiarize themselves with this knowledge by seeing each part of the heavens in each part of the glass. But if they cannot understand how parts which are so small as to be imperceptible to us can be divided as much as the firmament, then there is no better remedy than to have them look at them through glasses which magnify so delicate a point until it becomes a prodigious mass. In doing this, they will readily conceive that with the aid of another still more carefully ground glass, those points could be increased in size until they equaled the firmament whose extent they admired. And now that these objects seem to them to be very easily *divisible*, let them remember that nature is capable of doing infinitely more than art does. For, after all, who has proved to them that those glasses may not have changed the natural size of the objects, or conversely that they have re-established the true size which the form of our eye had changed and foreshortened as glasses do which diminish.

It is annoying to spend time on such trifles, but there are times for trifling. To clear thinking minds one need merely say on this subject that two "nothings of extent" cannot make an extent [geometrical magnitude]. But because there are some people who seek to avoid this insight by making the strange reply that two "nothings of extent" may just as well make an extent as two units, neither of which is a number, may be combined into a number, it becomes necessary to retort as follows: In like manner these people might well counter by saying that twenty thousand men make an army although none of them is an *army;* or that a thousand houses make a city although none is a *city;* or that the parts make a whole although none is the *whole;* or to confine the comparison to numbers, that two binaries form a quaternary, and ten tens make a hundred, although none be so. But by such illogical comparisons no clear intellect will confuse the immutable nature of things with their freely assigned names which depend upon the caprice of the men who have made them. For it is clear that to facilitate discussion the name *army* has been given to twenty thousand men, the name of *city* to many houses, and the word *ten* to ten units; and it is clear that from this freedom of designation arise the names *unity, binary, quaternary, a ten, a hundred,* all of them differing according to our fancy. And this has been done although these things are, in fact, of the same kind by virtue of their unalterable nature, and are all proportionate among themselves, and differ only in terms of more or less, and although in accordance with these designations a *binary* is not a *quaternary*, and a *house* is not a *city*, any more than a *city* is not a *house*. But though a house is not a city, it is nevertheless not a nothing [of a city]; there is a great difference between not being a thing and being nothing in [regard to it].

In order that we may understand the matter thoroughly, it is necessary to know the sole reason why unity is not listed as a number and why Euclid and the first writers on arithmetic excluded unity from the concept of number. They did this because they had various properties in mind that are to be found in all numbers save unity, and because they wished to avoid constant repetition of the fact that this applies to all numbers save unity. And they did this in accordance with the aforesaid existing liberty of making definitions at will. Moreover, if they had wished, they could similarly have excluded the binary and the ternary and anything else they desired, for everyone is his own master in such matters, provided he states what he is doing. And so, contrary to this usage, we include unity and fractions as well among numbers when we wish. In fact, we are forced to do so in general propositions in order to avoid saying each time: *in every number and in unity and in fractions such and such a property is to be found.* In everything that I have written I have taken it in this indefinite sense. Yet when Euclid himself — who deprived unity of the name of number, as he was entitled to do — wanted to make it understood that unity is not a nothing, but that on the contrary it is of the same class, he defined homogeneous magnitudes as follows: *Magnitudes,* said he, *are said to be of the same kind, when one can be made to exceed the other by being multiplied several times.* Consequently, since unity, by being multiplied several times, may exceed any number, it is of the same kind as numbers, because of its very essence and because of its immutable nature in the sense of Euclid himself who decreed that it should not be called a *number.*

An *indivisible* is different as regards extension. Not only does it differ in name, which is an arbitrary matter, but by its very definition it differs in kind. For no matter how many times an *indivisible* is multiplied, it is still far from exceeding any magnitude in space, since it can never become anything but a single and unique *indivisible* unit. This is natural and necessary, as has already been shown. And since this last proof is based on the definition of these two things, *indivisible* and *extent*, we shall complete and round out the demonstration.

An *indivisible* is that which has no parts, and an extent [geometrical magnitude] is that which has various separate parts. On the basis of these definitions, I say that two *indivisibles*, by being united, do not make an extent. For, when they are united, they touch in one part, and thus the parts where they touch are not separated, since otherwise they would not touch. Now, by their definition they have no other parts; hence they have no separated parts, and hence they have no extent by the definition of extent which bears on the separation of parts. On the same basis, we can show the same thing for all *indivisibles* which we may so join. Consequently an *indivisible*, no matter how often we multiply it, will never become an extent. Hence, by the definition of things of the same kind, it is not of the same kind as an extent.

This is how we demonstrate that *indivisibles* are not of the same kind as numbers. From this it follows that two units may indeed make a number, because they are of the same kind, and that two indivisibles do not form an extent, because they are not of the same kind. From this we see how little ground there is for comparing the relation between unity and numbers with that between *indivisibles* and extent.

But if we wish to make a comparison among numbers which will properly represent what we are considering with regard to extent, it must be the relation of zero to numbers. For zero is not of the same kind as numbers, because even if multiplied it cannot exceed them, so that it is a veritable *indivisible* as a number, just as the *indivisible* is a veritable zero in extent. And we will find a parallel between rest and motion, and between an instant of time; for all these things are heterogeneous as regards their magnitudes, because even when multiplied infinitely they can never be anything other than indivisibles, any more than these indivisibles of extent, and for the same reason. And then we shall find perfect correspondence between these things; for all these magnitudes are infinitely divisible without becoming *indivisibles* of themselves, so that they always remain in the middle between infinity and nothing.

That is the admirable relation which nature has established between these things and the two marvelous infinities which she has offered to men, not to be conceived but to be admired. To conclude this consideration with a final remark, I shall add that these two infinities, though infinitely different, are nevertheless related, so that knowledge of the one necessarily leads to knowledge of the other.

As regards numbers, from the fact that they can always be increased, it follows absolutely and unmistakably that they can always be decreased. For, if, for example, we wish to multiply a number as much as 100,000 times, we can also take a one-hundred-thousandth part of it, by dividing it by the same number by which we multiply, and thus every factor in multiplication becomes a factor in division when the whole number is changed to a fraction. And so infinite increase necessarily also implies infinite division.

In space, the same relationship is seen between these two opposite infinities. That is to say that if a space can be infinitely extended, it follows that it can be infinitely reduced, as is seen from the following example. If we look through a glass at a vessel which is constantly moving directly away, it is clear that the diaphanous place where we see any chosen point on the vessel is always rising in constant flux as the vessel becomes farther removed. Now, if the course of the vessel is constantly extended even to infinity, this point will constantly get higher. Nevertheless, it will never reach the point from which the horizontal ray falls which leads from the eye to the glass, so that it will always approach it without ever reaching it and will always divide the space that remains horizontally under this point without ever reaching it. From this we see the necessary conclusion which is drawn from the infinity of the extent of the vessel's course to the infinite and infinitely small division of the small space that remains horizontally under this point.

Those who remain unsatisfied by these reasons and who continue in the belief that space is not infinitely divisible, can lay no claim to understanding geometrical demonstrations; although they may be enlightened in other matters, they are very slightly enlightened in these matters, for one may very easily be an able man and a bad geometrician. But those who clearly see these truths can admire the grandeur and the power of nature in this double infinity which surrounds us on all sides. And by the consideration of these wonders they may learn to know themselves, on seeing themselves placed between an infinity and a nothing of extent, between an infinity and a nothing of shade, between an infinity and a nothing of motion, between an infinity and a nothing of time. As a result, we may learn to estimate our own value and to make reflections which are worth more than all the rest of geometry itself.

I have felt obliged to enter upon this lengthy consideration for the benefit of those who, though they did not at first understand this double infinity, nevertheless are capable of being persuaded of it. And although there are those who have enough insight to do without it, it may nevertheless happen that this discourse, which is necessary to some, may not be altogether useless to others.

39. THE ART OF PERSUASION

[1658 or 1659] (?)

The art of persuasion is necessarily related to the way in which we secure agreement to what we propose to men and to the nature of the things which we wish to make men believe.

No one is unaware that there are two gateways through which opinions are received by the soul; these are the two principal faculties, namely, the understanding and the will. The more natural of these is the understanding, for we should agree with only those verities which have been demonstrated; but the more common of these, though it be contrary to nature, is the will, for all men are almost always led to believe not by proof but by sentiment. This voice is base, unworthy, and alien; the whole world disavows it. Everybody professes to believe, and even to like only what he knows to be deserving.

I am not speaking here of divine verities which I should by no means associate with the art of persuasion, for they have their place infinitely above nature. God alone can place them in the soul and do this in a manner pleasing to Him. I know that He has wished them to enter the mind from the heart and not into the heart from the mind. He has wished this in order to humble the superb power of reasoning which claims to be the judge of the things that the will chooses, and in order to cure this infirm will which is totally corrupted by its vile ties. Hence when speaking of things human, we say that we should know them before loving them — a saying which has become proverbial. Yet the saints, on the contrary, when speaking of things divine, say that we should love them in order to know them, and that we enter into truth only through love. Of this they have made one of their most useful maxims.

It now becomes apparent that God has established this supernatural order, and has made it quite the opposite of the order which was to be natural to men in things of nature. However, men have corrupted this order by making things profane which they should deem holy, because, in reality, we believe little excepting that which pleases us. For this reason we are so indisposed to accept the verities of the Christian religion that are entirely opposed to our pleasures. *Tell us agreeable things and we shall listen to you,* said the Jews to Moses, as if approbation were to determine belief. To punish this disorder by an order which conforms to Him, God sheds His light on minds only after having overcome the rebellion of the will by a most celestial sweetness which charms and wins.

Now I am speaking only of those truths within our reach; the mind and the heart, I say, are like gates through which they are received into the soul, but very few enter through the mind, though multitudes of them are introduced through the foolhardy caprices of the will without the counsel of reason.

Each of these faculties has its principles and the first motivating force of its actions. Those of the mind are natural verities and are known to everyone, such as that *the whole is greater than any of its parts.* In addition, there are several special maxims which are accepted by some but not by others; but, even though they be false, once they are adopted, they influence belief as powerfully as do those which are absolutely true. The powers of the will are certain natural desires common to all men, such as the desire to be happy which people are bound to have. In addition there are particular ends which everyone tries to achieve; since these are able to please us, even though they are really pernicious, they stimulate the will just as powerfully as if they made for its genuine happiness.

So much for the forces that lead us to assent. But the things of which we must persuade others have very diverse qualities. Some necessarily follow from common principles and admitted verities. These may lead infallibly to persuasion, for they must inevitably carry conviction when brought into relation with accepted principles; it is impossible for the soul to reject them, once we are able to link them with the verities which the soul has already accepted. There are some things which have a close union with the objects that give us satisfaction; these are also accepted with assurance, for as soon as we make the soul perceive that a thing may lead to what it loves supremely, the soul inevitably receives it joyfully. But there is nothing more certain in nature than the sureness of the effect produced by those things which have this full harmony among themselves and with accepted verities. And conversely, whatever has no relation to our beliefs or to our pleasures is irksome, false and absolutely foreign.

In all these cases there is nothing to doubt. But there are cases where the things which we should like to make people believe are well founded on known verities, yet at the same time they are contrary to the pleasures which are closest to us. And these cases are in great danger of showing by an experience, which is but too common, what I said at the outset, namely, that this imperious soul which boasted of acting only on reason follows, through shameful and foolhardy choice, whatever a corrupt will desires, no matter what resistance even the most enlightened mind may oppose. Then a dubious balance is effected between verity and voluptuousness, and the knowledge of the one and the consciousness of the other wage a combat whose outcome is very uncertain, for in order to judge it we would have to know everything that goes on within man, and man himself almost never knows this. Hence it seems that we must consider the person whom we wish to persuade of whatever it may be; we must know his mind and his heart, what principles he accepts, and what things he likes. Then we must note the relation of the thing in question to these avowed principles or to objects of delight on the basis of those charms commonly attributed to the thing under consideration. Thus the art of persuasion is just as much the art of being ingratiating as of being convincing; for men are governed so much more by caprice than by reason.

Now, I shall give rules only for the former of these two methods, which are respectively to convince and to please. And I shall do this only on the supposition that we have agreed on these principles and that we continue firmly to hold them; otherwise I do not know whether there would be any means of accommodating the evidence to the inconsistency of our caprices.

But the mode of pleasing is incomparably more difficult, more subtle, more useful, and more admirable. Moreover, if I do not discuss it, it is because of inability to do so; and I feel so utterly unsuited to it that I believe the matter to be absolutely impossible.

Not that I do not believe there are as definite rules for pleasing as for demonstrating, nor that anyone who knew and employed them perfectly could not succeed as surely in making himself loved by kings and all sorts of people as he could demonstrate the elements of geometry to those who have sufficient imagination to understand hypotheses. But I consider, and perhaps my weakness leads me to believe so, that it is impossible to succeed in this. At least I believe if any one is capable of doing so, it is people whom I know, and that no one else has as clear and abundant insight in the matter. The reason for this extreme difficulty is to be found in the fact that the principles of pleasure are not firm and not stable. They differ in all men, they vary so greatly in all individuals that no man differs more from another than he does from himself at various times. A man's pleasures are not like a woman's; a rich man and a poor man have different pleasures; a prince, a soldier, a merchant, a bourgeois, a peasant, the old, the young, the healthy, and the sick all differ, and the slightest happenings change them.

Now there is an art, and it is the one I am presenting, of showing the connection of verities with their principles either of truth or of pleasure, provided that the principles once agreed to remain fixed and are never contradicted. But there are few principles of this kind, and, apart from geometry which considers only very simple figures, there is scarcely a truth upon which we always agree, and there are even fewer objects of pleasure toward which we do not constantly change. Consequently I do not know whether there is any way of giving fixed rules to bring discourses into agreement with the inconstancy of our caprices.

This art, which I call the art of *persuading*, and which rightly is but the direction of methodically perfect proofs, consists of three essential parts: the defining of terms which must be used for clear definitions; the advancement of principles or evident axioms for proving the matter in question; and constant mental substitution, in the demonstration, of definitions for things defined.

The reason for this method is evident, for it would be useless to propose what we want to prove, and to undertake its demonstration, if we had not clearly defined all the terms that are not intelligible. Similarly, the demonstration must be preceded by the demand for obvious principles which are necessary to it, for if we do not secure the foundation, we cannot secure the edifice; finally, in demonstrating we must mentally substitute definitions for the things defined, for otherwise we might misuse the various meanings of terms. It is easy to see that in using this method we are sure of convincing. For the invincible force of reasoned conclusions cannot fail to produce its effect when all terms are understood and entirely freed from ambiguity by definitions, when there is agreement on principles, and when in demonstration we always mentally substitute definitions for things defined.

Consequently there can never be the slightest doubt about a demonstration in which these conditions are observed; moreover where these are not observed, no demonstration can be valid. Hence it is very necessary to understand and to be in possession of them. For this reason, and in order to make things easier and more explicit, I shall briefly sum them all up in a few rules which will include all that is necessary for the perfection of definitions, axioms, and demonstrations, and consequently the whole method of geometric proofs of the art of persuading.

Rules for Definitions

I. Do not undertake to define any things which are so well known in themselves that clearer terms to explain them are lacking.

II. Do not leave undefined any terms which are a bit obscure or ambiguous.

III. In the definition of terms use only words which are perfectly well known or which have already been explained.

Rules for Axioms

I. Do not omit any necessary principle, no matter how clear and evident it may be, without having asked whether it is granted as such.

II. Regard as axioms only those things which are perfectly self-evident.

Rules for Demonstrations

I. Do not undertake the demonstration of any things which are so self-evident that no greater clarity is gained by proving them.

II. Prove all propositions that are a bit obscure, and in proving them use only very obvious axioms or propositions which have already been agreed to or demonstrated.

III. Always mentally substitute definitions for the things defined, so as not to be deceived by the ambiguity of terms which definitions have restricted.

These are the eight rules which contain all the precepts of sound and immutable proofs; three of them are not absolutely necessary, and may be neglected without error. It is even difficult and almost impossible always to observe them exactly, though it is far better to do so as far as possible; these three are the first ones of each of the three divisions.

As regards definitions: Define no terms that are already perfectly well known.

As regards axioms: Do not fail to ask for any axioms which are perfectly evident and simple.

As regards demonstrations: Do not demonstrate any things that are very well known in themselves.

For without doubt it is not a great fault to define and to explain things clearly, though they be very clear in themselves; nor is it a great fault not to fail to demand in advance axioms which cannot be rejected where they are necessary; nor, finally, is it a great fault to prove propositions which one would accept without proof.

But the other five rules are absolutely necessary, and we cannot dispense with them without serious shortcomings and often without error; for this reason I am taking them up again in particular.

Necessary rules for definitions. Do not leave undefined any terms which are a bit obscure or ambiguous. In the definition of terms use only words which are perfectly well known or which have already been explained.

Necessary rule for axioms. Regard as axioms only those things which are perfectly evident.

Necessary rules for demonstrations. Prove all propositions, and in proving them use only very obvious axioms or propositions which have already been agreed to or demonstrated. Never take advantage of the ambiguity of terms by failing mentally to substitute for them definitions which restrict and explain them.

This is what the art of persuading consists of, and it may be summed up in these two principles: Define all the terms that are introduced; prove everything by mentally substituting definitions for the things defined.

Here it seems proper to meet three principal objections that may be raised. One is that there is nothing new about this method; another is that it is very easy to learn without the necessity of studying the elements of geometry, since it consists of these two words which one can learn at the first reading; the final one is that this method is quite useless, since its use is confined almost entirely to mere matters of geometry. Consequently it becomes necessary to point out that there is nothing so unknown, nothing more difficult to practice, and nothing more useful and more universal.

As for the first objection, which is that these rules are common to the world, *that it is necessary* to define everything and to prove everything, and that logicians themselves have included them in the precepts of their art, I wish that all this were true; I wish it were so well known that I should not have had the trouble of seeking so carefully the source of all the shortcomings of reason which, indeed, are common. But this is so far from being the case that, if we except merely the geometricians whose numbers are so limited that they are unique in a whole nation and in long spans of time, we see no one else who knows this. It will be easy to make this intelligible to those who have comprehended perfectly what little I have said about it; but if they have not comprehended it perfectly, I confess they will learn nothing from it. But if they have entered into the spirit of these rules, and if these have made a strong enough impression to take root and to become firmly fixed, they will perceive what a difference there is between what is said here and what some logicians may have written about it in a haphazard approach in some places in their works. Those who have a discerning mind know what a difference there is between similar words, depending on the places and the accompanying circumstances. Does anyone really believe that two persons who have read and learned by heart the same book know it equally? Let us assume that the one undertakes it in such a manner as to know all the principles, the force of consequences, the replies to the objections that may be raised, and the whole economy of the work; on the other hand let us assume that for the second person the words are dead, and the seeds, though they be like those which have produced such fertile trees, have remained dry and barren in a sterile mind which has received them in vain. All those who say the same things do not possess them in the same fashion; that is why the incomparable author [i.e. Montaigne] of the *Art of conferring* devotes so much care to making clear that we must not judge the capacity of a man by the excellence of a "bon mot" which we hear him say. Instead of extending the admiration of a good discourse to the speaker, let us penetrate, says he, into the spirit from which it comes, let us find out whether he owes it to his memory or to some lucky chance, let us receive him with coolness and with scorn in order to see whether he will feel that we are not according his words the esteem which their quality merits. In most cases we shall see that we will make him disavow them at once, and we will draw him very far from this thought which is better than he believed, merely to toss him to another thought which is very base and ridiculous. We must therefore ascertain how this thought was lodged in its author; how and from what source he has obtained it, and to what extent it is his; otherwise a precipitous judgment will be deemed foolhardy.

I should like to ask fair-minded people whether the two principles: *matter is by nature utterly incapable of thought* and *I think, therefore I am* are in effect the same in the mind of Descartes and in the mind of Saint Augustine who said the same thing twelve hundred years earlier. Indeed, I am far from saying that Descartes was not their real author, even if he learned them only by reading this great saint; for I know what a difference there is between writing a word by chance, without longer and more extended reflection on it, and noting in this word an admirable chain of consequences that prove the distinction between material and spiritual nature, and make of it a firm principle supported by an entire system of physics, as Descartes claimed he was doing. For without examining whether he succeeded effectively in his pretention, I am assuming that he did, and on this assumption I say that this word is as different in his writings from the same word as used by others, who merely happened to use it, as a man full of life and vigor is different from a dead man. Someone will say a thing about himself without comprehending its excellence; or someone else will understand a marvelous sequence of events which makes us say boldly that it is no longer the same word, and that he no longer owes it to the man from whom he learned it, that an admirable tree does not belong to the man who tossed the seed thoughtlessly and ignorantly on fruitful soil which thereby profited from its own fertility. The same thoughts sometimes grow very differently in someone else than in their author; barren in their natural field, they thrive when transplanted. But it happens much more often that a good mind brings its own thoughts to all the fruition of which they are capable, and that subsequently others who have heard these thoughts praised, borrow them and adorn themselves with them but without recognizing their excellence; it is then that the difference of the same word in various mouths becomes most apparent.

In this way logic has perhaps borrowed the rules of geometry without understanding their full meaning, and so when people include these rules at random among their own, it does not follow that they have penetrated into the spirit of geometry. If they give no evidence other than casual mention, I should be far from comparing them with this science which teaches the veritable method of guiding reason. But on the contrary, I should be strongly disposed to exclude them from this science and almost irretrievably so. For there are those who say a thing casually and, unmindful of all it means, and instead of following its lights, they lose themselves utterly in useless quests, running after what these offer but cannot give. All this clearly shows that they are not very discerning, and all the more so if they failed to follow these lights because they had not noticed them. Everybody is seeking a method that will prevent going astray. The logicians profess to show the way, but only the geometricians succeed, and aside from their science and whatever imitates it, there are no veritable demonstrations. Its whole art is contained in the sole precepts that we have stated; they alone suffice and they alone prove; all other rules are useless or harmful. That is what I know from long experience with all sorts of books and persons. And on that I pass the same judgment as those who say that the geometricians give them nothing new by their rules, because in effect they have them, though they are mingled with a multitude of other useless or false rules from which they cannot distinguish them. They are like those people who seek a diamond of great value among a large number of artificial ones, but who are unable to distinguish between them. Yet since they have them all together they boast of possessing the genuine diamond just as much as he who, without pausing before this wretched heap, puts his hand on the choice stone which they are seeking and for which they would not throw away all the rest.

The flaw in false reasoning is a malady which can be cured by these two remedies. Another has been compounded from an infinite number of useless herbs, where the good ones are covered over and remain ineffective because of the evil qualities of this mixture. In order to discover all the sophisms and all the ambiguities of captious reasonings, they have invented barbarous names which astound those who hear them. Instead of being able to disentangle all the windings of this tangled knot merely by pulling the ends assigned by the geometricians, they have marked a strange number of others in which those are included, and without knowing which is the right one. And so, since they show us a number of different routes which they say will lead us where we wish, even though but two of them will take us there, one must know how to mark them in particular. People will claim that geometry, which designates these routes with certainty, merely gives what we already had from others; because in effect these gave the same thing and more; but such people overlook the fact that this present lost its value by its very abundance, and that addition meant loss. Nothing is more common than good things; it is only a matter of discerning them, and it is certain that they are all natural and within our reach, and even known to everyone. But people do not know how to distinguish them. This is universal. Excellence of any kind is not to be found in extraordinary and bizarre things. We climb to reach it, and we merely become farther removed from it; most often we need to bend down, instead. The best books are those which their readers believe they could have written. Nature, which alone is good, is quite familiar and common. Hence I do not doubt at all that these rules, being true, must be simple, naïve, and natural as they are. *Barbara* and *baralipton* do not mold reasoning. It is not necessary to strain the mind; strained and labored manners fill it with silly presumption through queer affectation and vain, ridiculous inflation instead of with solid, vigorous nourishment.

One of the principal reasons why those who enter the realm of knowledge are carried so far from the true course they should follow is their first notion that good things are inaccessible. That is why they call them grand, high, elevated, sublime. This undoes everything. I should like to call them low, common, familiar; these suit them better; I hate swollen words . . . [sentence incomplete].

40. THREE DISCOURSES BY PASCAL ON THE STATION OF NOBLEMEN [REDACTION BY NICOLE]

[End of 1659] (?)

FIRST DISCOURSE

If you would enter into genuine understanding of your station, consider it in this image.

A man was tossed by a tempest on an unknown island whose habitants were at a loss to find their lost king, and since in body and in face he had marked resemblance to this king, he was taken for him and was recognized in that capacity by all the people. At first he did not know what to do about it, but he finally resolved to yield to his good fortune. He accepted all the homage which people wished to confer, and let himself be treated as king.

But since he could not forget his natural station, at the same time that he accepted this deference, he remembered that he was not the king for whom the people were searching and that this kingdom did not belong to him. Thus he had two ways of looking at things; the one according to which he acted as king, the other by which he recognized his real state, and that it was mere chance that had put him in the place where he was. He hid this latter thought and brought the other to light. By the former he dealt with his people, and on the basis of the latter he dealt with himself.

Don't imagine that you possess the riches of which you find yourself master by any smaller degree of chance than that through which this man found himself a king. By virtue of yourself and of your nature you have no right to them any more than he had; and you are not merely the son of a duke but you find yourself in this world only as the result of an infinite number of fortuitous events. Your birth depends on a marriage or rather on the marriages of all those from whom you are descended. But on what do these marriages depend? On a chance visit, on a casual statement, on a thousand unforeseen incidents.

You say that you have your riches from your ancestors, but did not your ancestors acquire them and conserve them through a thousand chance happenings? Do you imagine, too, that these possessions have passed from your ancestors by some natural law? That is not true. This order is based merely and solely on the will of legislators who may have had good reasons, but none of these is derived from a natural right which you may have to these things. If it had pleased them to ordain that, after having been owned by the Conscript Fathers during their lifetime, these goods should revert to the republic after their death, you would have no cause for complaint.

Therefore the whole title by which you own your goods is not a title by nature but by human institution. Another orientation of the imagination of those who made the laws would have made you poor, and it is only this chance encounter which has caused you to be born with the caprice of laws favorable to you that puts you in possession of all these goods.

I do not wish to say that they do not belong to you legitimately and that anyone other than you should be permitted to rob you of them; for God, who is Master over them, has permitted societies to make laws for sharing them, and once these laws are established, it is wrong to violate them. This is what distinguishes you somewhat from this man who owned his kingdom only because of an error on the part of the people; because God did not authorize that possession and would oblige him to give it up, whereas He does authorize yours. But what you have quite in common with him is that this right, which you have to it, is founded no more than his on some quality and on some merit which may be in you and which renders you worthy of it. Your soul and your body are equally indifferent to the station of a boatman and to that of a duke. There is no natural tie which links them to one station rather than to another.

What follows from this? It follows that, like the man of whom we were speaking, you must have two ways of looking at things; that if you deal outwardly with men in accordance with your rank you must recognize by a more hidden but more rightful way of thinking that you are not by nature above them. If public opinion raises you above the common run of men, let the other humble you and keep you in perfect equality with all men, for that is your natural station.

The people who admire you probably do not know this secret. They believe that nobility is a genuine greatness, and they almost consider the great as being of a different nature from others. Do not reveal this error to them, if you wish, but do not abuse this elevation insolently, and above all do not delude yourself by believing that your being has something more elevated than that of the others.

What would you say of that man who had been made king through an error of the people, if he came to forget his natural station to such an extent that he fancied this kingdom to be his due, that he merited it, and that it rightfully belonged to him? You would wonder at his stupidity and at his folly. But is there any less of this in persons of rank who live in such strange forgetfulness of their natural state?

How important this opinion is! For all the self-exaltation, all the violence, and all the vanity of the great come from the fact that they do not recognize what they are. For it is difficult for men to treat others with insolence if they regard themselves inwardly as the equals of all men, and if they are persuaded that nothing in them merits these little advantages which God has given them over others. To treat others insolently, one must forget himself in this particular, and believe that he has some genuine excellence over them. The illusion, which I am endeavoring to reveal to you, consists in just this.

SECOND DISCOURSE

It is well, Sir, for you to know what people owe you, so that you may not presume to demand from men what is not your due, for this is a visible injustice. Nevertheless, it is very common in those of your station because they are ignorant of its nature.

There are two kinds of greatness in the world, for there is greatness which has been established and natural greatness. Established greatness depends on the will of men who have thought it reasonable to owe honor to certain estates and to attach a certain respect to them. Power and nobility are of this kind. In one country people honor nobles, in another commoners; in this one they honor the first-born, in that other the younger. Why this? Because it is men's pleasure to do so. The matter was one of indifference before it was established; after its establishment it became just, because it is unjust to disturb it.

Natural greatness is that which is independent of the fancy of men, because it consists in the genuine and effective qualities of the soul or of the body which make the one or the other more worthy of esteem; such are the sciences, the light of the intellect, virtue, health, strength.

We owe something to both of these kinds of greatness, but inasmuch as they are of a different nature, we consequently owe them different respect. As regards established greatness, we owe it conventional respect; that is to say, certain outward ceremonies which must however be accompanied with reason by inward recognition of the justice of this order, but which do not make us conceive of some real quality in those whom we thus honor. We must speak to kings on our knees; we must stand in the chamber of princes. It is stupidity and baseness of spirit to refuse them this homage.

But as for natural respect, which consists in esteem, we owe that only to natural greatness, and conversely we owe contempt and aversion to qualities that are contrary to natural greatness. It is not necessary that I esteem you because you are a duke; but it is necessary that I salute you. If you are a duke and a gentleman, I render what I owe to both of these qualities. I shall not refuse you the courtesies which you merit in your quality of duke nor the esteem which you merit as a gentleman. But if you were a duke without being a gentleman, I should still do you justice; for in rendering you the outward homage which the order of men has attached to your birth, I should not be lacking in the inward contempt for you which the baseness of your spirit merited.

The justice of this homage consists in just this. And the injustice consists in attaching natural respect to established greatness, or in exacting established respect for natural greatness. Monsieur N. is a greater geometrician than I. In this quality he wishes to walk ahead of me; I shall say to him that he does not understand the situation. Geometry is a natural greatness, it demands preference based on esteem, but men have attached no outward preference to it. I shall walk ahead of him, and I shall esteem him more highly than myself in the matter of geometry. Similarly, if as duke and peer you are not content with having me stand with bared head before you, and if you wish in addition that I should esteem you, I should beg you to show me the qualities which merit my esteem, and I could not justly refuse it. But if you did not do so, you would be unjust in demanding it of me, and assuredly you would not succeed, though you were the greatest prince in the world.

THIRD DISCOURSE

I wish to acquaint you, Sir, with your true station, for it is one thing in the world of which people of your kind are most ignorant. In your opinion what is it to be a great lord? It means being master of several things after which men lust, and thus to be able to satisfy the needs and the desires of some men. It is these needs and these desires that draw them to you and which make them submit to you; without this they would not even look at you. But through these services and the deference they bestow upon you, they hope to obtain from you some share of these goods they desire, and which they see at your disposal.

God is surrounded by people full of benevolence who ask of him the blessings of benevolence within his power; consequently he is properly the king of benevolence.

Similarly you are surrounded by a small number of people over whom you reign in your own way. These people are full of covetousness. They ask you for the gifts they covet. It is covetousness that attaches them to you. Therefore you are properly a king of covetousness; your kingdom is of a rather limited extent, but in this respect you are the equal of the greatest kings of the earth. Like you they are kings of covetousness. They derive their strength from such covetousness, that is to say, from the possession of things which the cupidity of men desires.

But in knowing your natural station, make use of the means it gives you, and do not claim to reign in any way other than that which makes you king. It is not your strength and your natural power which make all these people subject to you. Therefore do not claim to dominate them by force, nor treat them with severity. Satisfy their just desires, relieve their wants, derive your pleasure from doing good, raise them as much as you can, and you will be acting like a true king of covetousness.

What I am saying to you does not carry very far; if you remain there, you may lose out, but at least you will lose out as a gentleman. There are people who as stupidly damn themselves by avarice, by brutality, by debauchery, by violence, by passions, by blasphemy. The means I open up for you are doubtless more honest, but in truth it is always great folly to damn oneself. And that is why one should not stop there. One should scorn covetousness and its rule, and aspire to this kingdom of benevolence, where all subjects breathe benevolence alone and desire only the blessings of benevolence. Others than I will tell you the way; it will suffice for me to have turned you from this brutal life into which I see that some persons of your station have allowed themselves to be led out of ignorance of the true nature of their station.

41. LETTER FROM PASCAL TO FERMAT

From Bienassis, August 10, 1660.

Sir:

You are the most gallant man in all the world, and certainly I am one of those who are in a position to recognize such qualities and to admire them infinitely, above all when they are combined with the talents which you have to so unusual a degree. All this obliges me to express in writing my gratitude for the offer you are making to me; I am doing this in spite of the great effort which reading and writing still cost me. However, the honor which you are doing me is so dear to me, that I cannot reply too promptly. And so I shall say to you, Sir, that if I were in good health, I should have hastened to Toulouse, and I should not have permitted a man like you to take as much as a single step to come to a man like me. I shall also say to you that although I consider you to be the greatest geometrician in all Europe, it is not this attribute which has attracted me; but I find so much penetration of mind and integrity in your conversation that I am seeking you out because of them. For to speak to you frankly about geometry, I consider it to be the highest exercise of the mind, but at the same time I know it to be so unprofitable that I make little distinction between a man who is merely a geometrician and a skillful artisan. Therefore I call it the most beautiful trade in all the world, but after all it is only a trade, and I have often said that it is good to test but not to employ our capacities, so that I would not take two steps for geometry. I am sure that you are very much in the same mood. Yet at present there is this further consideration: I am engaged in studies so remote from such preoccupations that I can scarcely remember that they actually exist. A year or two ago I had occupied myself with it for a very special reason; having satisfied the same, I am in danger of never thinking of it again. Moreover, my health is not yet good enough, for I am so weak that I cannot walk without a stick, nor ride a horse. Moreover, I can ride but three or four leagues at most in a carriage, and consequently it took me twenty-two days to come here from Paris. The physicians ordered me to take the waters at Bourbon for the month of September. I have spent the past two months, as my condition permitted, in going by water from there in Poitou to Saumur in order to remain until Christmas with the Duke of Rouannez, Governor and Lieutenant General of Poitou, who has an affection for me which I do not merit. But since I shall pass through Orléans in going to Saumur by river, if my health does not permit me to proceed further, I shall go from there to Paris. This, Sir, is the whole state of my present life, of which I believe I should give you an account in order to assure you how impossible it is for me to receive the honor which you deigned to offer me. With all my heart I hope some day to make some return for this honor to you or to your esteemed children, to whom I am deeply devoted, since I have a particular veneration for those who bear the name of the first man in the world. I am, etc.

42. LETTER FROM PASCAL TO MADAME DE SABLÉ ABOUT MONSIEUR MENJOT

[End of 1660] (?)

Although I am greatly embarrassed, I can no longer defer sending you many thanks for having presented me to Monsieur Menjot, for beyond doubt I owe my acquaintance with him to you, Madame. Although I already esteemed him highly because of the things my sister had said of him, I am unable to express to you with what joy I received the favor which he wished to do me. One need merely read his letter to see how much wit and judgment he has. Although I am incapable of understanding the heart of the matters which he treats in his book, I shall say to you nevertheless, Madame, that I have learned much from the way in which with a few words he harmonizes the immateriality of the soul with the power that matter has of altering its functions and of causing delirium. I am most eager to have the honor of a conversation with you on this subject.

For Madame de Sablé

43. WRITING ON THE SIGNATURE OF THOSE WHO SUBSCRIBED TO THE CONSTITUTIONS IN THIS MANNER: I SUBSCRIBE TO THESE CONSTITUTIONS ONLY INSOFAR AS FAITH IS CONCERNED, OR SIMPLY: I SUBSCRIBE TO THE CONSTITUTIONS BEARING ON FAITH, QUOAD DOGMATA

[*End of November or December, 1661*] (?)

Since the whole question of today centers around these words, *I condemn the five propositions in the sense of Jansen*, or *the doctrine of Jansen on the five propositions*, it is of extreme importance to see how we subscribe to them.

First of all we must know that in truth there is no difference between condemning the doctrine of Jansen on the five propositions and condemning efficacious grace, Saint Augustine, and Saint Paul.

It is solely for this reason that the enemies of this grace are endeavoring to have this clause passed.

We must know furthermore that the way they have chosen of defending themselves against the decisions of the Pope and of the bishops who have condemned this doctrine as interpreted by Jansen, has been so subtle that although fundamentally it is true, it has been so lacking in frankness and so timid, that it does not seem worthy of the true defenders of the Church.

The basis for this mode of self-defense has been to say that in these utterances there is a fact and a doctrine; and that they promise credence for the one and respect for the other.

The whole quarrel centers about knowing whether a fact and a doctrine are separate, or whether right alone exists; that is to say, whether Jansen's interpretation which is expressed there, does anything but indicate the doctrine.

The Pope and the bishops are on one side, and they claim that it is a matter of doctrine and of faith to say that the five propositions are heretical in the interpretation of Jansen. Alexander VII declared in his constitution, *that in order to be in the true faith, one must say that the words in the interpretation of Jansen express only the heretical meaning of these propositions*, and that thus it is a fact which entails a doctrine, and which forms an essential part of the profession of faith; just as when one says, *the opinion of Calvin on the Eucharist is heretical*, this certainly is a matter of faith.

A very small number of persons who are constantly writing little pamphlets, say that by its nature this fact differs from doctrine.

Finally it should be noted that the words *fact* and *doctrine* are to be found neither in the pronouncement nor in the constitutions, nor in the formulary, but only in some writings which have no necessary relation to this signature; in view of all this one should scrutinize the signature that can conscientiously be made by those who believe they are obliged by their conscience not to condemn the interpretation of Jansen.

My opinion on this is that, since the interpretation of Jansen has been expressed in the pronouncement, in the bulls, and in the formulary, it must necessarily be formally excluded from the signature; otherwise one does not fulfill his duty. For it is a pure illusion to claim that it suffices to say that one does not believe what is in the faith in order to claim thereby to have indicated sufficiently that one does not condemn the interpretation of Jansen; and all this for the simple reason that people imagine there is a fact in this which is separate from doctrine. Many proofs can be given to show that this is a pure illusion.

This one proof may suffice. Since the fact and the doctrine are things which are not mentioned at all in all that is to be signed, these two words bear no relation whatever to each other that would make reference to the one imply the exclusion of the other.

If it were stated in the pronouncement or in the constitutions or in the formulary that one must believe not only in the faith but also the doctrine; or that the fact and the doctrine alike are to be subscribed to; and finally that these two words *fact* and *doctrine* were formally indicated therein — then perhaps one might say that by simply stating that one agreed to the doctrine one would indicate sufficiently that he were not agreeing to the other. But these two words appear only in our discussions and in some writings that are quite separate from the constitutions which may be destroyed, whereas the signatures remain; they are neither related nor opposed to each other; nor are they implicit in the nature of the thing, where faith is not naturally opposed to the fact, but to error; nor are they in what is to be signed. Consequently it is impossible to claim that an expression of faith necessarily entails exclusion of the fact.

For although when in saying that we accept the faith alone, we thereby indicate that there is some other thing which we do not accept, it does not follow that this thing which we do not accept is necessarily the interpretation of Jansen. That may mean many other things such as the enumerations which are made in the statement and the prohibition of reading and writing.

Moreover since the word faith is extremely ambiguous, and since some people claim that the doctrine of Jansen entails a point of faith and others claim that it is only a pure fact, it is indubitable that in simply saying that one accepts the faith, without saying that he does not accept the terms of Jansen's doctrine, he does not thereby indicate that he does not accept it; on the contrary, he indicates thereby that he accepts it. For the avowed intent of the Pope and of his bishops is to make the condemnation of Jansen a mark of faith, with everyone saying it publicly, and nobody publicly daring to say the contrary.

It is beyond doubt that this profession of faith is at least equivocal and ambiguous, and consequently wicked.

From the above I conclude that those who merely sign the formulary without reservation sign the condemnation of Jansen, of Saint Augustine, and of efficacious grace.

Secondly, I conclude that whoever formally excludes the doctrine of Jansen, saves Jansen and efficacious grace from condemnation.

Thirdly, I conclude that those who sign while speaking only of faith, and without formally excluding the doctrine of Jansen, are taking a middle course which is abominable before God, despicable before men, and utterly useless to those whom one would like to send to perdition.

44. PRAYER BY PASCAL ASKING GOD TO USE ILLNESSES TO A GOOD END

[Between 1659 and 1661] (?)

I

Lord, whose spirit is so good and so gentle in all things, and who art so compassionate that not only all prosperity but even all afflictions that come to Thine elect are the results of Thy compassion: grant me grace that I may not do as the pagans do in the condition to which Thy justice has reduced me; grant that as a true Christian I may recognize Thee as my Father and as my God, in whatever estate I find myself, since the change in my condition brings no change in Thine own. For Thou art the same, though I be subject to change, and Thou art God no less when Thou dost afflict and when Thou dost punish, than when Thou dost console and when Thou dost manifest indulgence.

II

Thou hadst given me health that I might serve Thee, and I have profaned it; now Thou dost send me illness to correct my ways: do not permit me to use it to anger Thee by my impatience. I have misused my health, and Thou hast justly punished me for it; do not suffer me to misuse Thy punishment. And since the corruption of my nature is such that it renders Thy favors pernicious, grant, O my God, that Thine omnipotent grace may render Thy chastisements salutary to me. If my heart was filled with love for the world while it had some vigor, annihilate this vigor for my salvation, and render me incapable of enjoying the world not only through the weakness of my body, but rather through the ardor of a love which will render me capable of delight in Thee by rendering me capable of delight only in Thee.

III

O God, before whom I must give an exact accounting of my life unto the end of my life and unto the end of the world! O God, who dost permit the world and all things of the world to be, only that they may train Thine elect and punish sinners. O God, who dost leave hardened sinners in the delightful and criminal ways of the world and in the pleasures of the world. O God, who dost make our bodies to die, and who in the hour of death dost detach our soul from all that it loved in the world. O God, who dost wrest me in the final moment of my life from all things to which I had attached myself, and to which I had given my heart. O God, Thou who on the day of judgment must consume the earth and all creatures contained therein, to show to all men that Thou alone dost live, and hence that Thou alone art worthy of love, since nothing can endure without Thee. O God, Thou who must destroy all these vain idols and all these deadly objects of our passions, I praise Thee, my God, and I shall bless Thee all the days of my life, that Thou hast deigned to predispose this dread day in my favor, by destroying for my sake all things in the feebleness to which Thou hast reduced me. I praise Thee, my God, and I shall bless Thee all the days of my life because it has pleased Thee to lessen me so that I no longer have the capacity for enjoying the sweetness of health and the pleasures of the world. And I bless Thee for having somehow annihilated to my advantage the deceptive idols which Thou wilt indeed annihilate to confound the wicked on the day of Thy wrath. Give me, Lord, the strength to judge myself in the wake of destruction that Thou hast made with regard to me, so that Thou mayest not judge me Thyself after the complete destruction which Thou wilt make of my life and of the world. For, Lord, just as at the moment of my death I shall find myself separated from the world, devoid of all things, alone in Thy presence to answer to Thy righteousness for all the impulses of my heart, so, Lord, grant that I may consider myself in this illness as in a kind of death, separated from the world, devoid of all the objects to which I am enslaved, alone in Thy presence to implore Thy mercy for the conversion of my heart; and thus may I find unbounded consolation in Thy sending me now a kind of death to exercise Thy mercy before Thou dost in fact send me death to exercise Thy judgment. Grant then, O my God, that as Thou hast anticipated my death, so may I anticipate Thine appalling sentence, and may I examine myself before Thy judgment in order to find mercy in Thy presence.

IV

Grant, O my God, that I may worship in silence the order of Thy providence in the guidance of my life; may Thy rod comfort me, and, having lived in bitterness during peace, may I taste celestial sweetness during the salutary ills with which Thou dost afflict me. But I recognize, my God, that my heart is so hardened and so filled with the thoughts, cares, anxieties, and ties of the world, that neither illness any more than health, neither discourses, books, Thy holy Scriptures, Thy Gospel, Thy most holy Mysteries, alms, fasting, mortification, miracles, partaking of the Sacraments, the sacrifice of Thy Body, neither all my efforts nor those of the whole world together can be of any avail in beginning my conversion, if Thou dost not accompany all these things with the quite extraordinary aid of Thy grace. That is why, my God, I address Thee, omnipotent God, to ask of Thee a gift which all creatures combined are utterly unable to grant me. I should not presume to address my cries unto Thee, if anyone else could grant my petition. But, my God, since the conversion of my heart which I ask of Thee, is a work that surpasses all the efforts of nature, I can but turn to the Author and omnipotent Master of nature and of my heart. To whom shall I cry, Lord, and to whom shall I have recourse [if not to Thee]? Nothing that is not God can fulfill my expectation; it is God Himself whom I ask and whom I seek. O God, it is Thee whom I ask, and it is to Thee alone that I turn to find Thee. Open my heart, Lord, enter into the rebellious place which vices have occupied and which they hold in subjection; enter as into a strong man's house, but first bind the strong and powerful enemy who masters it, and then take the treasures which are there. Lord, take my affections which the world had stolen; do Thou Thyself steal this treasure, or rather take it back, since it belongs to Thee, as a tribute I owe Thee, since Thine image is engraved upon it. Thou hadst formed it, Lord, in the moment of my birth, but it has become quite effaced, the image of the world is so engraved upon it, that the thought of Thee is no longer recognizable. Thou alone hast been able to create my soul; Thou alone canst create it anew. Thou alone hast been able to form Thine image, Thou alone canst reform it and imprint upon it anew Thine effaced image, that is to say, *Jesus Christ*, my Saviour, who is Thine image and the character of Thy substance.

V

O my God, how happy is a heart which can love so charming an object that does not dishonor it, and whose attachment is so salutary to it. I feel that I cannot love the world without displeasing Thee, without harming myself, and without dishonoring myself; and yet the world is still the object of my delights. O my God, how happy is a soul whose delight Thou art, since it can abandon itself to love Thee, not only without any scruple, but even with merit. How firm and enduring is its happiness, since its hope will not be frustrated; because Thou wilt never be destroyed, and neither life nor death will ever separate it from the object of its desires, and the very moment which carries away the wicked with their idols in common ruin will unite the just with Thee in common glory. Just as these will perish with the perishable things to which they are attached, so the others will continue eternally in the eternal and abiding object to which they have closely joined themselves. Oh, how happy are those who with full freedom and with the invincible inclination of their will love perfectly and freely what they are obliged to love of necessity.

VI

O my God, achieve the good impulses Thou hast given me. Be their end even as Thou art their beginning. Crown Thine own gifts. For I recognize that they are Thy gifts. Yes, my God, and far from claiming that my prayers have merit which obliges Thee to grant them of necessity,

I recognize very humbly, my God, that, having given to creatures my heart which Thou hadst formed for Thyself and not for the world nor for myself, I can expect no grace but from Thy mercy, since I have nothing within me which can bind Thee to such grace, and since all the natural impulses of my heart, which incline toward creatures or toward myself, can but anger Thee. I therefore render thanks unto Thee, my God, for the good impulses which Thou dost give me and even for the desire Thou givest me to render thanks unto Thee.

VII

Touch my heart that it may repent of its errors, because without this inward pain, the outward ills with which Thou dost touch my body would be a new occasion for sin. Grant that I may well recognize that the ills of the body are both but the outward image and the punishment of the ills of the soul. But, Lord, grant also that they be their cure, by making me behold in the pains which I feel the pain which I did not feel in my soul, though my soul is quite ill and covered with ulcers. For, Lord, the greatest of its maladies is this insensibility and this extreme weakness which have taken from it all sense of its own miseries. Grant that I may feel them keenly, and may whatever portion of life remains for me be continual penitence for the transgressions of my past life.

VIII

Lord, although my past life has been exempt from great crimes, whose occasion Thou hast kept from me, nevertheless it has been very odious to Thee by its continual negligence, by my persistent repugnance to Thine inspirations, by ill use of Thy most august Sacraments, by contempt for Thy Word, by the idleness and utter uselessness of all my acts and of my thoughts, by the complete loss of the time Thou hadst given me only to adore Thee, to search in all my occupations the means of pleasing Thee, and to do penance for the errors which are committed every day and which are common even to the most just, so that their life should be one continual penance without which they become unjust and sinners. Thus, my God, I have gone counter to Thee.

IX

Yes, Lord, until now I have always been deaf to Thine inspirations; I have scorned all Thine oracles; I have judged contrary to Thy judgments; I have contradicted the holy maxims which Thou hast brought to the world from the bosom of Thine Eternal Father, and according to which Thou wilt judge the world. Thou sayest: Blessed are ye that weep, and woe unto ye that have received your consolation. And I have said: Woe unto them that mourn; happy are those who enjoy an advantageous fortune, a glorious reputation, and robust health. And why did I deem them happy if not because all these advantages provided them with very ample facility to enjoy creatures, that is to say, to offend Thee. Yes, Lord, I confess that I esteemed health as a good thing; not because it is an easy means of serving Thee usefully, of devoting more care and more vigils to Thy service and to the aid of my neighbor, but because, thanks to my health, I was able to abandon myself with less restraint to the abundant delights of life and to enjoy its baneful pleasures all the more. Grant me grace, Lord, that I may reform my corrupted reason and that I may bring my sentiments into harmony with Thine, that I may esteem myself happy in affliction, and that my impotence to act outside of Thee may so purify my sentiments that they may not be repugnant to Thine, and that thus I may find Thee within me, since I cannot seek Thee outside because of my weakness. For, Lord, Thy Kingdom is in Thy faithful, and I shall find it within me if I find Thy Spirit and Thy sentiments.

X

But, Lord, what shall I do to constrain Thee to shed Thy spirit on this miserable earth? All that I am is odious to Thee, Lord, and I find nothing in me that may be pleasing to Thee. I see nothing there, Lord, but only Thy grief. Consider therefore, God, the ills that I suffer, and those which threaten me. Look with a merciful eye upon my wounds which Thy hand has made. O my Saviour, Thou who hast loved Thy sufferings even in death: O God, Thou who hast made Thyself man only to suffer more than any man for the salvation of mankind: O God, Thou who hast become incarnate only after men have sinned, and Thou who hast taken a body only to suffer in it all the ills that our sins have merited: O God, Thou who so lovest bodies which suffer, that Thou hast chosen for Thyself the body most afflicted with sufferings in all the world, mayest Thou find my body pleasing not because of itself nor because of all it contains, for everything in it is worthy of Thy wrath, but because of the ills it endures which alone may be worthy of Thy love. Love my sufferings, Lord, and may my ills invite Thee to visit me. But to achieve the preparation for Thine abode, grant, O my Saviour, if my body have in common with Thine that it may suffer for my offenses, that my soul may also have in common with Thine that it be saddened by the same offenses, and that thus I may suffer with Thee and as Thou dost, in my body and in my soul for the sins which I have committed.

XI

Grant me the grace, Lord, to join Thy consolations to my sufferings, so that I may suffer as a Christian. Lord, I do not ask that I be exempt from pains, for that is the reward of saints; but, Lord, I ask that I may not be abandoned to the pains of nature without the consolations of Thy Spirit, for that is the curse of Jews and pagans. I do not ask to have fullness of consolation without any suffering, for that is the life of glory. Neither do I ask to be in fullness of ills without consolation, for that is an estate of Judaism; but I ask, Lord, that I may feel together the pains of nature for my sins and the consolations of Thy Spirit by Thy grace, for that is the veritable estate of Christianity. May I not feel pains without consolation, but may I feel pains and consolation together, so that finally I may come to feel only Thy consolations without any pain. For, Lord, Thou hast left me in the world to languish in natural sufferings without consolation before the coming of Thine only Son. Now Thou consolest the sufferings of Thy faithful by the grace of Thine only Son, and Thou crownest Thy saints with pure blessedness in the glory of Thine only Son. These are the admirable degrees by which Thou dost conduct Thy works. Thou hast raised me from the first degree; grant that I may pass from the second to arrive at the third. Lord, this is the grace I ask of Thee.

XII

Do not permit, my God, that I be so far removed from Thee, that I may consider Thy soul sorrowful unto death, and Thy body overwhelmed by death through my own sins, without my rejoicing at suffering in my body and in my soul. For what is there more shameful and nevertheless more common in Christians and in me than that while Thou dost sweat blood for the expiation of our offenses, we live in delights; Christians who profess to belong to Thee; those who by Baptism have renounced the world to follow Thee; those who have sworn solemnly before the Church to live and to die with Thee; those who profess to believe that the world has persecuted and crucified Thee; those who believe that Thou hast exposed Thyself to the wrath of God and to the cruelty of men to redeem their crimes; those, I say, who believe all these verities, who consider Thy Body as the living offering freely given for our salvation; those who consider their pleasures and the sins of the world as the sole reason for Thy sufferings, and the world itself as Thy hangman, who indulge their bodies with the same pleasures in this same world; those who could not without trembling with horror see a man caress and cherish the murderer of his father who had given himself to give him life — all these can live, as I have done, with the fullness of joy in the world which I know veritably to have been the murderer of Him whom I recognize as my God, and as my Father, who has given Himself for my own salvation, and who has borne in his person the punishment for my iniquities. It is just, Lord, that Thou hast interrupted a joy as criminal as that in which I was reposing within the shadow of death.

XIII

Then take from me, Saviour, the sadness which love of self might arouse for my own pains, and the things of the world which do not succeed in accordance with the inclinations of my heart and which do not concern Thy glory. But place within me a sadness in conformity with Thine; that my pains may serve to appease Thy wrath; make of them an occasion for my salvation and my conversion so that henceforth I may wish for health and desire life only to employ and to end it for Thee, with Thee, and in Thee. I ask of Thee neither health, nor sickness, nor life, nor death, but that Thou wouldst dispose of my health and my sickness, of my life and my death for Thy glory, for my salvation, and for the welfare of the Church and of Thy Saints to whom [I hope through Thy grace] I belong. Thou alone knowest what is meet for me; Thou art the sovereign Master; do as Thou wilt. Give me, or take me, but make my will conform to Thine; grant that in humble and perfect submission, and in holy confidence, I may prepare myself to receive the commands of Thine eternal providence, and that I may adore equally everything that comes to me from Thee.

XIV

Grant that in constant equanimity of spirit I accept all happenings, since we do not know what we should ask, and grant that I may not presume to desire one rather than another, and that I may not make myself judge and be responsible for consequences which Thy wisdom has justly desired to conceal from me. Lord, I know that I know but one thing, namely, that it is good to follow Thee, and that it is evil to offend Thee. Beyond that I do not know what is the best or the worst of all things. I do not know whether health or illness, wealth or poverty, nor any things in the world are profitable to me. This is a discernment which surpasses the strength of men and of angels, and which is hidden in the secrets of Thy providence which I adore, and which I do not desire to probe.

XV

Grant then, Lord, that I may conform to Thy will, just as I am, that, being sick as I am, I may glorify Thee in my sufferings. Without them I cannot attain to glory; without them, my Saviour, even Thou wouldst not have risen to glory. By the marks of Thy sufferings Thou wert recognized by Thy disciples, and likewise by their sufferings Thou dost recognize those who are Thy disciples. Therefore recognize me as Thy disciple by the ills that I endure, in my body and in my spirit, for the offenses which I have committed. And since nothing is pleasing to God unless it be offered to Him by Thee, unite my will with Thine and my sufferings with those that Thou hast suffered; grant that mine may become Thine. Unite me with Thee; fill me with Thee and Thy Holy Spirit. Enter into my heart and into my soul, there to bear my sufferings and to continue in me that part of the suffering of Thy passion which yet remains to be endured, which Thou art yet completing in Thy members until the perfect consummation of Thy Body, so that it shall no longer be I who live and who suffer but that it shall be Thou who dost live and suffer in me, O my Saviour. And thus, having some small part in Thy suffering, I shall be filled wholly by Thee with the glory which it has brought to Thee, the glory in which Thou dost dwell with the Father and the Holy Spirit, forever and ever. Amen.

45. PASCAL'S WILL

[August 3, 1662]

Present in person was Blaise Pascal, esquire, ordinarily residing in Paris, outside of and near the gate Saint Michael, parish of Saint Cosme, being at present in bed, sick of body, in a room in the third story of a house located in Paris on the moat between the gates of Saint Marcel and of Saint Victor, in the parish of Saint Etienne du Mont, in which resides Maître Florin Perier, councilor of the king in his board of excise of Clermont-Ferrand in Auvergne. Pascal was still sound of mind, memory, and understanding as it seemed to the undersigned notaries from his words, gestures and bearing. Mindful that there is nothing more certain than death nor anything more uncertain than the day and the hour of death, and being desirous not to be taken without having made his testament, for this and other reasons that move him thereto, he has made, dictated and given to the undersigned his testament and disposition of his last will in the form and manner which follow.

Firstly as a good Christian, Apostolic and Roman Catholic, he has commended and commends his soul to God, praying to Him that by the merit and the precious blood of our Saviour and Redeemer Jesus Christ it may please Him to pardon his faults and to join his soul, when it shall leave this world, to the number of the blessed, imploring to this end the intercessions of the glorious Virgin Mary and of all the saints of paradise.

Item, he wills and orders that all his debts be paid, and that all errors, if there be any, be adjusted and corrected by the undersigned executor of his will.

Item, he desires his dead body to be interred in the said church of Saint Etienne du Mont of the said City of Paris. As regards the ceremonies of his funeral procession, service, and burial, together with the masses, prayers, and alms for the repose of the soul of the said testator, he leaves and gives over all of it to the discretion and will of his aforesaid undersigned executor, or, if the latter is then absent from this city of Paris, to the discretion of Demoiselle Gilberte Pascal, the latter's wife and the sister of the said testator.

Item, he gives and bequeaths to Françoise Delfante (*sic*), wife of Monsieur Pinel, the sum of twelve hundred pounds, payable in one sum.

Item, he gives and bequeaths to Anne Polycarpe, chambermaid of the said Demoiselle, the sum of one thousand pounds, payable in one sum.

Item, he gives and bequeaths to one Esdune, kitchen maid of the said testator, the sum of one hundred pounds tz., pension for each year during the life of this Esdune.

Item, he gives and bequeaths to the nurse who was the wet-nurse of Estienne Perier, nephew of the said testator, the sum of thirty pounds pension for each year during the life of the said nurse who lives in Normandy.

Item, he gives and bequeaths to Blaise Bardout, godson of the said testator, the sum of three hundred pounds to be employed in having him taught a trade, and until that time it shall remain in the hands of the said executor of this testament, who will pay him interest for it.

Item, he gives and bequeaths to the said Etienne Perier, his nephew, the sum of two thousand pounds tz., payable in one sum.

Item, the said testator gives and bequeaths to the general hospital of this city of Paris one fourth of the rights belonging to the said testator in the public coaches, recently established in the said city of Paris, but subject to this agreement: If it happens that instead of owning the share of the said carriages which the Provost Marshal now owns, the said Provost Marshal shall in future own one sixth of the total number of them, then instead of such a sixth of the total of the said carriages which now belong to the said testator, there shall belong to him only one sixth as opposed to the remaining five sixths; this on condition that the said hospital contribute in due proportion to the same expenses and charges, and hold to the same stipulations and conditions to which the said testator was held.

Item, the said testator gives and bequeaths (under the conditions stated above for the general hospital of Paris) another quarter of the same rights, unless the said hospital of Clermont within the three years following upon the death of the said testator prefers to take the sum of three thousand pounds (payable in one sum) for the said portion; if the latter is done, the said portion shall return to the said Demoiselle, sister of the said testator, who shall have no claim to the interest which the said hospital shall have had from the said portion during the said time.

Item, the said testator gives and bequeaths under the conditions previously announced for the hospital of the city of Paris to Maître Jean Domat, advocate of the king in the presidio of the said Clermont, another fourth of the above said rights to be enjoyed during his lifetime, and after his death the said fourth shall return to the said Demoiselle.

Item, the said testator desires that restitution shall be made for the two thirds for which he might be held (on account of the property of his deceased father) of the arrears and interests received without just title by his said father (and for the total of those which have been thus received by the said testator) the total of which shall be agreed upon and determined, both as to the sum and as to the persons to whom it shall be distributed, by the said Florin Perier, the said Demoiselle, his wife, and by the said Sire Daumat (*sic*). This shall be settled within six months at the latest by all of them or at least by those living at the said time, and it shall be executed by the said undersigned executor of this testament at the latest within one year after the death of the said testator.

And to execute and carry out the said present testament the said testator has named and chosen the said Florin Perier, his brother-in-law, whom he entreats to be willing to undertake the task; the said testator revokes all other testaments and codicils which he may have made before this one, the only one he declares valid, as being his intention and last will. As such it was done, dictated and given by the said testator to the said notaries, then read and re-read to him by one of these notaries present, until he said he well understood it, in the said room, the third day of August 1662, before noon, and signed:

PASCAL

QUARRÉ   GUNEAU

www.ingramcontent.com/pod-product-compliance
Lightning Source LLC
Chambersburg PA
CBHW060623250426
43670CB00056B/1944